The Dreamer and the Dream

NEW SUNS:

RACE, GENDER, AND SEXUALITY IN THE

SPECULATIVE

Susana M. Morris and Kinitra D. Brooks, Series Editors

The Dreamer and the Dream

Afrofuturism and Black Religious Thought

Roger A. Sneed

THE OHIO STATE UNIVERSITY PRESS

COLUMBUS

Library of Congress Cataloging-in-Publication Data
Names: Sneed, Roger A., author.
Title: The dreamer and the dream : Afrofuturism and Black religious thought / Roger A. Sneed.
Other titles: New suns: race, gender, and sexuality in the speculative.
Description: Columbus : The Ohio State University Press, [2021] | Series: New suns: race, gender, and sexuality in the speculative | Includes bibliographical references and index. | Summary: "Analyzes the interplay of Black religious thought with science fiction to illuminate Afrofuturism as an important channel for Black religion and spirituality, drawing from Octavia Butler's *Parable* books, Janelle Monáe's Afrofuturistic saga, *Star Trek*'s Captain Benjamin Sisko, Marvel's *Black Panther*, and Sun Ra and the Nation of Islam" —Provided by publisher.
Identifiers: LCCN 2021016237 | ISBN 9780814214794 (cloth) | ISBN 0814214797 (cloth) | ISBN 9780814281574 (ebook) | ISBN 0814281575 (ebook) | ISBN 9780814258064 (paper) | ISBN 0814258069 (paper)
Subjects: LCSH: Afrofuturism. | African Americans—Religion. | Religious thought. | Science fiction.
Classification: LCC PN3433.6 .S64 2021 | DDC 700.4/52996073—dc23
LC record available at https://lccn.loc.gov/2021016237

Cover design by Black Kirby
Composition by Stuart Rodriguez
Type set in Palatino

CONTENTS

In some respects, this book began the first time I laid eyes on a comic book, the first time I watched an episode of *Star Trek,* the first time I saw the redesigned USS *Enterprise* streak into warp speed. It began when I found other nerds like me, but they didn't look like me, and I was told that my love of science fiction in general and *Star Trek* in particular was "a white thing." Coincidentally, I was also told that being gay was a "white thing." The book began when I realized that while my mother and my community had Christianity, I had *Star Trek, Superman,* and *Star Wars.* My first hero was Superman, my first crush was on Aquaman, and my first role model was Mr. Spock.

Growing up in Tulsa, Oklahoma, in the 1970s and '80s was a bundle of contradictions and contestations. As most gay folk say when they talk about their emerging awareness of their sexuality, I knew that I was different. My mother said that she and my grandmother were concerned that at the age of five I hadn't started talking. When I did, she said that all I ever did was talk to myself.

However, by the time I was in first grade, I was talking a lot, and reading even more. When I went from reading Little Golden Books to reading comic books, I entered a new world. My grandmother would take me to the grocery store with her after she got off work, and she would let me pick out a comic book. If I remember correctly, the first comic book my grandmother bought me was a Batman comic; however, I remember the first Superman comic I got. I became obsessed with comic books and the superhero genre—especially Superman and Action Comics. I also remember seeing television commercials for *Star Trek: The Motion Picture*. While I did not get to see the movie until much later, the images of the redesigned USS *Enterprise* on television and in print stayed with me. I would make sure that I stayed up on Friday nights to watch the original *Star Trek,* which was in syndication at this point. I remember missing an episode and thinking that I would never get a chance to see it again—this, of course, was well before VCRs and streaming services.

Amidst my burgeoning nerd life was the church. Sunday mornings and evenings and more than a few Wednesdays were spent at North Peoria and Young Street Church of Christ. There, I learned about God and my own place in the world. I would perform readings of Scripture and serve communion. I was special. I was part of a community . . . that did not have room for gay people.

I came of age in the middle of the HIV/AIDS crisis. I heard that AIDS was God's punishment for living a "wicked lifestyle." The same God I had been told loved me did not actually love me. I begged God to fix me, to make me "straight." I heard that liking comic books and science fiction made me gay. I heard that I was too smart and that I "talked white." I was too light, and my walk wasn't correct. I was a sissy, homo, queer, weirdo, fag.

By the time I got to college, I assumed that if I did all the right things and acted the right way, then I could successfully eliminate my same-sex attractions. Sublimation was the name of the game. I threw myself into "respectability politics" and nearly any and every activity that signaled acceptable Blackness. I joined the university's gospel choir—even though I have never been able to sing. I pledged Alpha Phi Alpha, reasoning that the first Black college fraternity and the fraternity of the Reverend Dr. Martin Luther King Jr. was the perfect fraternity for me.

I subscribed to the respectability politics of the day, hoping to fashion myself into the proper model of a Black man. I even continued to go to church every Sunday, mostly to please my mother. But something gnawed at the edges of my life. I let it become anger, telling myself that it was righteous anger at injustice and apathy.

Finally coming out was, to put it bluntly, traumatic. Friends were no longer friends. Some friends did their best to walk with me through the tumult, but I had no real resources. I had only seen *Tongues Untied* once—I was thoroughly scandalized. I had yet to encounter Essex Hemphill or James Earl Hardy. I had read just an excerpt from E. Lynn Harris's *Just as I Am.* I had only recently (at that time) encountered Cornel West's *Race Matters*, but I knew nothing about Black liberation and womanist theologies. I had never even heard of a Black science fiction writer, though I had thankfully been exposed to the Milestone line of comics and Dwayne McDuffie's ground-breaking writing and centering of Black and Latino superheroes.

When I decided to attend seminary in order to answer my existential questions regarding my sexuality, I knew virtually nothing about theology and next to nothing about Black cultural criticism. I also did not know much about divinity schools or schools of theology—I nearly applied to Oral Roberts University, until I saw that their application demanded a statement that the applicant would not participate in homosexual activity. I moved to Atlanta two weeks after the end of the 1996 Summer Olympics. The city was awash in the afterglow of the international spotlight and an influx of people into the city. My years in Atlanta were not uniformly excellent, but they were transformative. I was out in every conceivable way.

I would argue vehemently with conservative classmates, devour James Cone's insistent, passionate writings, struggle with my Old Testament class, and endure Supervised Ministry; on the weekends, I would go to Loretta's, Traxx, and the Castle. Each club had their particular day. Loretta's on Fridays, Traxx on Saturday evenings, and the Castle on Sunday. I encountered house music and the freedom of letting my body go on the dance floor. I'd eat dinners with other Black gay men at Mick's or, if we had the money, Houston's. Sundays, I'd go to a small AME church in Decatur led by Reverend Kathi Martin, an out Black lesbian. I became part of a discussion group for Black gay men and joined a small writing collective.

Despite having a vibrant social life, the days I spent in classes were increasingly frustrating. My professors possessed vast knowledge of the Christian theological tradition, but they could not speak to my experiences as a gay man. Indeed, Emory University itself had reached a compromise with the United Methodist Church regarding allowing same-sex commitment ceremonies to happen in the churches and chapels that were part of the university.[1] I recall going to chapel one Wednesday because a classmate was going to deliver the sermon. As they preached, naming marginalized groups and how God stood with them, I waited for the preacher to mention gays and lesbians. That moment did not arrive in that sermon. Out of frustration, I penned a poem called "Speak My Name," concluding that I had to be the one to speak my name, since no one else would. By my final

1. http://www.umaffirm.org/cornews/emory3.html

year at Candler, I decided that I would focus on getting ready to apply for doctoral programs.

Stumbling across Victor Anderson's *Beyond Ontological Blackness* was intellectually transformative. I had finally found a critique of Black liberation theology that "spoke my name." Certainly, I had read Renee Hill's and Elias Farajaje Jones's respective critiques of the silences in Black liberation and womanist theologies, but what I needed and found in Anderson's work was not only a sustained philosophical and theological assessment of Black liberation theology but also a potential mentor.

Vanderbilt University's Graduate Department of Religion was not just another step on an academic path. It was the place where it all seemed to come together. Reading Cornel West and bell hooks alongside James Cone and Kelly Brown Douglas prompted me to ask, "Where and when and how do Black gays and lesbians enter into these conversations?" That question became the basis of the first book, *Representations of Homosexuality: Black Liberation Theology and Cultural Criticism.* I argued that we entered into Black liberation and womanist theology and cultural criticism as tragic figures, requiring the pity of Black heterosexuals. I turned to Black gay men's writings to inform Black liberation theology and cultural criticism.

This book began when I was writing the dissertation and somehow stumbled across Samuel Delany and Octavia Butler. I was a graduate student, supposedly near the peak of academic achievement, and had never heard of, much less read Delany and Butler. After the dissertation, after landing the coveted tenure-track job, after publishing my first book, I told myself that my next book would be about science fiction and ethics. I had planned on writing a treatise in which science fiction served as a source for doing Christian ethics.

Then Trayvon Martin. Michael Brown. Eric Garner—we were the same age. Renisha McBride. Sandra Bland.

Tamir Rice. He was only twelve. Philando Castille. Alton Sterling. Terence Crutcher. He was from my hometown. I knew the street he died on.

Week after week, a new name. A new video of another Black person running away, complying, begging not to be shot, begging for air, dying anyway. Week after week, I retreated into the world of *Star Trek*—on demand via Netflix, to the amazement of my nine-year-old self. I was drawn specifically to the sixth-season *Deep Space Nine* episode "Far Beyond the Stars," in which Benjamin Sisko lives the life of a 1950s Black science fiction writer named Benny Russell who creates "Deep Space Nine." The climax of the episode in which Benny experiences a crushing rejection of his story "Deep Space Nine" would always leave me in tears. His simple "I'm a human being, dammit!" and the prophetic "I created it! And it is real!," along with the enigmatic Prophet telling him that he is the Dreamer and the Dream—these would be what I needed to cope with the piling trauma of seeing more Black death and pain in a system of white supremacy. African American life has been the record of bearing all forms of pain. What Orlando Patterson calls "social death," and what Debra Walker King understands as a "culture of pain" has framed and continues to frame Black life in America.[2] To be Black in America is to experience, in some form or another, the debilitating, insidious, and destructive nature of white supremacist thinking and action. White supremacy is a pervasive, death-dealing, nihilistic force that is interwoven into every institution in American life. As King points out, Black people are subjected to both overt and symbolic forms of violence.[3] Black people experienced the communal pain and the constant reminder that Black bodies are not safe, and that no amount or measure of middle-class "respectability" can save one from police violence and any other form of physical violation.

Black people also know that our bodies and spaces are subject to virtual violence. For example, comedian Leslie Jones, star in the recent version of *Ghostbusters*, was harassed on Twitter to the point of temporarily driving her away from the social media platform. Not content with barraging her Twitter account with racist vitriol, a hacker hacked her account and posted nude pictures of her along with racist images. Such incidents prompted other Twitter users to start supportive hashtags like #LoveForLeslieJ. Leslie Jones's experience of racist abuse is not an isolated incident. Black people individually and collectively experience the pain of white supremacy and its imaginings of blackness as dangerous, docile, and subject to domination and death. Debra Walker King's concept of "blackpain" is not merely a response to discrete incidents. Rather, it is a response to the systemic and institutional deployment of white supremacist thinking and action. She notes that "blackpain exists outside of time . . . it is time—mythic time—and a memorial to the wounds and traumas some Americans wish to deny and discard."[4] Further, King contends, "We must disrupt the pervasive marking of race that codes black bodies in pain as an ordinary event of everyday life."[5] King's work is an attempt at disrupting that pervasive marking. Further, we may see Black Lives Matter, and Black protests in Ferguson, the University of Missouri, Yale University, and other cities across the nation, as well as other interventions via social media as attempts by Black people

2. Patterson, *Slavery and Social Death*, 34.
3. King, *African Americans and the Culture of Pain*, 34.
4. Ibid, 21.
5. Ibid.

as means of addressing blackpain. I contend that the power of Afrofuturism is to disrupt that pervasive marking of race and the destructive coding of Black bodies and existence as inferior. Afrofuturist productions exist outside of ordinary time.

I had to write. I had to "write the words," as the Prophet told Benny Russell. This book represents an endeavor to merge science fiction as expressed in Afrofuturism with Black religious thought. The earliest iterations of this book focused on being a "corrective" to Black liberation theology. Indeed, one of the essays that appears in this book was initially conceived and presented as a "prolegomena to an Afrofuturistic theology." However, after presenting, rewriting, and submitting that piece to a few academic journals and reading the reviewers' comments, I came to a conclusion: I am not writing theology. While my academic training and much of my teaching has been in the orbit of Black liberation theology, this book is not that. While I am not antagonistic toward theology, this book's arguments benefit from a wider focus on Black religious thought. In focusing on Black religious thought, I hope to broaden the scope of an argument regarding Afrofuturism.

ACKNOWLEDGMENTS

I have often seen people describe the process of writing a book as a lonely endeavor. I have been fortunate in that writing this book, I have not been alone. This is not merely "acknowledgments"; rather, I think of this as overdue gratitude. I have had the support of family, friends, and colleagues from the beginning to the end of this project. I have a cloud of witnesses both present and passed on who've cheered me on, sat with me, cried and laughed with me, and counseled me. First, this project would not have been possible without the support of The Ohio State University Press and the editors of the New Suns: Race, Gender, and Sexuality series, Kinitra D. Brooks and Susana Morris. The Furman Humanities Center and its director, Michele Speitz, contributed financial resources, encouragement, and an invaluable opportunity to share part of my work with a larger audience via the Tolle, Lege summer series of public lectures.

My friends, colleagues, and students in the Furman University Religion Department have been supportive in ways that I cannot describe. I have also been lucky to have cherished friends across the university who've been part of this process: Michael Svec, Brandon Inabinet, Laura Morris, Gretchen Braun, TJ Banisaukas, Mary Alice Kirkpatrick, Jason Hansen, Carolyn Day, Michelle Horhota and Geoffrey Gunn, Cherie Maiden, Onarae Rice, Teresa Cosby, Michael Jennings, and Paul Thomas—just to name a few. Further, this project would not have been possible without the inquisitive minds I have had the honor of teaching in my many years at Furman.

The Swamp Rabbit Brewery and the Tasting Room deserve special mention, as they have been a second office or a second home. My thanks go out to the proprietors of those establishments. Ben and Teresa Pierson, Andrew and Caitlin Pierson Myers, Evan Rutter, and Christine Seiler created spaces that were welcoming and conducive to the writing process. Rowe Carenen, Josh Mathis, and Michael Svec spent many a beer or glass of wine discussing this book with me and helping me untangle many of its premises.

I also owe my dear friends Rima Abunasser and Darin Bradley a debt of gratitude for over a decade of friendship. During a conversation about this book, it was Rima who suggested that I title the book *The Dreamer and the Dream*. Darin published an early piece in the journal *Bahamut* that was a seed for the book. Our many, many conversations about *Battlestar Galactica* and *Star Trek* (and that summer we plowed through all the *Star Trek* movies) helped lay the foundations for me to talk about *Trek* at length during speaking engagements.

Nyasha Junior, Rhon Manigault-Bryant, and Lisa Allen-McLaurin have been longtime friends and I am indebted to the Wabash Center for Teaching and Learning in Religion for providing the space in which I was able to meet these wonderful Black women. Their encouragement has been invaluable.

My California friends have also been a delight. Prior to the COVID-19 pandemic, my frequent trips to the Huntington Library to conduct research in the Octavia Butler archive were made all the more enjoyable by being able to relax with Darnise Martin, Daniel Johnson, Jeffrey Guhin, Reggie Tucker-Seeley, Jessica Tinkleberg and Jeremy Schneider, and Melissa Wilcox. Special thanks to Jeffrey and Melissa, who graciously extended invitations to present my work at their institutions.

Molly and Ray Kaplan, Meredith Hammons, Vicky Schooner, Heather McMurray, and Craig Johnson have all been the dearest of friends, whose support and encouragement has sustained me through the years.

And finally, this book would not have at all been possible without my family: my mother Ruth Sneed, my sister Kim Peigne, my nieces Ashley, Candis, and Kindil, and nephew Joshua. I write for them.

There has been a renewed interest in Black speculative fiction in the form of Afrofuturism. The massive success of Marvel Studios' 2018 *Black Panther* sparked several articles and thinkpieces about Wakanda, Afrofuturism, and renewed visions of Black futures. The phrase "Black speculative fiction" itself functions as an umbrella term that encompasses science fiction, fantasy, and horror. In the latter part of the twentieth century and in much of this current century, Black peoples have embraced not only science fiction, fantasy, and horror but also what we might call "nerd culture." *Black Panther,* along with Jordan Peele's unprecedented success with his movies *Get Out* and *Us,* has ushered in an interest in telling Black stories via the Black speculative. Further, these movies and the writing they inspired have played an important role in the emergence of the "Blerd," a portmanteau of "Black" and "nerd." This emergence of the Blerd has been facilitated largely by the technological marvel that is the internet. This inquiry and subsequent analysis is rooted squarely in the form of the Black speculative that encompasses science fiction. Even then, the forms of Black science fiction take on different descriptions—such descriptions themselves defy the notion that Black people have not engaged in science fiction productions. At times, this form of the Black speculative has been termed "Astro Blackness" or, in a more mundane fashion, "Black science fiction." Contemporaneous with this rise of publicly displayed interest in Black speculative fiction is the emergence of critical Black analyses of religion and intersections with popular culture.

In academic discourses, people like Anthony Pinn and Monica Miller have spearheaded innovative ways of viewing Black cultural productions in conjunction with Black religions. They have charted paths laid down by Black cultural critics like Michael Eric Dyson, bell hooks, and Cornel West in order to expand Black religious thought. However, these essays, articles, and books have largely ignored Black speculative fictions, preferring to look at drama, and Black literary productions. Jon Gill uses Afrofuturism as part of his studies of Black religion, theology, and hip-hop. Indeed, this book will later reference his review of Marvel's *Black Panther*.

This book proceeds from the assertion that an Afrofuturistic consciousness yields a vision of Blackness that, while it may respond to white supremacy, is not bound by whiteness. Further, Afrofuturism is not bound by a conception of a Christian God who stands over and against us. Nor does that God stand "with" us. As Anthony Pinn has articulated in several of his works, part of the enduring problem that Black liberation theology has not adequately addressed is the problem of Black suffering. The vision of God that I argue Afrofuturism might lead us toward is closer to Victor Anderson's conception of God as articulated in *Creative Exchange: A Constructive Theology of African American Religious Experience*. He claims, "God names the totality of the World itself, which is the union of life in all of its concrete actualities (finitude) and ideal potentialities (transcendence)."[1] While Anderson seeks to ground this conception of God within institutions such as the Black church and Black families (in all their multiple iterations), I argue that, like Octavia Butler's Lauren Olamina, God is not to be found in those institutions. Rather, if God is "the totality of the World itself," then as the fictional Earthseed religion that Olamina creates argues, God is change. Change is God. We shape that change, and that change shapes us. As James Cone argued in his early foundational works, God is Black. To that, I add that God is Black insofar as that Blackness itself is part of a universe shaped by and shaping change. Further, to limit the encounter with God to institutionalized religious organizations is to rob us of the creative possibilities inherent in the encounters with God-as-world. Ruby Sales, a veteran of the modern civil rights movement, put it quite succinctly during the plenary session at the 2015 meeting of the American Academy of Religion when she noted that there is a distinction between "black religion" and "the Black church." She contended that the difference between Black religion and the Black church is that the Black church as it emerged out of Black religion

---

1. Anderson, *Creative Exchange*, 134.

became an institution that reinscribed hegemonic narratives, to wit, the primacy and authority of the (male) Black preacher, while Black religion is and has been an organic response by Black peoples not only to racist oppression, but also to the possibilities of Blackness in this world.[2] To this point, I turn to Black imaginations as shaping that change and shaping God.

As Anderson "suggest[s] that God names the totality of the World itself," I counter with a suggestion informed by the Earthseed verses outlined in Octavia Butler's *Parable of the Sower* and *Parable of the Talents,* namely that we as human beings name (and shape) God. We imagine and reimagine the divine. For the Afrofuturist, this requires a prophetic imagination that sees Blackness in multiple dimensions. We bear witness to the dehumanization of Black bodies, but we do not live in that dehumanization. We see ourselves as agents of change, and that change shapes us. Thus, God-as-world understood via Afrofuturism is indeed Black. It is that Blackness between the stars that encompasses all known reality. It is that Blackness from whence we came. As we understand, the universe is constantly expanding. God-as-world is then understood as constantly changing.

Religion in Science Fiction and the Turn to Afrofuturism

Star Trek creator Gene Roddenberry represents science fiction's skepticism and, at times, outright antagonism toward religion and religious belief.[3] He describes religion as "nothing more than a substitute for a malfunctioning brain." *Star Trek* in most of its incarnations held religion at arm's length, and at times was altogether dismissive of it. For example, *Star Trek: The Next Generation*'s third-season episode "Who Watches the Watchers?" focuses on an alien society that begins to worship Captain Jean-Luc Picard as a deity. Upon the suggestion that he fulfill (at least in some limited sense) the Mintakans' view of him as a god, Picard says the following:

> Horrifying. Dr. Barron, your report describes how rational these people are. Millennia ago, they abandoned their belief in the supernatural. Now you are asking me to sabotage that achievement, to send them back into the dark ages of superstition and ignorance and fear? No![4]

---

2. Sales, "Racial Injustice and Religious Response from Selma to Ferguson."
3. Pearson, "From Thwarted Gods to Reclaimed Mystery?"
4. Directed by Robert Wiemer, written by Richard Manning and Hans Beimler. Aired October 14, 1989.

It is clear that Picard, as the representative of the ideals of the United Federation of Planets as well as that of an enlightened humanity, believes that a crowning achievement for any humanoid species is the renunciation of religion and the embrace of a secular rationality, as typified in the empirical sciences. Picard's view—as an extension of Roddenberry's—is reflective of a progressive, linear view of human history and achievement. In this view, human societies would progress from superstition to religion to science. In *Star Trek*'s linear progressive view of history, religion is suspect, fraught with human error, and an impediment to human progress. Further, Picard as representative of this linear progressivism characterizes religious belief as a basis for culture is also the basis for discrimination, holy wars, and atrocities. Another example of such a view is the fourth-season episode "Devil's Due." In this particular episode, the *Enterprise* responds to a distress call from researchers on the planet Ventax IV. Apparently, an entity named Ardra has returned to fulfill a millennia-old contract in which the Ventaxans pledged their planet to her in return for resolving the planet's crises. At first, it seems that Ardra is the "real deal," performing feats that the intrepid crew of the *Enterprise* cannot explain. However, they uncover that she is, indeed, a "flim flam artist," deploying sophisticated technology in order to deceive the Ventaxans.[5] With the exception of *Deep Space Nine*, which will be discussed at length in chapter 4, and perhaps a smattering of *Star Trek: Voyager* episodes, the franchise under Roddenberry's guidance treated religion and its attendant deities, gods, and so forth as easily explained and disposed tricks of science.

That said, contemporary forms of televised and cinematic science fiction have appeared to take religion more seriously. For example, *Babylon 5*, a serialized "five season novel for television," took religion far more seriously than either *Star Trek: The Original Series* or *Star Trek: The Next Generation*. As the first serialized science fiction show to introduce series-long character arcs, this series showed that human religions existed in that show's imagination of the twenty-third century. Indeed, religion as well as larger mythological arcs are integral to the series' five-year arc. The reimagined *Battlestar Galactica*, which aired from 2003 to 2009, also took a far more serious approach to religious belief—one of the series' central questions was whether or not the Cylons worshipped an actual deity. By the end of the series, it is rather strongly implied that *some kind of entity* was responsible for the events of the series . . . and events 150,000 years later.[6] Ronald

5. Directed by Tom Benko, written by Phillip Lazebnik and William Douglas Lansford. Aired February 4, 1991.

6. Directed by Michael Rymer, written by Ronald D. Moore. Aired March 20, 2009.

Moore, the creator of the 2003 version of *Battlestar Galactica* (*BSG*), said that the series' religious themes were "reflective of [his] religious views in that [he doesn't] have really firm religious views."[7] Despite having been raised Catholic, Moore said that he dabbled in Eastern religions and was "open to various ideas." Such ideas made their way into the series: The humans of the Twelve Colonies of Kobol were polytheistic, worshipping multiple gods (some of whom were clearly influenced by Eastern religious traditions, and some were influenced by Greek/Roman religious mythologies).

An obvious example of the intersection of religion and science fiction is the *Matrix* trilogy. The first movie alone is rife with religious symbolism. From the name Neo functioning as an anagram for "the one" to Carrie Anne Moss's Trinity literally breathing new life into Neo after his battle with Agent Smith to Lawrence Fishburne's Morpheus and the late Gloria Smith's Oracle, the movie trades upon several mythological and religious themes in order to craft a cyberpunk mythology that stood on its own and virtually redefined the science fiction film. The subsequent movies *The Matrix Reloaded* and *The Matrix Revolutions* joined the first movie in constructing a trilogy that incorporated even more Christian thematic elements. Mark D. Stucky outlines how each of the movies "parallel the New Testament collection":

- The Matrix is the Gospel of Neo, the coming of age of the postmodern messiah, his death, and his resurrection.
- The Matrix Reloaded perhaps corresponds to the Acts of the new messiah and his disciples, chronicling the next stage of their struggle with the machines.
- The Matrix Revolutions concludes the trilogy with the Apocalypse According to St. Neo, where during the apocalyptic final battle between humanity and the machines, Neo ends the war and brings the final realization of the messianic age of peace between humanity and machines.[8]

Stucky's outline of the *Matrix* movies is not the only one that examines the Christian (especially the gnostic influences) and Buddhist influences that are shot throughout each movie. For example, the *Journal of Religion* published

7. Clayton Neuman, "Ronald D. Moore on the Meaning of God in Battlestar Galactica's Finale—an AMC Interview," Slice of SciFi, March 24, 2009, https://www.sliceofscifi.com/2009/03/24/ronald-d-moore-on-the-meaning-of-god-in-battlestar-galacticas-finale-an-amc-interview/.

8. Stucky, "He Is the One," 2.

a 2006 essay that argued that the trilogy shifts from Western conceptions of religion to Eastern views.[9]

The current interest in Afrofuturism is tied to the growth of science fiction in general. The emergence of science fiction movies (and, to some extent, television shows) as part of the mainstream speaks to a desire to find new ways to engage the world. Many descriptions of science fiction point to both the "sense of wonder" and its power to critique current social problems.[10] In a 2017 Den of Geek article concerning a London exhibition on science fiction, curator Patrick Gyger articulates why science fiction has entered into the mainstream:

> As we become ever more reliant on technology in our everyday lives, sci-fi has become a logical means of making sense of an increasingly complex, interconnected world.
>
> "Then science fiction helps us read the world we're in," Gyger says. "It doesn't shape the world we're in, but it helps us read the world we're in. And we're in a world where there doesn't seem to be many alternatives. . . . It's a very strong tool to approach reality. And science fiction is a strong one, because it takes one perspective, and transforms it in an exaggerated manner. It puts it in the future or the near future to see what happens when you're dependent on your phone. Or it can record what you see, like in *Black Mirror*. That's why *Black Mirror* is such an important show. It doesn't say, 'This is what is going to happen,' of course—it talks about the present."[11]

Science fiction may be described as prophetic and predictive. As it critiques our society and its problems, it may, as Octavia Butler pointed out in discussing the *Parable* series, identify "If this, then."

Television science fiction may also perform the function of disrupting other iterations of white supremacist imaginaries. Ytasha Womack mentions "Trekkies," or fans of the *Star Trek* franchise, asking why and then writing or envisioning Black peoples in the future. Further, Womack articulates that Afrofuturism is "often the umbrella for an amalgamation of narratives . . . [and] values the power of creativity and imagination to reinvigorate culture and transcend social limitations."[12] This umbrella involves more than

9. Wittung and Bramer, "From Superman to Brahman," 11.

10. Gerlach and Hamilton, "Introduction: A History of Social Science Fiction," 163.

11. Ryan Lambie, "How Sci-Fi Went Mainstream," *Den of Geek*, July 7, 2017, http://www.denofgeek.com/uk/movies/into-the-unknown/50481/how-sci-fi-went-mainstream

12. Womack, *Afrofuturism*, loc. 315, Kindle.

literary productions. We point to musical productions like those of Sun Ra, George Clinton and Funkadelic, and Janelle Monáe as representative of musical Afrofuturism, but we can also point to comic books and other forms of visual art as well as television and film as presenting Afrofuturistic visions.

Outline of the Book

Scope is what drives Afrofuturism and informs the layout of this book. While scholars like Paul Youngquist and Ytasha Womack point to Sun Ra and P-Funk as the genesis of Afrofuturism and Mark Dery as the person who coined the term "Afrofuturism," Sheree Thomas goes back to W. E. B. Du Bois's 1920 short story "The Comet" as the first science fiction narrative written by a Black person. One might even contend that enslaved Black peoples who subscribed to an apocalyptic vision of divine retribution against white slave owners formed a kind of proto-Afrofuturism. Afrofuturism does not limit itself to conceptions of "the future" as a primary site. I present the following chapters as case studies in the intersection of Afrofuturism and Black religious thought.

The first two chapters are "foundational" chapters. Chapter 1 explores representations of Blackness in science fiction and then moves to descriptions of Afrofuturism. When looking at major science fiction franchises (*Star Trek* and *Star Wars*, for example), we see certain reproductions of racial stereotypes. Further, we see Black people in these franchises as adjunct to the "central" white male characters. Afrofuturism serves as a corrective to the perceived white, cishet maleness of science fiction.

Chapter 2 traces Black religious thought as a productive field in which Afrofuturism can work and will examine the possibilities for unions between Afrofuturism and Black religious thought. In general, science fiction has had an ambivalent relationship to religion, ranging from approving to hostile. However, Afrofuturism in its multiple facets has a mostly comfortable relationship with religion, even as some of its formulators and contributors may themselves hold ambivalent views.

Chapters 3 and 4 turn to two Afrofuturists, Octavia Butler and Janelle Monáe. Both chapters regard these Black women Afrofuturists as not only foundational but also intersectional. These chapters draw on Kimberlé Crenshaw's description of intersectionality and the interlocking matrices of race, class, gender, and sexual orientation. Both Butler and Monáe use Afrofuturism as a lens to critique the intersections of oppressions. They do not engage in hierarchical rankings of oppression; rather, they demand attention to the ways in which identities intersect, inform, and influence each other. These chapters also position Butler and Monáe as Afrofuturistic prophets. Chapters 3's focus on the *Parable* series situates Butler's use of dystopian settings as a way of saying "If this, then that." Octavia Butler's work casts an eye back to slavery but throws us forward to dystopian moments in which our hope rests in the enduring power of Black women drawing on the teachings of their foremothers. Butler is an architect of intersectional Afrofuturism, showing us, as Samuel Delany did, that science fiction need not center white cisgender heterosexual men as the be-all and end-all. Indeed, all of the protagonists in Butler's works are Black women. Further, Butler used her writing to interrogate religion. The *Parable of the Sower* and the *Parable of the Talents* situate an unlikely creation of a holistic religion, Earthseed.

Chapter 4 focuses on musical artist Janelle Monáe as a queer Afrofuturistic savior and traces the development of queer themes in her Afrofuturistic saga. Her two full-length albums and her first EP feature an android living in the future. However, her work draws on prior musical motifs. Cindi Mayweather is a futuristic android, but through Monáe, she emulates James Brown's frenetic stage presence, Michael Jackson's charisma, and Prince's eclectic musical stylings. As she blends these prior influences with an Afrofuturistic saga, she creates a narrative that critiques misogyny, homophobia, racism and white supremacy, and classism. Monáe's Afrofuturism becomes a vehicle by which she can reinvent her own self, culminating in a revelation of her own self as pansexual vis-à-vis her latest album *Dirty Computer*.

Chapters 5 and 6 turn to Afrofuturistic television and film. An unlikely entrée in a book on Afrofuturism, *Star Trek* offers a window into how Black people can repurpose science fiction to address the existential concerns of Black life. *Star Trek* has a history of centering white, cisgendered, heterosexual men. Captains Kirk and Picard were the "heart" of *Star Trek,* but when *Star Trek: Deep Space Nine* premiered, it was decidedly different from the series that preceded it. Indeed, *Deep Space Nine* (*DS9* for short) was decidedly not the crown jewel of the *Star Trek* franchise. However, it distinguished itself as the most emotionally complex series. Like the prior chapters, chapter 4 centers *Star Trek: Deep Space Nine*'s Captain Benjamin Sisko as prophetic. Of special interest here is the sixth-season episode "Far Beyond the Stars," in which Sisko lives the life of a Black science fiction writer living in 1950s New York. This chapter centers Sisko and his 1950s counterpart's experience of racism and white supremacy as well as the collapse of time and space between the 1950s and the twenty-fourth century. Benny Russell's prophetic creation of *Deep Space Nine* informs Sisko's role as captain, Emissary to the Prophets, and leader in the struggle against the totalitarian

Dominion. Central to understanding this episode is how a Black prophetic imagination frames how we see a collision of the past, the present, and the future.

Chapter 6's focus on the movie *Black Panther* centers Wakanda as an Afrofuturistic utopian ideal. Within this ideal, the viewer sees the emancipatory possibilities inherent in a society where Black men and women are free from white supremacy and its attendant toxic masculinities and desires for empire. The scope of Afrofuturism reaches into the realm of superhero comic books and movies based on them. *Black Panther*'s "surprising" success is not just due to Marvel Studios' excellent marketing campaign. Rather, it is also due to the desire to see a Black superhero who is not bound by white supremacy. Further, *Black Panther* gave us something else: a vision of a society, an entire culture that never experienced slavery and colonialism. *Black Panther* and the vision of Wakanda is, quite literally, the "what if" of Black life. The "what if" within *Black Panther* also points beyond toxic masculinity, as we see the women of Wakanda as savior figures, their wit and wisdom functioning to save Wakanda from invasion and destruction.

Chapters 7 and 8 are callbacks to the first two chapters and are experimental. If Black religious thought is a productive field for Afrofuturism and vice versa, then these chapters are a thought experiment: What might Afrofuturism say about eschatology? What might we say about Afrofuturism and Black religious identities? As a form of religious criticism, Afrofuturism may be able to articulate visions of Black life via a "what if" that takes us to an eschatological view of Afrofuturism. What can Afrofuturism tell us about hope in the future? This chapter turns to jazz musician and Afrofuturist pioneer Sun Ra and the Nation of Islam (NOI) as examples of Afrofuturistic eschatology. Both Sun Ra and the Nation developed visions of a Black future tied to a mythical Black past. Africa, Egypt, and a Black planet all figure in the respective eschatological dreams presented by Sun Ra and the NOI. While Sun Ra's eschatology would embrace all peoples—with Black peoples leading the way—the NOI's eschatology was far more apocalyptic, drawing on a science fictional interpretation of Ezekiel's Wheel. This apocalyptic eschatology situates the Mother Wheel as a supremely powerful vehicle that has at times disgorged other smaller vehicles described as UFOs. For the NOI, this Mother Wheel was prophesied in Ezekiel and will return at some point to destroy the forces of white supremacy. This chapter also points to how *Black Panther* combines both Sun Ra's and the NOI's visions into an Afrofuturistic eschatological vision.

Chapter 8 continues the thought experiment further by teasing out the possibilities for an Afrofuturistic religious identity. Building upon the Judith Weisenfeld's work on Black religious identity during the Great Migration (the period in which both Sun Ra and the Nation of Islam emerged and flourished) and Anthony Pinn's ongoing work to center humanism as part of African American religious experience and identity, I argue that Afrofuturists can center their love of Black speculative fictions as part of constructing new religious identities.

The book ends with a conclusion and postscript that point toward future directions for Afrofuturistic religious thought. Because the terrain of Afrofuturism is constantly shifting, this conclusion will also incorporate brief excurses into more current developments and productions and attempt to tie those into the overall thrust of the book. As this book argues that Afrofuturism functions as a focusing lens for Black religious thought and can shape how Black scholars and laypersons can re-vision Black religious lives and experiences, I am keenly aware that there may be an author or producer of Afrofuturistic visions that this book has not addressed. In early drafts of this work, reviewers noted that the book does not address Jon Gill's work. That oversight is not intentional, nor is it a commentary on Gill's fusion of Afrofuturism with hip-hop. Indeed, I anticipate future works that might build upon this and take Gill's work up as part of another examination of Afrofuturism and Black religion. This book is not an exhaustive examination of Afrofuturistic productions, as the book would never be finished. Rather, it is an examination of representative productions and how they may be interpreted via Black religious thought and vice versa.

PART I

Foundations

CHAPTER 1

Race in Science Fiction

A People living in a distant world and time encounter a strange new alien race, complete with different language, religion, and technology. These first contacts with the alien race are utterly disastrous. Possessing superior technology, the aliens abduct millions of the people and herd them onto vessels capable of crossing vast gulfs of space. The abducted do not know what these aliens want with them. Perhaps they have captured them in order to eat them?[1] After endless days and nights in which the prayers to the gods have gone unanswered, during which the People have endured unimaginable abuse, during which some of the People have been lost to that cruel and unforgiving void, those who are yet alive arrive in a new and alien world. Over countless years, the culture, the language, and the gods of the People are lost. The People endure torture, rape, and murder and are sold as animals to others of this alien race. Generations later, after the physical enslavement of the People has ended, nearly all memory of the homeworld is lost. Occasional attempts at rebellion are put down—often violently. Further, the People endure decades of social, cultural, educational, and economic disenfranchisement at the hands of the aliens, while the aliens continue to blame

---

1. Such a scenario was depicted in the classic *Twilight Zone* episode "To Serve Man" (airdate: March 2, 1962).

many of their world's social and cultural problems on the People. Further, the People forget the gods of their homeland and adopt the religions of the aliens who enslaved them and adapt it to what is left of their cultures and folkways. In some cases, a few of the People go so far as to say that it was the will of those alien gods that they be kidnapped and enslaved, since their homeland was irrevocably "heathen" and "savage." Attempts at retrieving the narratives of the homeworld are almost always fragmentary. A few of the People begin to use forms of fiction in order to reconstruct a sense of what the homeworld might have been like, and what a new homeworld free from the influence of the aliens might be like.

The African encounter with Europeans, the transatlantic slave trade, chattel slavery, segregation, and so forth can, if described differently, read like a dystopian science fiction/horror narrative. Indeed, Cornel West calls this encounter "The Absurd," calling to mind popular science fiction's penchant for using monolithic and imposing terminology to characterize invading alien entities.[2] These five-century-long encounters with white supremacy seem so all-encompassing, so pervasive, they threaten to completely short-circuit any imagination of a Black life beyond it. Our scholarly works are endeavors to show that Black folks have a history, have art, have sciences, and have religious worldviews independent of whiteness; nevertheless, those endeavors are responses to white supremacist claims of Black deficiencies. Indeed, our writings and other cultural productions are inextricably tied to the Absurd, the five-century white supremacist project that has positioned whiteness as inherently superior and any Black cultural production as inherently deficient, any Black history as insufficient, and any Black science as virtually nonexistent.

This chapter is a brief introduction into representations of African Americans in science fiction and Afrofuturism. This chapter will set the stage for later chapters and the examination of Afrofuturism's intersections with Black religious thought. Further, I will explore why this book will focus on Black religious thought instead of Black liberation and womanist theologies.[3] In short, this book seeks to engage Black religious thought as an expansive

---

2. *Star Trek* is not alone in this penchant: the Borg, or the Dominion, for example. *Doctor Who* has the Daleks and the Cybermen. *Star Wars*, of course, has the Sith and the Empire.

3. A note about nomenclature. While this book uses the term "Black religious thought and criticism," it is not different from West and Glaude's use of the term "African American religious thought." Further, this book capitalizes "Black" in reference to African Americans. This capitalization is intentional and has now been recognized by the Associated Press as the way to address Black peoples in the African diaspora.

intellectual field that incorporates Black liberation and womanist theologies but also other forms of Black religious experience, criticism, and thought.

Race in Science Fiction

When it comes to the presence of Black people in science fiction, the average layperson might say that there aren't many Black people in science fiction. Indeed, legend has it that when Whoopi Goldberg was a child and saw Lieutenant Uhura as part of the crew of the USS *Enterprise*, she ran to her mother and exclaimed that there was a Black woman on television, and she wasn't a maid.[4] Not only have Black people struggled to be represented in science fiction, they have struggled for recognition as producers and consumers of science fiction.

Unfortunately, depictions of Black people in science fiction film and television often follow the deeply problematic tropes found in other fiction genres. All too often, Black men and women are depicted in ways that conform to long-held stereotypes and caricatures. As Adilifu Nama put it in *Black Space: Imagining Race in Science Fiction Film*, "the structured absence of blackness has historically been a signature feature of the genre."[5] This structured absence is itself part and parcel of the (mis)representations of Black people in popular culture. As Nama goes on to state, even when Black people are absent in science fiction, their presence is keenly felt. Indeed, as Isaiah Washington notes in *Race in American Science Fiction*, American science fiction and its overwhelming concern with aliens, be it alien invasion, alien conversion, or some other form of alien encounter, may be read through the lens of America's obsession with race.[6]

Washington notes an example of that obsession in Philip K. Dick's *Do Androids Dream of Electric Sheep?* However, we can carry that obsession with race on into the film adaptation, the classic *Blade Runner* (1982). Throughout the film, set in a dystopian Los Angeles in the year 2019, we see that this future society has taken on an almost pan-Asian flavor. Stories-high advertisements feature Asian women, the street vendors are generally Asian men and women, and the dialect spoken is clearly informed by Chinese. However, there are no Africans or African Americans in the movie at all. What does such a complete erasure of Black people signify about how the pro-

---

4. "Goldberg," *Star Trek,* https://www.startrek.com/database_article/goldberg-whoopi.

5. Nama, *Black Space*, 10.

6. Lavender, *Race in American Science Fiction*, 26.

ducers of *Blade Runner* saw the existence of nonwhite persons in the future? Clearly, they saw the existence of Asians in a dystopian 2019, but where did all the Black people go? Did the producers not perceive the presence of Black people in 1982 Los Angeles?

This absence is problematic enough. However, when we consider the sparse presence of Black people in science fiction film and television, such sparse representations may be as troubling as complete erasure. Consider the presence of Lando Calrissian in *Star Wars: The Empire Strikes Back.* As will be mentioned briefly in a later chapter, Octavia Butler did not think much of his presence in the *Star Wars* saga. To examine his presence in *The Empire Strikes Back* is revealing. He is introduced as a "friend" of Han Solo and a last resort when Han, Leia, Chewbacca, and C-3PO are on the run from Darth Vader. However, it becomes readily apparent that he is not only flamboyant but also a liar, out to protect his own ill-gotten interests. Further, he betrays Han, Leia, and Chewbacca to the Empire. Billy Dee Williams's Calrissian is a stereotypical pimp, his capes and suave/predatory demeanor toward Leia signaling competition and threat to Han Solo. His presence in the sequel, *Return of the Jedi,* is supposedly a form of redemption after he betrayed Han, Leia, Chewbacca, and C-3PO to the Empire. In *Return,* Lando flies the *Millennium Falcon* and helps destroy the new Death Star. That said, he has very little character development in the original trilogy. Further, the recent standalone *Star Wars* movie, *Solo,* was supposed to hint at Lando's pansexuality, but no such reference made it into the final cut of the film. Again, the bulk of the character development was left to Han Solo.

That said, Nama contends that Lando Calrissian's roles in the original trilogy signify a "shifting and uncertain status of African Americans in the early 1980s."[7] Further, Nama reads Calrissian as a tokenized figure who represents white ambivalence toward Black upward mobility. If Calrissian represents such anxiety for white people, certainly that anxiety must be quelled. Nama notes that Calrissian is different from other Black characters in science fiction cinema in that he does not die: He survives to the end of *Return of the Jedi* and appears again in *The Rise of Skywalker,* the final episode of the *Skywalker Saga.*

More than surviving to the end of the original trilogy, Lando Calrissian garnered such interest as to be all but assured a prominent role in Lucasfilm's 2018 standalone *Han Solo* feature film. To that end, speculation ran wild regarding who would be cast as Lando. The announcement that Donald Glover would play the flamboyant scoundrel was met with great antici-

---

7. Nama, *Black Space,* 32.

pation. Indeed, in an interview with Ellen DeGeneres, Glover noted that his own mother cautioned him not to "mess it up."[8] While the movie itself received mixed reviews, Glover's performance was charming and inspired.

The recent *Star Wars* sequel trilogy (Episodes VII–IX) has been more visible in terms of racial representation. Trailers for the much-anticipated Episode VII began with the face of John Boyega playing a Stormtrooper. In *Star Wars: Episode VII: The Force Awakens*, Boyega's Finn (formerly designated FN-2187) defects from the First Order (a totalitarian entity that arose from the ashes of the defeated Empire in the original trilogy), rescues Resistance pilot Poe Dameron, and joins the Resistance. In the final movie, *The Rise of Skywalker*, we learn that Finn is "Force sensitive," something that had been hinted at in *The Force Awakens*, but not explored in the second movie, *The Last Jedi*. Additionally, the sequel trilogy added to its racial diversity by casting Guatemalan American actor Oscar Isaacs as Poe, Daisy Ridley as Rey, and Kelly Marie Tran as Rose Tico.[9]

The *Star Trek* franchise seems to have fared somewhat better than the Star Wars saga in terms of consistent racial representation. As will be detailed in the fourth chapter, nearly every series in the franchise has included African Americans as part of the series, beginning with Nichelle Nichols as Lieutenant Nyota Uhura in the original series on through the current series *Star Trek: Discovery*. However groundbreaking Nichols's appearance as a series regular was—and we cannot underestimate the impact of her presence on the bridge of the Federation starship *Enterprise*, since NBC executives wanted Gene Roddenberry to axe her from the show—Nichols nearly quit the series. In what is now a legendary narrative, worthy of the mythological status the series and the cast now occupy, Nichols encountered the Rev. Dr. Martin Luther King Jr. at an NAACP banquet, where he urged her to remain on the show. According to a *Vulture* article that referenced a Reddit Ask Me Anything that Nichols participated in,

---

8. Whitbrook, "Donald Glover's Mom Warns Him."

9. However, the nature of other forms of representation in *Star Wars* has been contested. For example, after *The Force Awakens*, some fans began producing fan art and fanfiction that explored the on-screen chemistry between Finn and Poe. Despite fan interest in seeing Finn and Poe become an on-screen couple, the characters barely interacted in *The Last Jedi*, the aforementioned Rose Tico served as a kind of love interest for Finn, and *The Rise of Skywalker* introduced a female bounty hunter as a prior love interest of Poe's. Indeed, Oscar Isaac pushed for an on-screen romance, but studio executives refused. See Laura Prudom, "Star Wars: Oscar Isaac Says 'Disney Overlords Weren't Ready' for Finn/Poe Romance," *IGN*, December 23, 2019, https://www.ign.com/articles/2019/12/23/star-wars-finn-poe-romance-star-wars-gay-rise-of-skywalker-oscar-isaac-disney.

King said something along the lines of "Nichelle, whether you like it or not, you have become a symbol. If you leave, they can replace you with a blonde-haired white girl, and it will be like you were never there. What you've accomplished, for all of us, will only be real if you stay."[10]

As a result of her role, NASA asked her to help recruit minorities into the space agency. Again, the legendary nature of the show and Nichelle Nichols's role as a nonstereotypical Black woman was cemented when astronaut Mae Jemison became the first African American woman to travel in space. She describes herself as a fan of *Star Trek* and, according to her entry on the *Star Trek* wiki page Memory Alpha, would begin each shift on the space shuttle *Endeavor* by "informing Mission Control in Houston that 'hailing frequencies were open,'" which was Lieutenant Uhura's signature phrase.[11]

This is not to say that *Star Trek* in all its incarnations has never had a problem with representations of race. Indeed, detractors of the series point to Lieutenant Uhura's diminished role by the show's third and final season and called the character little more than a glorified telephone switchboard operator. This kind of criticism is perhaps best exemplified in a sketch on the 1990s sketch comedy *In Living Color* called "The Wrath of Farrakhan." As a parody of *Star Trek II: The Wrath of Khan,* Louis Farrakhan (played by Damon Wayans) beams onto the bridge of the *Enterprise* in order to liberate the rest of the crew from Captain Kirk (played by Jim Carrey). When he turns to Uhura (played by Kim Wayans), he says, "Oh, my Nubian princess! How long have you placed his calls? I've watched this show every week and all I see is the back of your nappy wig!" Uhura responds to Carrey's Kirk indignantly and tells him to, in so many words, place his own calls.

I contend that such criticisms ignore that at least in the first two seasons, Uhura had more than just one simple line. Further, for the time period, her role was revolutionary in that she was not completely submissive, incompetent, or docile. I point to a first-season episode, "The Naked Time," in which the crew becomes infected with some kind of virus that causes them to act in an intoxicated fashion and the ship is imperiled as it spins out of control toward a disintegrating planet. An infected crewman seals off the engineering section and takes over control of communications, and begins flooding all the channels with his drunken singing. Eventually, Captain Kirk snaps at Uhura to turn off the unceasing noise, to which she replies, "I've been

---

10. Fitz-Gerald, "Read How Martin Luther King Jr. Affected *Star Trek*."
11. "Mae Jemison," Memory Alpha, https://memory-alpha.fandom.com/wiki/Mae_Jemison.

trying! Don't you think that if I could I would!!"[12] Such an outburst from a Black person to a white person—a commanding officer, no less—would have been unthinkable in the 1960s. Further, Captain Kirk actually apologizes to Lieutenant Uhura for his impatience. Another example of how Uhura was a revolutionary character was in the episode "Who Mourns for Adonais?," in which an entity that called itself Apollo jammed communication frequencies between the *Enterprise* and the landing party. Uhura was tasked with rewiring the communications circuitry in order to break through the interference and informed Commander Spock that her task was delicate work, for which Mr. Spock said, "I can think of no one better equipped" to handle the bypass work.[13]

The point of such an extended analysis of Uhura is to show that race in science fiction is not quite simply described. To be sure, television science fiction, including *Star Trek*, still had problematic relationships with presentations of Black characters. For example, the fourth episode of the 1987 revival of *Star Trek, Star Trek: The Next Generation*, was a deplorable representation of an all-Black planet. Indeed, this episode had the ruler of this planet inciting a fight between his consort, a Black woman, and Tasha Yar, a blond-haired white woman.[14]

Twentieth- and twenty-first-century television and cinematic science fiction has presented a conundrum regarding the representations of Black peoples. On the one hand, to have at least one Black person in a supposedly nonstereotypical role may be groundbreaking. However, that role may still be presented within and through the white stereotypical gaze. In other words, such presentations of Blackness are typically presented vis-à-vis the aegis of white supremacy. Any number of low- and big-budget science fiction movies in the twentieth and twenty-first centuries present Black bodies as disposable—so much so that science fiction had begun to follow the trope of Black bodies in horror films being the first to die. For example, the critically acclaimed and fan favorite movie *Star Trek II: The Wrath of Khan* has only one other Black character besides Commander Uhura. Captain Clark Terrell (played by the late Paul Winfield) commands the ill-fated USS *Reliant*, which is taken over by the twentieth-century genetically modified

12. *Star Trek*, "The Naked Time," directed by Marc Daniels, written by John D. F. Black, aired September 29, 1966, on Desilu Productions.

13. *Star Trek*, "Who Mourns for Adonais?," directed by Marc Daniels, written by Gilbert Ralston and Gene L. Coon, aired September 22, 1967.

14. The website Den of Geek describes "Code of Honor" as "quite possibly the worst piece of *Star Trek* ever made." James Hunt, "Revisiting Star Trek TNG: Code of Honor," *Den of Geek*, September 28, 2012, https://www.denofgeek.com/tv/revisiting-star-trek-tng-code-of-honor/.

supercriminal Khan Noonien Singh (played by Ricardo Montalban).[15] Khan implants mind-controlling Ceti eels in both Terrell and his first officer, Pavel Chekov. In a dramatic display, Terrell, having been ordered to kill Admiral Kirk, turns his phaser around and vaporizes himself. Certainly, to the cursory viewer, it would appear that *Star Trek* itself is not free from the narrative of the Black person being first to die—and doing so in order to save white people.[16]

What Is Afrofuturism?

Afrofuturism is Black people throughout the African diaspora taking science fiction, horror, fantasy, and other forms of speculative fiction and repurposing them into the service of more fully describing Black lives, experiences, and concerns.[17] Those concerns tend to revolve around the appropriation and appreciation of racial, sexual, and gender difference; technological interventions that determine the regulation and distribution of social services and basic human needs; and how such technologies (DNA markers and genetic testing, for example) are deeply informed by racism, sexism, and homophobia and further oppressive forms of social control.

Simply put, Black people were not supposed to imagine the future, much less write or sing about it. Indeed, Black people's songs about a future were to be confined to the spirituals and gospel music as part of the life of the church. Even then, those pleas were to be addressed to a white God, a white church, and a white Jesus. Afrofuturism is another element in Black people's history of taking the scraps left by white supremacist structures and institutions and turning them into enduring cultural productions. Like what Black people did with clothing, cuisine, and religion, science fiction was never supposed to be a space for Black people.

The term "Afrofuturism" was coined by Mark Dery in "Black to the Future: Interviews with Samuel R. Delany, Greg Tate, and Tricia Rose." Dery's claims regarding Black producers of science fiction may be problematic. For example, he asserts that there are few African Americans who write science fiction, an assumption that gives way upon deeper explora-

---

15. Khan first appears in the first-season episode, "Space Seed." Harve Bennett, the producer of *Wrath of Khan*, watched this episode and decided to bring this character back and center him as the main villain of the movie.

16. Nicholas Meyer, *Star Trek II: The Wrath of Khan* (June 4, 1982; USA: Paramount Home Video, August 6, 2002), DVD.

17. Anderson and Jones, *Afrofuturism 2.0*, x.

tion, which yields far more than a "few" African Americans who have written science fiction. Nevertheless, the term that he coined has persisted and taken hold in a way in such a way as to become the primary way in which we describe African American, African, and other diasporic African science fiction works.[18]

An example of the productive use of the term is found in Ytasha Womack's *Afrofuturism: The World of Black Sci-Fi and Fantasy Culture*. Describing herself as an Afrofuturist "before the term existed," Womack argues that

> any sci-fi fan, comic book geek, fantasy reader, Trekker, or science fair winner who ever wondered why black people are minimized in pop culture depictions of the future, conspicuously absent from the history of science, or marginalized in the roster of past inventors and then actually set out to do something about it could arguably qualify as an Afrofuturist as well.[19]

Her description of the Afrofuturist is far-ranging. Womack's description of Afrofuturism is not only wide-ranging, it is democratic, critical, and visionary. The "any" is diagnostic, in that any person who wishes to center Black lives and experiences through speculative fiction is an Afrofuturist. Such a conception of the Afrofuturist has been used to read Black science fiction literary productions back into African American literary history.

While Dery may have been the first person to coin the term, it is Alondra Nelson's pioneering use of a then-young internet to gather African American voices together as well as produce a more productive interpretation of the term. In 1998, Nelson founded an online community, and out of that community later emerged a special edition of the journal *Social Text*, in which some of the online contributors were able to further tease out the implications and meanings of "Afrofuturism" as a nascent term. In the introduction of that special issue, Nelson notes that "Afrofuturism can be broadly defined as 'African American voices' with 'other stories to tell about culture, technology, and things to come.'"[20]

Martin Delany's *Blake; or, The Huts of America* stands as a form of literary Black speculative fiction that predates contemporary Afrofuturism. This novel, which was initially published as a serial in the *Anglo-American Magazine*, might be one of the first forms of Black speculative fiction that engages the genre of alternate history. As a genre of speculative fiction, alternate

---

18. Dery, "Black to the Future," 179.
19. Womack, *Afrofuturism*, loc. 87, Kindle.
20. Nelson, "Introduction," 9.

history focuses on "what could have been"—Harry Turtledove's novels in which the Axis powers won World War II are an example of this genre.

In the case of Delany's novel, Blake tells the story of Henry Blake and his successful slave rebellion and subsequent founding of a Black nation in Cuba. For Samuel Delany (no relation), this narrative "is about as close to an sf-style alternate history novel as you can get."[21] This novel and its central figure embody a vision of a world in which a Black revolution not only occurs but is also successful. Here, we see a Black writer using speculative fiction in order to line up with a political agenda. Alex Zamalin describes "Blake" as imagining "Black liberation on Black terms."[22] Delany's fictional rebellion mirrors Delany's own quest for a Black nationalism.

Sheree Thomas's edited volume *Dark Matter: A Century of Speculative Fiction from the African Diaspora* includes W. E. B. Du Bois's apocalyptic short story "The Comet" as another pioneering work in Black science fiction. This short story appeared seventeen years after the publication of the landmark *Souls of Black Folk* in the collection *Darkwater: Voices from within the Veil*. It outlines the aftermath of Earth passing through a comet's tail, the devastation it wreaks, and the journey of two survivors of the devastation. In the case of this story, the first survivor we encounter—from whose point of view this story is told—is a Black man. In the moments before the disaster, he is a messenger, sent by a white bank president into the dank, disgusting, and dangerous vaults beneath the bank to retrieve old records. The story begins by establishing his position in the social order of New York: "Few noticed him. Few ever noticed him save in a way that stung. He was outside the world—'nothing!' as he said bitterly."[23] His "nobodiness" is clearly reinforced by the demand that he go into the lower vaults: "It was too dangerous for valuable men."[24] However, that dangerous work appears to be what saves him from the disastrous effects of the approaching comet's tail, for once he ascends out of the vaults, he sees that everyone is dead. Apparently, no one heeded the warnings splayed across newspapers that cautioned people to close their doors and windows and "seek the cellar."[25] Wandering the dead-strewn streets of Manhattan, Jim presently encounters another survivor of the comet, a young white woman. What follows might call to mind a form of re-creation story, a hopeful moment in which the two survivors of

21. Samuel R. Delany, "Racism and Science Fiction," *The New York Review of Science Fiction*, no. 120 (August 1998), https://www.nyrsf.com/racism-and-science-fiction-.html.

22. Zamalin, *Black Utopia*, 21.

23. W. E. B. Du Bois, "The Comet," 5.

24. Ibid.

25. Ibid, 7.

this disaster can become a new Adam and Eve, remaking the world beyond its racist foundations. Amidst this death and destruction, Jim and Julia seem ready to embrace a new destiny:

> A vision of the world had risen before her. Slowly the mighty prophecy of her destiny overwhelmed her. Above the dead past hovered the Angel of Annunciation. She was no mere woman. She was neither high nor low, white nor black, rich nor poor. She was primal woman; mighty mother of all men to come and Bride of Life. She looked upon the man beside her and forgot all else but his manhood, his strong, vigorous manhood—his sorrow and sacrifice. She saw him glorified. He was no longer a thing apart, a creature below, a strange outcast of another clime and blood, but her Brother Humanity incarnate, Son of God and great All-Father of the race to be.[26]

Du Bois weaves a religious sentiment into this narrative. Julia is not just going to be the Eve, mother of a new creation; Jim is now both the Incarnation and Odin. Here, Du Bois transforms a "white" god and recasts it in the form of a Black man. Julia—most likely through her own inheritance of white supremacy—saw herself as part of a prophecy. Julia is ready to shed herself of the racism that the old order had imposed upon her, and Jim is ready to walk into a new world in which his possibilities are not constrained. Indeed, this form of ending is a standard trope in more than a few apocalyptic science fiction movies and stories.[27] The new Adam and new Eve will usher in a new era for humankind, free of the oppression that preceded it. Du Bois's prose is lyrical and appears to build toward a consummation. However, in this case, the utopia that Jim and Julia envision is rudely interrupted. They are not the only survivors of this apocalypse. It was only New York City that experienced the destructive force of the comet. The survivors that Jim and Julia encounter immediately resurrect the violent and virulent racism that was supposed to have been part of the extinguished old order.

While Thomas herself does not employ the term "Afrofuturism" in the volume's introduction, I think her intention to foreground the voices of diasporic African writers as producers of science fiction is clearly within Womack's broad description of the work of the Afrofuturist. Until Thomas's anthology appeared, Du Bois's short story had not been widely invoked as an example of early Black science fiction. Like the dark matter that Thomas

---

26. Ibid, 15.

27. An example of such a trope is the 2009 science fiction mystery/thriller *Knowing*, in which aliens rescue the Earth's children from an extinction-level event. The final scene of the movie is a boy and girl being deposited on an Earth-like planet.

invokes in her anthology, the contributions of Black writers to the [science fiction] genre have not been directly observed or fully explored. For the most part, literary scholars and critics have limited their research largely to examinations of work by authors Samuel R. Delany and Octavia E. Butler, the two leading Black writers in the genre. This particular claim may be interpreted as an implicit critique of Dery's assertion that there are not many African Americans who produce science fiction. By presenting an array of literary work that spans a century, Thomas shows that Afrofuturism extends far beyond Samuel Delany and Octavia Butler. This collection of literary works by Africans in the diaspora is more than simply a descriptive collection. It is a form of resistance to a literary white supremacist imaginary that renders Black bodies as "spectres."

That said, Afrofuturism is not limited to literary visions. An interdisciplinary, multiformat field, Afrofuturism engages nearly every form of cultural production. As Womack puts it, Afrofuturism is "an intersection of imagination, technology, the future, and liberation."[28] It is a field of experimentation in which the Afrofuturist can engage music, art, or any other form of cultural production in order to center and reimagine Black lives and experiences. Returning to Dery's assertion that "so few African Americans write science fiction," the essay in which this assertion appears attends to the then-new Milestone Comics, founded and created in 1993 by Dwayne McDuffie, Denys Cowan, Michael Davis, and Derek T. Dingle. As an imprint of DC Comics, Milestone Comics featured Black, Latino, women, and gay superheroes. Sadly, Dery only mentions Milestone, but says nothing of its creators, who sought to diversify the overwhelmingly white superhero comic landscape. The subsequent conversation with Samuel Delany only refers to Milestone, but then swiftly moves back into the familiar terrain of canonical literary science fiction. When Dery poses a similar question to Greg Tate concerning the assumed "lack" of Black people writing and reading science fiction, Tate corrects him:

> I don't know that that's necessarily true; I've read SF [science fiction] since I was about twelve years old and I know a lot of black people who read it. Also, in comic book fandom, which is certainly a related field, 25 percent of the readership is black, which is pretty high. . . . According to the people at Milestone, the industry also knows that 50 percent of the comic readership is nonwhite—black, Latino, and Asian American. So I would argue

---

28. Womack, *Afrofuturism*, loc. 110, Kindle.

that the visionary vistas of SF contained in comics are definitely attracting black readers.[29]

Again, Dery appears to assume that Black people are absent en masse from science fiction either as consumers or producers. While we may credit Dery with coining the term that has become pervasive in describing and cataloging Black creative endeavors in the various forms of speculative fiction, it is fascinating that as he incorporates a discussion of Milestone Comics, he glosses over comic books as a viable avenue of science fiction. Tate's corrective is also interesting, as neither Tate nor Dery acknowledges that in interviews Octavia Butler expressed at least passing familiarity with and fondness for comic book characters like Superman.

Mark Bould's "The Ships Landed Long Ago" takes a different approach. He says that it is not his intention to "incorporate Afrofuturism into" science fiction. Rather, Bould contends that science fiction has "much to learn from the experience of technocultures that Afrofuturistic texts register across a wide range of media."[30] He does not want to position Afrofuturism as resistance. Instead, he wants to position Afrofuturism as joining with science fiction studies as part of a project of transformation. This piece, published in 2007, may be read as anticipating the emergence of a media-savvy figure like Janelle Monáe, who, as a later chapter will argue, wields capitalism in her presentation of self as a model of a liberated Black queer sexuality:

Afrofuturism tends towards the typical cyberpunk acceptance of capitalism as an unquestionable universe and working for the assimilation of certain currently marginalized peoples into a global system that might, at best, tolerate some relatively minor (although not unimportant) reforms, but within which the many will still have to poach, pilfer, and hide to survive.[31]

Thus, we might consider the early 1990s as the period in which Afrofuturism was in its latency. Consider that in this period, the Nation of Islam and its attendant racial mythologies experienced a brief but powerful resurgence, emergent technologies like the internet exposed Black people to other Black peoples (much like the Great Migration exposed Black refugees from the South to diasporic religions and cultures), and industries like the comic book industry saw prototypical forays into revising the dominant narratives.

---

29. Dery, "Black to the Future," 207.
30. Bould, "The Ships Landed Long Ago," 182.
31. Ibid.

One might expect Afrofuturism to be uniformly antagonistic toward or skeptical of religion. However, while some Black science fiction producers throughout the diaspora utilize Afrofuturism to critique religion, others also use Afrofuturism to retrieve religious practice and belief from monolithic descriptions. In a sense, Afrofuturism is a corrective to the larger field's presentation of and engagement with religion by showing that speculative fiction need not be hostile to religion. Afrofuturists from Samuel Delany to Octavia Butler to Nnedi Okorafor to Janelle Monáe center African and diasporic religious and spiritual practices as part of their Afrofuturistic landscapes.

Contemporary full-length examinations of Afrofuturism do not necessarily focus on the intersections of Afrofuturism and religion. As this book will later explore, several essays and book chapters have outlined connections between Afrofuturism and Black religious thought. However, a recent work examines the concept of utopia in Afrofuturism. While Alex Zamalin's *Black Utopia: The History of an Idea from Black Nationalism to Afrofuturism* is not solely an exploration of Afrofuturism and religion, it is an intriguing examination of several Afrofuturists and how they approach utopia as a political project. Zamalin's later chapters are of particular interest here, as they explore Sun Ra's and Octavia Butler's respective presentations of Blackness and utopia. Zamalin does not explore eschatology as Christophe Ringer does in his essay on the movie *District 9*. Rather, Zamalin focuses on Afrofuturism as a decidedly political project that is part and parcel of other African American attempts at achieving utopia. Indeed, the closest that Zamalin comes to describing what this book considers an eschatological approach is in the introduction:

> Utopia is like religion not because of the dogmatic theology or secular truths it postulates, but because it conjures powerful, irrepressible, sometimes ecstatic feelings: of salvation, of being at home in the world, and of reconciliation with strife. For this reason, utopia is as fruitful a site from which to test the value of our extant political formulations as it is a horizon toward which we might look to improve our lives.[32]

While Zamalin describes utopia as like religion, I want to posit Afrofuturism as providing visions of utopia that are part of religion and may be understood as part of Black religious thought.

---

32. Zamalin, *Black Utopia*, 6.

CHAPTER 2

Black Religious Thought and Afrofuturism

Curtis Evans's *The Burden of Black Religion* argues that Black religion has borne a great burden in shaping larger views of African Americans. Evans addresses the narrative that Black religion in general and the Black church in particular points to a "naturally religious" nature of Black people. While Evans's book is a genealogy and a refutation of this burden, we might ask about the nature of Black religious criticism in the twenty-first century. The epilogue appears to do that. Following Robert Orsi's warning to adopt different views of religion and culture, Evans hopes that Black religious thought will be released "from the dichotomous interpretations of black religion that continue to be driven by past debates and [will be] a bit more modest in [an] appraisal of how people work within a culture that is always working on them. Newer work must movie beyond the black church and free up scholars to construct more interesting and empirically grounded narratives, thereby partially lifting the burden that has weighed so heavily on histories and interpretations of African American religion."[1]

Michael Eric Dyson describes Black cultural criticism as a Black intellectual project and constellation of Black activity that resists monolithic presentations of Black identity. As one of the standard bearers for late

---

1. Evans, *The Burden of Black Religion*, 280.

twentieth-century Black cultural and religious criticism, Dyson's early works are "concerned to examine the redemptive and unattractive features of African-American culture, to pass fair but critical judgment on a variety of cultural expressions and historic figures."[2] As Victor Anderson notes in *Beyond Ontological Blackness,* cultural criticism in general "will be both culturally enlightening and emancipatory."[3] Both Dyson's and Anderson's claims hold that Black cultural productions (including Black religious life and productions) can be paradoxical. They can be enlightening and emancipatory as they present manifold visions of Black identities and Black cultures. However, they can be simultaneously problematic if and when they reinforce cultural stereotypes and promote homophobia, classism, and sexism.

This chapter will further outline the contours of Black religious thought. This chapter also will engage Black religious thought's approaches to Black popular culture. Finally, this chapter will introduce the potential connections between Black religious thought and Afrofuturism.

We may trace what we describe as Black religious thought back to W. E. B. Du Bois's foundational *Souls of Black Folk,* particularly Du Bois's assessment of the Sorrow Songs. Indeed, Du Bois himself describes the work as sketching the spiritual world of African Americans.[4] This work, along with Du Bois's foundational sociological work regarding Black communities, lays the foundation for later scholars of Black religion. Black religious thought and criticism may include and interrogate Black liberation and womanist theological claims, but it is not wholly bound by those claims. The Black religious and cultural critic may be informed by a different array of intellectual and cultural sources and may seek to describe Black religious lives and experiences through those sources.

Examples of the above are found in the work of scholars like Cornel West, Michael Eric Dyson, Anthony Pinn and Monica Miller, Victor Anderson, and bell hooks. Their analyses of rap, rhythm and blues, movies, and television grounded their work and made their scholarship "popular," or accessible to general audiences. As Anderson noted, Black cultural and religious criticism, is, at its heart, a set of emancipatory projects. West, hooks, Cone, Delores Williams, Katie Cannon, Dyson, and a host of Black and womanist theologians and cultural critics engage African American religious traditions and cultural life in order to present alternatives to pervasive and systemic white supremacy. These attempts at presenting alternatives to systemic white supremacy are at their best when they engage the Western

2. Dyson, *Reflecting Black,* xxv.

3. Anderson, *Beyond Ontological Blackness,* 21.

4. Du Bois, *The Souls of Black Folk,* 3.

philosophical and theological tradition. They are at the height of academic prowess when they engage with Black popular cultures and deconstruct the histories of white supremacist thought.

In *African American Religious Thought: An Anthology*, editors Cornel West and Eddie Glaude set forth the trajectory of Black religious thought. In the introduction, West and Glaude explicitly state, "We do not hold the view that theological education frames the entire enterprise of African American religious studies."[5] This claim is based upon seeing Black religious thought and criticism as dynamic, fluid, and responsive to shifts and changes within African American religious experiences. West and Glaude's primary approach in the anthology is a "historical periodization" using history, theology, and cultural criticism as framing disciplines.[6] Their third point regarding African American religious studies is instructive and informs the outline of this book:

> African American religious studies critically engages the way "black religion" is understood—extending the analysis beyond an assessment of the place of black religion and its institutions in American society to a more critical analysis of the discursive and ritualistic formations that question traditional scholarly categories and *open up new sites for investigation.*[7]

West and Glaude's approach to Black religious thought is a project that assesses "black religion" with an eye toward expanding "black religion" beyond the Black church. Their explorations of Black religion might be better framed by using the plural "religions." They represent an intellectual trajectory that might be expanded to find Black religious formation in areas *other* than the "traditional Black church." Indeed, for West, Dyson, and others, it is Black popular culture that stands as a "new site for investigation." Following these scholars, Black religious thought and criticism in the case of this project does not focus on the Black church or other institutionalized religions as the only way to understand Black religious life. To the last part of their assessment of the usefulness of African American religious studies, their claim that expanding the analysis beyond Black religious institutions means opening up new sites for investigation is provocative. It also informs this book's centering Afrofuturism and a Black science fiction imagination. If Glaude and West are right in their assertion that Black religious thought is at a crossroads and the anthology is intended to bring the field into the

---

5. West and Glaude, *African American Religious Thought*, xii.

6. Ibid., xxiv.

7. Ibid., xxv; my emphasis.

future, it might be appropriate to ask how Afrofuturism as part of Black popular culture may interact with this field. Examples of this trajectory in Black religious thought are manifold. Judith Weisenfeld's *Hollywood Be Thy Name* and *New World A-Coming,* Barbara Savage's *Your Spirits Walk Beside Us,* and LeRhonda Manigault-Bryant's *Talking to the Dead* speak to the critical function of Black religious thought's use of multiple forms of Black cultural productions. These works call into question the reliance upon African American Christianity as the primary lens through which we understand African American religious lives.

As a partner of Black religious thought, Black liberation and womanist theologians have begun to substantively address Black popular culture in their work. *The Spirituals and the Blues,* one of James Cone's early foundational works, explored the spirituals and the blues as a source for doing Black liberation theology. Womanist theologians routinely explore Black women's literature as a source for womanist theological reflection. For example, Robert Patterson's 2014 essay "Do You Want to Be Well? The Gospel Play, Womanist Theology, and Tyler Perry's Artistic Project" represents a typical academic interrogation of Tyler Perry's work. Patterson suggests that Perry's representations of Black women would be better served through a closer attention to womanist theology. Ronald Neal's examination of Perry in his 2016 essay "Spike Lee Can Go Straight to Hell! The Cinematic and Religious Masculinity of Tyler Perry" explores how Perry's productions reproduce particular images of Black masculinity. Neal focuses on Perry's presentation of masculinity, "juxtaposing Perry and [Spike] Lee and their differing conceptions of Black masculinity."[8] While Neal's piece does not address Black women, the volume *Womanist and Black Feminist Responses to Tyler Perry,* coedited by LeRhonda Manigault-Bryant, Tamura Lomax, and Carol Duncan, is a showcase of womanist and Black feminist critiques of Tyler Perry's oeuvre. This volume might appear as though it would be a thoroughly negative assessment of Perry's works. However, in keeping with the function of Black religious thought, this volume asks a critical question: "Is Perry's work life-giving or death-dealing to Black women and girls?"[9] As Emilie Townes notes in the foreword, this interdisciplinary volume takes Perry and his impact on African American cultural and religious life seriously.[10] Tamura Lomax's 2018 book *Jezebel Unhinged: Loosing the Black Female Body in Religion and Culture* is an examination of the "jezebel trope in the

8. Neal, "Spike Lee Can Go Straight to Hell!," 139.

9. Manigault-Bryant, Lomax, and Duncan, *Womanist and Black Feminist Responses to Tyler Perry,* 1.

10. Ibid., xiv.

black church and in black popular culture, showing how it is pivotal to reinforcing men's cultural and institutional power to discipline and define black girlhood and womanhood."[11] This book is a corrective to what Lomax perceives as a gap in Black feminist scholarship on the representations of Black women's bodies. As she notes in the introduction, Black feminists have laid out "robust critical discourse[s] on race, gender, sexuality, and representation." However, Lomax is concerned that these scholars have not significantly engaged religion. Again, from the introduction, she notes:

> Though Harris-Perry and a few others have taken up religion, there is no book-length black feminist study on the powerful functionality of race, gender, and representation within black religion. And there is no study that critically underscores the significant and collaborative work of discourse, which includes a range of speech acts such as talking and modes of writing and representation, circulating between black religion and black popular culture.[12]

Further, Lomax wants to engage in this study on the intersections of race, gender, and representation using the tools gained from both Black feminist scholarship and womanist theological scholarship. She sees her work as bridging gaps and challenging these particular intellectual modes of analysis.

In terms of Afrofuturism and Black religious scholars bridging gaps and presenting new connections, this is where scholars like Monica Coleman and Michael Brandom McCormack enter. Through their analyses of Octavia Butler's science fiction, Coleman and McCormack have signaled a new pathway for Black religious scholars, theologians, and critics. Coleman's discussion of Octavia Butler in *Making a Way Out of No Way* and a 2014 conference on Afrofuturism and Black religion and a subsequent special issue of the journal *Black Theology* represent initial engagements with Afrofuturism and Black theology. These engagements often function to broaden Black theological descriptions of God. These particular works highlight what I think is a shift in Black theological and religious thought.

Coleman's *Making a Way Out of No Way* is the continuation of her work in *Ain't I a Womanist?: Third Wave Womanism*. In this book, Coleman seeks a constructive womanist theology, partially as a continued response to the critiques of her 2016 essay "Must I Be a Womanist?" The introduction to

---

11. From the description of the book on the Duke University Press website: https://www.dukeupress.edu/jezebel-unhinged.

12. Lomax, *Jezebel Unhinged*, 4.

Ain't I a Womanist situates her search for a "postmodern womanist theology" within the context of working with Black women who are at the margins of society. Coleman seeks a womanist theology that can make use of multiple intellectual and cultural sources, including process theology and Black women's science fiction. Further, she is concerned that Black liberation and womanist theologies are primarily preoccupied with and dominated by Christianity. Her concern is that such a rigid alliance with Christianity does not speak to the diversity of Black women's religious experiences. This concern is, as mentioned above, an ongoing response from "Must I Be a Womanist?" and her argument that womanist theology only takes Black Christian experiences seriously and as a focus for theological engagement.

Regarding her use of Black women's science fiction, Coleman characterizes it as postmodern. As we take her description of postmodernity, Black women's science fiction fits neatly with the aims and goals of the book. She examines Octavia Butler's *Parable* series as a lens into a communal theology. This theology that Coleman constructs is not concerned with esoteric discussions about a remote God who theoretically sides with the oppressed. After discussing two Black women's experiences, one traumatic and demanding an answer from the God of Christianity, the other joyful but not rooted in Christianity, Coleman notes:

> I believe that insights from womanist theology and process theology can give me an answer to Lisa's questions about the problem of evil and Maria's declarations about survival, healing, and salvation. In a postmodern womanist theology, I can find a language that has a rich past, resonates with spirit and memory, and evokes images particular to the experiences of black women. . . . A postmodern womanist theology can explain why salvation is found both among black women braiding hair in a church on a rainy night and black women dancing to a drumbeat in an old warehouse on a sunny Sunday morning. A postmodern womanist theology is able to talk about how we can make a way out of no way.[13]

Coleman wants to construct a theology that speaks to the "constant sense of change in the world and how we exist in the midst of stability and instability."[14] Change exists at the heart of Coleman's theological project. Based on her work with Black women at the margins, she concludes that she needed a postmodern womanist theology that is not thoroughly rooted in

---

13. Coleman, *Making a Way Out of No Way*, 8–9.
14. Ibid., 45.

the Christianity of mainline churches. In a sense, the *Parables'* Lauren Olamina's discomfort and rejection of her father's church and God parallels Coleman's own quest for a more inclusive theology.

The 2016 issue of *Black Theology: An International Journal* contains several essays that emerged from the 2014 Vanderbilt Divinity School symposium on Afrofuturism and Black Theology. According to Terrence Dean and Dale Andrews, the essays sought to address Afrofuturism as "an evolving field of study in Black cultural studies" in connection with Black religion and theology.[15] At the symposium, I presented a paper on the *Star Trek: Deep Space Nine* episode "Far Beyond the Stars" but did not submit it for the journal—this essay will appear in a heavily modified form later in this book. I will focus on two essays that I think have critical bearing on this book.

Christophe Ringer's "Afrofuturism and the DNA of Biopolitics in the Black Public Sphere" is an intriguing piece. Here, Ringer centers the 2009 movie *District 9* as an example of the intersection between race, religion, and biopolitics. His argument is that emerging technological interventions using DNA build upon the prior racial order created in and through chattel slavery. Simply put, DNA-mapping technology is in no way free of the racial and racist assumptions regarding Black bodies that was inscribed through the attempts at cultural and religious justification of the transatlantic slave trade, chattel slavery, and subsequent racial discrimination. To that end, Ringer proposes transcendence through eschatology as a remedy. Ringer shifts the discussion concerning religion and eschatology away from traditional understandings. For him, eschatology is "an interpretive frame to engage Afrofuturism."[16] Further, he says:

> Transcendence of the past is the effect of the experience of the new possibilities in the present. As such, eschatology provides a hermeneutical bridge between religious discourses and contemporary theorists and theories concerned with the persons who are rendered as mere bodies, bare life, flesh and meat.[17]

Given the above, it makes sense that Ringer would turn to the movie *District 9*, since the movie is clearly a science fiction parable regarding racial anxiet-

---

15. Terrance Dean and Dale P. Andrews, "Introduction: Afrofuturism in Black Theology—Race, Gender, Sexuality, and the State of Black Religion in the Black Metropolis," Taylor&Francis Online, April 3, 2016, https://www.tandfonline.com/doi/full/10.1080/14769948.2015.1131499.

16. Ringer, "Afrofuturism and the DNA of Biopolitics," 57.

17. Ibid., 59.

ies about the body and social class. Drawing on Paul Tillich, Ringer establishes that global capitalism is the religion that centers *District 9*. Thus, the movie and the transformation of the central character Wikus is a "horrific racial tragedy rooted in biopolitics."[18] If this movie is a horror film rooted in racial biopolitics, then our emerging understandings of DNA and the ability to trace our ancestral roots may offer an eschatological balm to such horror. Ringer notes:

> Afrofuturism in its imaginative capacity may prove an important resource for science and technology to become an integral part of theological reflection. As commercial advances in genomic technology aimed at consumers increase, the insights of science will become far more acute if theology is to have a voice in our understanding of what it means to be human.[19]

As compelling as that statement is, Ringer's theological argument is somewhat underdeveloped. The analysis of *District 9* as a science fictional representation of our deep ambivalence regarding the body and race is compelling, but it also lacks a deeper connection of this movie to Afrofuturism. Indeed, it is not clear what might qualify this movie as Afrofuturism, except that the movie is set in a near-future South Africa and the white South African Wikus serves as a stand-in for the oft-dehumanized Black body. Nevertheless, Ringer's claim that Afrofuturism is an imaginative resource also points to the possibilities of Black theological approaches that utilize imaginative and creative aspects of Black cultural productions.

Another compelling essay in the special issue is Michael Brandon McCormack's "Your God Is a Racist, Sexist, Homophobic, and a Misogynist . . . Our God Is Change: Ishmael Reed, Octavia Butler, and Afrofuturist Critiques of (Black) American Religion." McCormack situates Reed's play "The Preacher and the Rapper" and Butler's *Parable* books as Afrofuturist critiques of the respectability politics of the 1980s and '90s that emanated from conservative forms of Black Christianity and policed Black popular culture. The play reverses the centrality of Christianity by shifting from the 1990s to the future (2014), by which time a former rapper has now become a practitioner of Santeria. By this imagined 2014, the not-so-subtly-named Rev. Jack Legge is in disgrace. When he meets again with Ogun (formerly named 3 Strikes), Ogun says that Legge's god is "racist, sexist, homophobic, and a misogynist."

---

18. Ibid., 63.
19. Ibid., 67.

Indeed, the racist, sexist, misogynistic, and homophobic God of "The Preacher and the Rapper" is also present in Butler's *Parable* series. McCormack notes that Butler's dystopian America is the counterpunch to Reed's multicultural, multifaith future. Further, McCormack explicitly situates the *Parables* as religious criticism, since Lauren Olamina rejects her Baptist father's God. Further, McCormack positions Earthseed as a "pragmatic naturalist theology" that, through its focus on the stars as part of human destiny, gives humankind an eschatological hope.[20]

Both McCormack and Coleman use Afrofuturism as a way to move beyond Black Christianity as the center of Black religious experience. I would argue that McCormack and Coleman find in Butler—and, by extension, in Afrofuturism—the cultural resources necessary to push beyond Black theologies rooted in the church. In *Making a Way out of No Way,* Coleman notes:

> Using black women's science fiction as a theological resource stretches both womanist theology and postmodern metaphysics in new directions. Because black women's science fiction includes elements of traditional African religions, it helps womanist theology to include the non-Christian religious dimensions of black religion in its scope. Black women's literature can also have a prophetic function in theology. Black women's science fiction can provide concrete images, models and proposals for what could happen or what should happen.[21]

This stretching of womanist theology using Butler is an imaginative way for Coleman to succinctly critique womanist theology without leveling controversial charges. In this way, Lauren Olamina's critique of her father's God can function as Coleman's critique of the all-powerful, all-loving God of Black liberation and womanist theology.

Michael Brandon McCormack's thesis closely echoes this book's thesis. In the introduction to his essay, McCormack argues

> that a more substantive engagement with Afrofuturism is consistent with trajectories in Black and womanist religious thought, which have long privileged Black cultural courses (i.e. spirituals, slave narratives and folk tales) as data for critical analysis and constructive religious reflection, while posing emancipatory visions for communities of color.[22]

20. McCormack, "Your God Is a Racist," 22.
21. Coleman, *Making a Way Out of No Way,* 131.
22. McCormack, "Your God Is a Racist," 8.

Both Coleman and McCormack represent a potential shift in Black theological and religious thought. They represent a growing number of Black religious scholars who want to push their work beyond repeated analyses of the Black church and traditional Black liberation and womanist theologies as the primary frameworks by which we understand Black religious experiences. Coleman focuses on Octavia Butler's *Parable* books, as this book will as well. As I will discuss in the next chapter, Butler's *Parable* series represents what I will call "intersectional Afrofuturism." Intersectional Afrofuturism critiques and revises our views of gender, sexuality, and race. As the central figure of the *Parable* books, Lauren Olamina does not function as a heroic figure. My proposal of an intersectional Afrofuturism contends that it is not preoccupied with the heroic narratives offered by traditional science fiction and Black cultural criticism. Further, similar to what McCormack teases the reader with via an analysis of Ishmael Reed and Octavia Butler, this book delves into in a deeper fashion via extended analyses of other forms of Afrofuturism and Black science fiction.

The essays in the special issue of *Black Theology* were mostly concerned with literary Afrofuturism. Indeed, Ringer's essay on *District 9* is the only piece that directly examines popular science fiction through an Afrofuturistic lens. This preoccupation with Afrofuturistic literary expressions emerges from a larger theological and cultural use of Black literature. Black liberation and womanist theologies as well as Black cultural criticism attend to Black literary productions as a productive means of interpreting Black life. This attention to Black literature mirrors dominant cultural theory that privileges literature, certain musical forms, art, and so forth as "high culture."

The conceit that undergirds privileging Afrofuturistic literature is that literary science fiction exists as a "better" form of cultural production than science fiction film and television, even if that acceptance was slow in coming.[23] However, as science fiction film and television programs gained cultural cachet—due, in large part, to science fiction fans "growing up" and ascending into positions of power, creative control, and influence—we have seen the emergence of terms like "classic science fiction" and online debates about the relative merits of movie franchises and television shows. Consider, for example, the online debates surrounding the latest *Star Wars* movies or *Star Trek: Discovery*, the latest in the venerable *Star Trek* franchise.[24] The ongoing debates, particularly concerning the second installment in the *Star Wars*

---

23. Tymn, "Science Fiction," 48–49.

24. An example is *"The Last Jedi* Killed My Childhood, and That's Exactly Why It's Great" (https://io9.gizmodo.com/the-last-jedi-killed-my-childhood-and-thats-exactly-wh-1821429836).

sequel trilogy and whether or not these movies are good or should be held in the same regard as the original trilogy and even the prequel movies, highlight the intersecting (yet oddly conflicting) critiques of the movies' merits in terms of storytelling, plot and character development, and diversity and inclusion. Similar arguments have swirled around *Discovery*, as some fans have decried the series as being "too dark" and too much a divergence from what they think *Star Trek* creator Gene Roddenberry would have envisioned.

As the aim of this book is a sustained critical engagement with Afrofuturism as a lens into Black religious and cultural thought, a reader may ask a second question: "Why not theology?" This project is not a theological project. That is to say, this particular project is not immediately concerned with presenting a theology based on Afrofuturism; rather, it is an analysis of Black religious life and thought that should, as West and Glaude indicate, plumb the depths of new sites of critical inquiry. Taking a cue from Butler, Monáe, *Star Trek*, and Wakanda, the project took shape around an endeavor to tease out as much as possible the possibilities inherent in Afrofuturistic religious thought.

These possibilities include expanded views of divinity and divinities that go far beyond Western monotheisms. They involve expanded views of Black identities that move beyond heroic and monolithic Blackness—Afrofuturism also gives some form of eschatological view that, while attending to white supremacy, is not bound by it. Those views of the future use the speculative to also critique current social problems. Afrofuturism joined with Black religious thought critiques not just white supremacy, but also homophobia, sexism, classism, and the exploitation of human beings through the misuses of technology.

Conclusion: The Possibility of Afrofuturism as Religious Thought and Criticism

This chapter has sketched brief histories and trajectories in Afrofuturism and Black religious thought. The following chapters will highlight several examples of Afrofuturist writers, musicians, and cultural productions as forms of Black religious thought and criticism. In keeping with Glaude and West, and Ringer, Coleman, and McCormack, the following chapters draw on broader understandings of Black religious thought. Further, as McCormack notes, Afrofuturism offers a wealth of resources with which to re-vision Black religious thought. However, different from his essay, I might want to go a step further and posit Afrofuturism *as* religious thought and criticism. Afrofuturistic religious thought does not necessarily center the Christian God and its attendant Western modes of description and thought or the centering of the Black Christian church as a primary node of religious experience. However, Afrofuturistic religious thought does not automatically exclude God or the church. Indeed, as this book will articulate, Afrofuturism often holds God and religious institutions in tension with Black experiences. Such tensions are hardly ever neatly resolved. Perhaps the God concept collapses in on itself in order to give rise to new ways of thinking and writing about matters of ultimate concern. We might say that Afrofuturistic religious thought is open to multiple forms of religious expressions or no religious expressions at all.

PART II

Intersections

CHAPTER 3

Octavia Butler as Architect of Intersectional Afrofuturism

Octavia Butler once said that she began writing about power because she "had so little of it."[1] A Black woman writing in a field deemed the province of white heterosexual men may have rightly concluded that she had little power. Being—as she described herself—"a comfortably antisocial hermit in Seattle" hints that a person who is a study in contrasts might have or wield little power. Both in her first year of college and again at a science fiction convention, Butler heard white men claim that the presence of Black characters in a story would somehow detract from the overall premise and power of a story.[2] The promise of Afrofuturism is its re-visioning of Black lives, and giving Black futurists a power denied them by white supremacy. White supremacy in science fiction continues the legacy of the transatlantic kidnapping, enslavement, and ongoing subjugation of Black bodies. By attempting to deny Black people any space in producing science fiction, white supremacy is upheld, and the white imaginary may proceed unchecked. As noted in the previous chapter, Afrofuturism is not a naively utopian project; Afrofuturists use multiple cultural forms to examine the possibilities of Blackness. The next two chapters will attend to Octavia Butler and Janelle Monáe

---

1. Sommerlad, "Octavia Butler."
2. Butler, "Lost Races of Science Fiction," 181.

as what I call "architects of intersectional Afrofuturism." By that, I contend that their respective writings and musical productions consciously center Black women who are also not necessarily gender-conforming. From Butler's *Parable* duology to Monáe's body of musical work, both acknowledge the necessity of telling more than a single story as they weave race, class, gender, sexual orientation, and religion to present complex and compelling futuristic narratives of Blackness.[3]

The task of this and the subsequent chapters is to situate and center producers and the productions of Afrofuturism as pointing toward greater possibilities—the "what if?"—of Blackness. In this particular chapter, Octavia Butler as a shaper of Afrofuturism, an architect of intersectionality within Afrofuturism, consciously sought to alter the terrain of Black cultural and religious life and thought. As Michael Brandon McCormack notes in his essay on Butler and Afrofuturism, her decision to situate religion as a central element in the *Parable* series offers readers "possibilities for imagining alternative emancipatory forms of Black theological discourse and religious practice."[4] Her autobiographical sketch, "Positive Obsession," printed as an addendum to *Bloodchild*, articulates the cultural mores that unconsciously worked against Black creativity and imagining multiple possibilities for Black life. I will quote her at length:

> So, then, I write science fiction and fantasy for a living. As far as I know I'm still the only Black woman who does this. When I began to do a little public speaking, one of the questions I heard most often was, "What good is science fiction to Black people?" I was usually asked this by a Black person. . . . But the answer to that was obvious. . . . A young Black woman once said to me, "I always wanted to write science fiction, but I didn't think there were any Black women doing it." . . . What good is any form of literature to Black people? What good is science fiction's thinking about the present, the future, and the past? What good is its tendency to warn or to consider alternative ways of thinking and doing? . . . At its best, science fiction stimulates imagination and creativity. It gets reader and writer off the beaten track, off the narrow, narrow footpath of what "everyone" is saying, doing, thinking—whoever "everyone" happens to be this year.[5]

3. TED, "The Danger of a Single Story: Chimamanda Ngozi Adichie," YouTube, October 7, 2009, https://www.youtube.com/watch?v=D9Ihs241zeg.

4. McCormack, "Your God Is a Racist," 24.

5. Butler, *Bloodchild*, 187–88a.

She ends the meditation by reiterating the question "What good is all this to Black people?"

Ytasha Womack quotes Alondra Nelson as saying that "Afrofuturism is a feminist movement."[6] Octavia Butler is the personification of this assessment. Her many novels and short stories featured Black women as central characters. Further, Butler's claim that she was writing about power because she had so little of it is a reference to the intersections of her identity as a Black woman (and science fiction writer). I do not think it a coincidence that Olamina is juxtaposed against a white (presumably heterosexual) male who initiates a theocratic regime. Butler's writings, like those of fellow pioneer Samuel Delany, interrogate race, gender, and sexuality via the field of science fiction.

This chapter draws on Susana Morris's essay on Butler's final published novel, *Fledgling*, and her linkage of Afrofuturism with Black feminist thought. Morris argues that both Afrofuturism and Black feminism are speech acts that "talk back," a concept that bell hooks notes is tied to "terms of coalition and power sharing."[7] This synthesis of Afrofuturism and Black feminism is productive in that it further fleshes out the liberating possibilities of Afrofuturism. Further, I turn to Kimberlé Crenshaw's intersectionalism as a focal point for understanding Octavia Butler. Crenshaw's landmark essays "Demarginalizing the Intersection of Race and Sex: A Black Feminist Critique of Antidiscrimination Doctrine, Feminist Theory and Antiracist Politics" and "Mapping the Margins: Intersectionality, Identity Politics, and Violence Against Women of Color" lay the intellectual groundwork for understanding the multiple vectors of oppression that Black women experience.

Butler repeatedly notes both to herself and others that she is writing out of the intersection of herself as a Black woman—and a fan of science fiction. How many other Black people wrote to Marvel Comics to express their concern after Jack Kirby left Marvel?[8] Perhaps many did—far more than would have been understood to have been science fiction/comic book fans. We might say that Blerds—especially Black women nerds—are automatically intersectional.

To describe Butler and Delany as pioneers in science fiction is not an understatement. Delany described himself as "the first broadly known

6. Womack, *Afrofuturism,* loc. 1262.

7. Susana Morris, "Black Girls Are from the Future," 154.

8. OEB 4072, letter to Stan Lee, 1970.

African American science fiction writer" and Butler as the second.[9] Their presence and work influenced and continues to influence Black science fiction and fantasy authors. For example, fantasy author Charles R. Saunders described Delany as a "formidable intellect" and Butler as a "storyteller" whose book *Wild Seed* "is the best evocation of the black experience in an SF [science fiction] setting."[10] Further, Saunders says, "One could also say that her work is more accessible than that of Delany, who sometimes writes on a more esoteric literary and intellectual plane. If there were only one reason why blacks should read science fiction, it would be the writings of Octavia Butler."[11] Indeed, in his introduction to "The Octavia Butler Papers," Gerry Canavan notes that Butler has been so extensively studied, it might appear that there is little if anything any scholar can say about Butler that has not already been said.[12]

However, I think that there can be just a bit more said about Octavia Butler in general, and the *Parable of the Sower* and *Parable of the Talents* books in particular. When speaking about Lauren Oya Olamina, the central character of the *Parable* series, Butler described her as the person she wanted to be. Butler also describes herself thusly: "I'm a pessimist if I'm not careful, a feminist, a Black, a former Baptist, an oil and water combination of ambition, laziness, insecurity, certainty, and drive."[13] I might posit Butler as the quintessential Black nerd. She describes her love of science fiction as having begun after watching a sci-fi movie and thinking that she could write a better story—and so she did. She mentioned reading superhero comic books—Superman and Marvel comics specifically—and her comments regarding Black presence in television shows like *Star Trek* and movies like *The Empire Strikes Back* are diagnostic. In a 1980 interview with Rosalie G. Harrison, Butler articulated what makes science fiction distinctive for her:

> *I think science fiction writers are a little bit more willing to use their minds.* They want different things to think about. They don't want to read about things as they are. They're bored with the present. Maybe they want to escape from the present. A lot of science fiction readers start out as the weird kid,

9. Cecilia D'Anastasio, "Samuel R. Delany Speaks," *The Nation*, August 24, 2015, https://www.thenation.com/article/samuel-r-delany-speaks/.

10. Bell, "A Charles R. Saunders Interview," 91.

11. Saunders, "Why Blacks Should Read (and Write) Science Fiction," in *Dark Matter*, 400.

12. Canavan, "The Octavia Butler Papers," 42.

13. Canavan, *Octavia E. Butler*, 1.

the out kid in junior high or grade school. . . . People who are, or were, rejects.[14]

In this interview, Butler is articulating how science fiction is able to harness the imagination in order to posit possible futures. At this level, Butler as the quintessential Black nerd, the Black nerd before "Blerd" became part of the cultural landscape, pointed to the larger experience of Black people as both outcasts and desiring not to be outcasts. It is an existential conundrum. A later interview illuminates her view that science fiction appeals to rejects and "weird kids" when she discusses having been called gay when she was younger. She noted:

I eventually wondered if they might not be right, so I called the Gay and Lesbian Services Center and asked if they had meetings where people could talk about such things. I wound up going down there twice, at which point I realized, Nope, this ain't it. I also realized, once I thought it over, that I'm a hermit. I enjoy my own company more than I enjoy most other people's— and going to parties or trying to meet Mr. or Mrs. Right or whatever simply doesn't appeal to me.[15]

We may infer from this that Butler viewed herself as asexual. However, her lack of a discussion of a personal sex life and sexual identity should not be taken as a declaration. Rather, I read it as another way in which Butler queers our expectations. In reading womanist thought, we see that Black women have historically been forced to define themselves over and against white and Black male heterosexual expectations.[16] Her refusal to do so may be read as a rejection of gendered and sexual binaries. This is just a peek into Butler's personality and the contestations that inform her writing. Butler began writing science fiction in a period in which there were no Black women writing science fiction, nor was there any science fiction that centered Black women. Further, her writings emerged in a period in which Black women's writing consistently challenged heteronormative notions and assertions. I find a kind of affinity in Butler, a sense of the self that seems always set just at the margins of society.

In describing Butler as "an architect of intersectional Afrofuturism," I am saying that her work precedes the conception of both Afrofuturism and intersectionality as coined by legal theorist Kimberlé Crenshaw by many

14. Harrison, "Sci-Fi Visions: An Interview with Octavia Butler," 4–5; my emphasis.
15. McCaffery and McMenamin, "An Interview with Octavia E. Butler," 14.
16. Lomax, *Jezebel Unhinged*, 2–4.

years. A 1990 interview with Randall Kenan traces Butler's understanding of her self and her writing as feminist. Further, as an intersectional Afrofuturist, Butler noted several times in several interviews that writing about Black people in science fiction does not mean centering racism and white supremacy: "I see science fiction as a way of disseminating the fact that we don't have only one kind of people, namely white males, in this world. They are not the only ones who are here; not the only ones who count."[17] For Butler, writing about Black people does not mean writing solely about racism—indeed, such a claim is reminiscent of Toni Morrison's noted critique of racism, that it functions as a distraction that "keeps us from doing our work."[18] Several documents in the Octavia Butler archive attest to the fact that Butler found many stories that supposedly centered Black people actually centering racism. As she pointed out in a 1981 letter to Pearl Parkerson Matthews, "Of course, racism is a facet of Black life, but it isn't the whole."[19] The distraction of focusing on white supremacy keeps an Afrofuturist from writing good science fiction. Butler clearly made a choice to not center racism and white supremacy, opting to use science fiction and Black characters to tell stories about the human condition. While it may appear that works like *Kindred* or the *Parable* series center white supremacy, it is equally possible that her vision is beyond it. Envisioning Black life beyond white supremacy is, I think, central to understanding Butler's work.

This chapter is informed by Susanna Morris's essay on Butler's final published vampire novel, *Fledgling*. In her examination, Morris links Afrofuturism with Black feminism to coin the term "Afrofuturistic feminism." She argues that both Afrofuturism and Black feminism are speech acts that "talk back" to systems of domination and oppression. Drawing on bell hooks's concept of "talking back," Morris contends that Afrofuturistic feminism is tied to "terms of coalition and power sharing," instead of reconstructing domination with Black faces and bodies.[20] The synthesis of Afrofuturism and Black feminism that Morris proposes is productive in that it further fleshes out the liberating possibilities inherent in Afrofuturism.

Where Morris focuses on *Fledgling* as an example of Butler's Afrofuturistic feminism, this chapter turns to the *Parable* books and the *Earthseed* verses that undergird them. I think that Butler as an architect of Afrofutur-

17. Francis, *Conversations with Octavia Butler*, 6.

18. Toni Morrison, lecture at Portland State University (1975), https://www.wweek.com/news/2019/08/07/one-of-late-writer-toni-morrisons-most-famous-quotes-about-racism-came-from-a-talk-at-portland-state-university-listen-to-it-here/.

19. OEB 4140, letter to Ms. Pearl Parkerson Matthews, March 9, 1981.

20. Morris, "Black Girls Are from the Future," 154.

istic feminism goes further than using Afrofuturistic writing to foreground Black feminism. I contend that her Afrofuturistic feminism performs libera- tive work that could be called Afrofuturistic feminist religious criticism. This chapter's aim is to explore the ways that Lauren Oya Olamina's Earthseed verses revise the God-concept and through the kind of revision possible through Afrofuturism, offer the reader new and creative ways of imagining the divine.

Also, this chapter focuses on the *Parable* books primarily because they explicitly center religion and its negative and positive potential. It would be all too easy to read the *Parable* books as some form of negative critique of religion in the same vein as Gene Roddenberry's critiques of religion. How- ever, Butler in the *Parable* books does not allow the reader such a dismissal of religion.

Butler's Work in General

As noted above, Butler said that she began writing about power because she had so little of it. As also noted above, being the lone Black woman writing science fiction and fantasy exposed the racism inherent in the genre. Further, Butler noted that many of her works focused on reconfiguring the human being. Further, I think Butler expanded her sense of a lack of power and connected it to other groups' lack of power. To make this clearer, I point to Butler's prolific letters to the *Los Angeles Times* as well as her own surviving research and subject files. Her archive at the Huntington Library contains a significant amount of newspaper clippings from the *Los Angeles Times,* some of which contain her own annotations and comments. In particular, I point to a 1978 letter to the editor written in response to an interview with California State Senator John Briggs, who, at the time, had introduced the Briggs Initiative (officially, Proposition 6), which would have banned gays and lesbians from serving as public school teachers. The interview is part of the archive and is quite lengthy. Butler's letter, however, is brief, but full of scorn regarding the then-state senator's antigay bias:

> The man's biggotry [sic], ignorance, and indifference to the rights of oth- ers are utterly transparent. It is amazing that he has managed to frighten so many people into supporting him—and so many who oppose him into silence. Remember when people could be frightened and/or silenced by the threat of being considered "niggerlovers"?[21]

21. OEB 4082, Letter to the Editor, *Los Angeles Times,* October 6, 1978.

I submit that her reactions to the manifold forms of oppression might frame the kinds of characters and situations she created in the *Parable* books. Briggs's virulent homophobia, Ronald Reagan's indifference toward the HIV/AIDS crisis, the imminent threats of nuclear war and climate change, and increasing antipathy and violence toward gays and lesbians I think played a role in Butler's work in general and the *Parable* series in particular.

This chapter follows McCormack's examination of Butler's *Parable* series and its exploration of religious thought. As McCormack points out, within African American religious thought (including Black liberation and womanist theologies),

> there has been scant attention to Afrofuturism, and its concerns with the intersections of spirituality, identity construction and struggles for social justice. . . . Among Black liberation theologians, in particular, the search for sources for emancipatory religious discourse and practice has typically involved a retrieval of resources from the past rather than a critical engagement with cultural resources that imagine alternative albeit (science-) fictional, possibilities for the future.[22]

Given that Black liberation and womanist theologies often situate Black people's literature as a site for doing theological reflection, it would seem that Butler (and Delany) would have received greater attention. However, I think Butler has not received greater attention among Black liberation and womanist theologians because it is difficult to situate her work within the emancipatory frameworks constructed by the Black theological academy. In short, her works do not fit within the kinds of heroic Blackness and confessional Black Christianity laid down by Cone and his students.

By saying that Butler's writing does not "fit" within the confessional frameworks of Black liberation and womanist theologies and the heroic Blackness those theologies contain, I contend that Butler's own meditations on race, sexuality, gender, and power routinely "fail" to confirm the rightness or efficacy of Black liberation theologies. This is not to say that we may interpret Butler's work as somehow intrinsically opposed to such theologies. Rather, we may problematize efforts from within Black liberation theological constructions to assimilate her science fiction into them.

Earthseed as presented in the *Parable* series is intersectional Afrofuturism at work. In the books, Lauren Oya Olamina, a sixteen-year-old Black girl, creates a new belief system. In *Parable of the Sower*, Lauren states, "At

22. Ibid.

least three years ago, my father's God stopped being my God. His church stopped being my church."[23] As Lauren is crafting this belief system that she later names Earthseed, the United States is falling apart socially and economically. Unattended climate change is wreaking havoc across the United States (and presumably, the globe). The small community that Lauren lives in is overrun by marauders, and soon, Lauren and a small group of other survivors are on a quest to establish a community. The social and economic decline of the United States is exacerbated by accelerating climate change and then the rise of a xenophobic, totalitarian, theocratic government. What assists in the creation of Earthseed is Lauren's ability to feel what others feel. Dubbed "hyperempathy," this condition emerges as a result of Lauren's mother's drug use. Lauren's hyperempathy or "sharing" is connected to her questioning her father's religion. Her connection to other people's feelings informs Earthseed's central tenets that God is change and that change shapes God. Consider the following:

> Intelligence is ongoing, individual
> adaptability. Adaptations that an intelligent
> species may make
> in a single generation, other species
> make over
> many generations of selective
> breeding and
> selective dying. Yet intelligence is
> demanding.
> If it is misdirected by accident or by
> intent, it can
> foster its own orgies of breeding and
> dying.[24]

Lauren's hyperempathy is the result of tragic circumstances; however, we may read the development of Earthseed as an intelligent adaptation. The demand of that intelligence lies in shaping the change so that it may be beneficial. The system called Earthseed is not a wholesale rejection of her father's beliefs; rather, I read this in the way that we might read Buddhism as emanating from Hinduism, or Christianity as an offshoot—or adaptation—of Judaism. In the question and answer section at the end of the *Par-*

---

23. Butler, *Parable of the Sower*, 7.
24. Ibid., 29.

able of the Sower, Butler contends that Earthseed is different from Buddhism in that Buddhism requires an avoidance of attachments in order to achieve Nirvana, while Earthseed requires us to pay close attention to all that is in our lives—we shape change not out of avoidance of attachment, but out of deep appreciation for our existence and intelligence as an adaptive part of change.

Lauren calls the collected writings "The Books of the Living." Again, this is paradoxical, as she is writing these verses and observations in a society ridden with decay, violence, and death. Indeed, the very notion of change that functions as the central tenet of Earthseed runs counter to the totalitarian, theocratic government of Christian America. Andrew Steele Jarrett, a fundamentalist Christian, rises to power based on promises that he and his strain of Christianity could "make America great again," but he and his followers initiate a campaign of terror and oppression that is rooted in death.[25] Jarrett's promises to "fix" America through an authoritarian turn to theocracy centers a God-as-king. This turn only engenders slavery, and a "Do unto others as God has done unto you" ethos. Indeed, as Earthseed gains followers, it eventually comes into conflict with Jarrett's extremist Christianity. By the end of the first *Parable* book, Olamina's Earthseed community Acorn is attacked by Jarrett's forces. Olamina's husband Bankole is killed, their daughter is kidnapped, and Olamina and other survivors are enslaved. Olamina's vision of religion is not religion as this form of extremist Christianity promotes. Rather, Earthseed centers an orientation and attitude towards humanity as part of a much larger whole. The genesis of Earthseed and calling those writings "The Books of the Living" is also a reaction to or revision of the Christianity and the God of Lauren's Baptist father, which appears rooted in death. The Christian narrative as presented in the *Parable* series sees transformation only in terms of suffering and death. Neither Olamina's father nor President Jarrett are capable of seeing their Christianity as a possible path for enhancing everyone's lives. Their visions of God are not productive. Instead, their visions are wholly destructive. Olamina's Earthseed does not avoid or ignore death and suffering; rather, it does not place death and suffering as a "consequence of sin" or as a precondition for religious belief and piety. Olamina is clear in her revision of her father's God—I say revision instead of rejection to highlight the point that Earthseed is adaptation in the face of change. Butler herself articulates both the promise and peril of religion and how it functions as part of the *Parable* series:

---

25. Butler, *Parable of the Talents,* 20.

[Lauren's] solution is—well, grows from another religion that she comes up with. Religion is everywhere. There are no human societies without it, whether they acknowledge it as a religion or not. So I thought religion might be an answer, as well as, in some cases, a problem. . . . I have people who are saying, well, here is another religion, and here are some verses that can help us think in a different way, and here is a destination that isn't something that we have to wait for after we die.[26]

Butler understands that religion—however we describe it—is foundational in human societies, which is a point that some elements within science fiction may ignore or underestimate. She further describes herself as having been raised by "strict Baptists whose views I never completely shared. Eventually, I became an ex-Baptist, but I never forgot the rousing services and the singing which I loved or the illogic and sometimes the religious biggotry [sic] which I hated. Do these things work their ways into my novels? Of course. They're a fundamental part of me." She further notes, "You say my work pleads for acceptance of differences. It should." Here, I will interpret this as saying that there is both a duty and a goal of her writing—which is at the heart of liberation theology/ethics—and that she views her ambivalent relationship to religion as part of the social and cultural critiques that lie at the center of her speculative fictions. While Butler may express ambivalence about organized religion, she understands that religion—however we describe it or experience it—is an inextricable element in human experience. She also understands that it is up to humans to shape religion to either productive or destructive ends. Butler's Earthseed is practical, without the trappings of elaborate religious ritual and rites of appeasement. The God of Earthseed does not require appeasement; rather, God-as-change requires our attention and conscientious action toward positive change.

The God of Change

In exploring the collected sayings of Earthseed as well as the *Parable of the Sower*, we see that through Lauren Olamina, Butler offers us a different way of seeing God. Orthodox Christian theologies present God as impassible, unaffected by humankind, and unchanging—wholly outside of human experience and comprehension. Also, Olamina—perhaps serving as a stand-in for Butler's own developing views of God and humanity—tries to make

26. Gonzalez and Goodman, "Science Fiction Writer Octavia Butler on Race, Global Warming, and Religion," 224.

sense of the nature of God. After reflecting on the various interpretations of God, ranging from God as big daddy, big cop, or king, ultimate reality or a big kid playing with his toys, Olamina asks, "But what if all that is wrong? What if God is something else altogether?"[27] Unlike the God of Christian theologies in general and liberation theologies in particular, the God of Olamina is indeed impassive—however, it is impassive in that it is not a discrete entity that stands over and against humankind breaking into history to side with the oppressed. It does not need to break into history, as it does not exist outside of history. Indeed, the change that is part of history is part of God itself.

> God is Change—
> Infinite
> Irresistible
> Inexorable
> Indifferent
> God is Trickster
> Teacher
> Chaos
> Clay[28]

In some sense, this God of Lauren Olamina's is more akin to the God as presented in the Hebrew Bible. Olamina's schema implicitly ignores the existence of a "Satan" or any other opposing entities.

Earthseed might be Black process theology. This is why Coleman sought to integrate the *Parable* series into *Making a Way Out of No Way*. Following the method laid down by Black liberation and womanist theologies, Coleman turns to Butler's Afrofuturism to enlarge theological descriptions of Black life. As such, this description of God necessarily includes Black queer existence and experiences, as those experiences are part of change. Reading Olamina, her verses, and the *Parable* series itself both implicitly and explicitly centers Black queerness as shaped by and shaping change.

Black and womanist theology at its core is an attempt at revolutionary theology, seeing God through the lens of Black peoples. This work of revision wants to subvert the distribution of power in and through theological discourse. However, these theological discourses do not change or challenge the fundamental tenets of Western Christianity: God is triune, and Jesus and

27. Butler, *Parable of the Sower*, 16.
28. Ibid.

the Holy Spirit are incarnations of the divine, and the Christian Church and its people are the conduits through which God performs the transformative work of saving humankind from sin.

The God of Butler's Earthseed is not driven by power or some notion of original sin that requires punishment and reconciliation. If there are any demands this God places upon us, it is that we attend to change, for change most certainly attends to us. We often fail to see how we are ourselves the product of change great and small. Butler's Black womanist theology can carry us to the stars, as it recognizes humanity as part of a much larger cosmos.

What makes it Black and womanist if it does not claim God as Black? I think that it is the imaginative emanation of a Black woman through the mind of a Black woman—one who is queer—that makes this a Black and womanist theology. Terrestrial Black theology cannot—it is built upon the bones of Christian theologies that are earthbound. Here, I might draw upon Barbara Holmes's *Race and the Cosmos* and expand Earthseed's god into the Blackness of the cosmos itself, or Thomas's use of dark matter as a metaphor for understanding Blackness. This is not the Blackness that whiteness creates; rather, it is the Blackness that the Blackness of the cosmos creates and nourishes.

The Importance of the Protagonist

Butler stated in several interviews that in crafting the character of Lauren Oya Olamina, she wanted her to be Butler's "better self."[29] Further, Butler noted, "In a very real way, my grandmother touched me and helped me to creat [sic] Lauren Olamina."[30] In creating Lauren, the reader sees a young, dark-skinned, not "conventionally attractive" Black girl developing an expansive and adaptive belief system. Throughout the *Parable* series, we see Lauren constantly having to respond to heteropatriarchy and its oppressive effects, first in the form of her father's response to finding out about her beliefs, and then later in the form of Andrew Steele Jarrett's oppressive Christian America. In creating Lauren Oya Olamina, Butler wanted her

> to be an intelligent, believable person. I didn't want to write satire, I didn't
> want to write about a hypocrite or a fool. I wanted her to believe deeply in

29. OEB Journal, "Journal," 1999, The Huntington Library, San Marino, California.
30. "Speech on Parable of the Sower and Parable of the Talents" (draft), Octavia E. Butler Papers, The Huntington Library, San Marino, California.

what she taught and I wanted her teachings to be reasonable, intellectually respectable. I wanted them to be something that someone I could admire might truly believe and teach. She didn't have to be always right, but she had to be reasonable.[31]

It is instructive that Butler replied that she wanted Olamina and the religion she created to be perceived of and understood as reasonable. As juxtaposed against both her father and the theocratic Steele, this religion in which God is simply that which we observe in ourselves and in nature may be more "reasonable" than a celestial entity who rewards some and punishes others.

All This Has Happened Before: Theorizing the *Parable* Series

What do these books tell us about Black religious thought? How may we interpret them so that they function as a resource for revising Black religious thought? As Michael Brandon McCormack points out,

> Butler's parables argue for radically different (though contiguous) forms of religious thought, practice and community which emphasize greater individual agency and communal solidary oriented toward a demystified (if still fantastic) "destiny."[32]

McCormack is right in reiterating the word "parables," as Butler's narrative in these books does not merely point toward a dystopian near-future; she draws on our present. Butler noted that she wanted "to look at where we are now, what we are doing now, and to consider where some of our current behaviors and unattended problems might take us."[33] Further, McCormack notes that Butler positions "Black youth as religious critics and innovators."[34] The key here is that Lauren is a young Black woman whose creation exists in a radically different imaging of the world and human possibilities. The "radically different forms of religious thought" that McCormack identifies in Butler's creation of Earthseed rely primarily on imagining Black life (and, by extension, all life) differently. As a young person revising and creating

31. "Questions and Answers Concerning Parable of the Sower and Parable of the Talents" (draft), Octavia E. Butler Papers, The Huntington Library, San Marino, California.
32. McCormack, "Your God Is a Racist," 24.
33. Butler, *Parable of the Sower*, 337.
34. Ibid.

new forms of religious thought and practice, the implicit critique is that the "established" or older forms of religious thought and practice have become staid and ineffective.

That said, it is clear that the world that Lauren Oya Olamina lives in is not a radically discontinuous world from our own. While Butler presents technological innovations that have the patina of science fiction (touch rings, holo screens, and the like), the *Parables* tell us about a world in which those innovations do not exist in order to make our lives better. Instead, they serve as stark markers of social class and prestige. Indeed, Lauren's hyperempathy is made possible because of her mother's tragic addiction to the drug Paraceto. Technology in Butler's *Parables* does not bring utopia. Instead, technology itself is employed by elites in order to exacerbate the existential pain of the underclasses.

Another theme pervasive in the *Parable* series and the ways that Butler talked about it is the repetition of history. During a conversation with Stephen Potts for the journal *Science Fiction Studies,* Butler responds to Potts's observation that Olamina's hopes for communal purpose echoed the hopefulness of the 1960s around the American space program by saying, "We keep playing the same record." While we may read the *Parable* series as a prediction of where this particular nation is going to go, Butler also recognized that this story is not unique to the United States.[35]

Theorizing Octavia Butler

Gerry Canavan, to whom this chapter referred above, was one of the first scholars to access the Huntington Library's massive archive of Butler's work. In the introduction to his *Masters of Science Fiction* text on her, Canavan provides a brief but scintillating biographical sketch. He describes Butler and her work according to her words, in which she described her work as a "positive obsession." To describe the work as such, Canavan observes that Butler's writing was a daily obsession, "a constant and daily devotion."[36] Her writing, her positive obsession was not merely part of a trope that fits science fiction fans. Rather, her work was part of a Black literary tradition in which Black people write themselves into existence. Butler saw herself as part of that tradition, but perhaps not as being part of the storied tradition of Langston Hughes, Zora Neale Hurston, Alain Locke, and the like.

35. Potts, "We Keep Playing the Same Record," 71.
36. Canavan, *Octavia E. Butler,* 5.

Octavia Butler's work, her thoughts, and so forth function as an intersectional Afrofuturistic trickster. The point of the trickster in mythological lore and narrative is to push characters into growth. I want to quote from Ayana Smith's essay "Blues, Criticism and the Signifying Trickster" as a way of understanding and describing Butler as a trickster:

> The trickster figure is often portrayed as one who lives outside the margins of society. He fits into no normalised pattern of social behaviour, and it is this rebel-like tendency that allows him to become the hero of the trickster tale. The trickster represents everything one would like to do but cannot. The trickster therefore presents an alternative, vicarious existence that contrasts with the strict boundaries of slave existence. In a society with limited roles available to African-Americans, the trickster provides an outlet for the expression of socially unacceptable themes.[37]

Such growth is hardly, if ever, smooth or without conflict. Indeed, the trickster's engagement with humans involves conflict. As such, describing Butler as an intersectional Afrofuturistic trickster is not a pejorative. She uses science fiction in order to disrupt our utopian visions and confirm our desires for transcendence. As Gerry Canavan notes, Butler's work holds forth utopia and dystopia at the same time.[38] The "If this, then" nature of her work also presents a "Yes, but" proposition. Humanity may reach the stars, but those stars are not necessarily welcoming. Further, simply inventing a means of traveling to different worlds and establishing colonies on those worlds will not itself usher in a wholly optimistic future. Humanity will almost certainly bring to the stars the problems that plagued them on this planet. Here, I want to draw attention to a telling exchange between Butler and H. Jerome Jackson in a 1994 interview for *The Crisis* magazine. *The Crisis* is the official magazine for the National Association for the Advancement of Colored People (NAACP), and as such, it focuses on issues relevant to African American communities. This particular interview appeared at the publication of the first *Parable* book. Jackson posed a few questions regarding Butler's role as an author and the nature of the *Parable of the Sower*. In response to the question regarding the novel and whether she was "trying to make a point," Butler responded with the problem of "throw-away labor" and American corporate rapaciousness in Mexico. The interviewer noted, "This sounds like it rattles you," with Butler responding, "It shouldn't be happening!"[39] The

---

37. Smith, "Blues, Criticism, and the Signifying Trickster," 180.
38. Canavan, "The Octavia Butler Papers," 52.
39. Jackson, "Sci-Fi Tales from Octavia Butler," 44–45.

interviewer followed up with, "But these are Hispanics. Don't black folks have enough problems?" The record of the interview notes that Butler took a long pause before responding. When she did, she said the following:

> I recognize that you're asking that only because you want to get a reaction. But if you only pay attention to what's happening to your own folk, by the time you notice, then it's creeping into your people too; and very well-entrenched.[40]

Butler as a visionary saw that race, while necessary to attend to, could not be the defining identity by which we address societal issues. Here, she puts Martin Niemoller's warning into plain words, warning the interviewer and the readers of *The Crisis* that social and political machinations and manipulations that are inflicted on one impoverished group of people won't stay with that group. In this interview, I read Butler as the trickster, using science fiction to disturb the neatly divided narratives that demarcate racial identity and racialized concerns. I also point to this exchange to highlight the trickster nature of Butler's Afrofuturistic intersectional feminism. In this interview, she refuses to be baited into a Blacks-only primacy and narrative. She understands the interconnectedness of oppressions and exploitation, apparently, in a way that the interviewer either does not understand or refuses to understand. As a trickster, Butler intimately understands and succinctly conveys the limited nature of the question.

Indeed, in drafts of the third *Parable* book, the figure of the Trickster figures prominently in Butler's vision for the series. As she was constructing the next *Parable* book, she initially thought it might be titled *Parable of the Trickster*. In describing the book's direction, she said that she wanted to show that humanity's ventures into space were not going to be easy. She wanted to examine how humanity would adapt to the massive struggles that we would face when moving out into a larger universe, cut off from the homeworld. Although the destiny of humankind is to leave the homeworld, that does not mean that human history is fulfilled.

In a sense, the unfinished *Parable* books are a refutation of the assumption of a linear, univocal "progress" of history. Indeed, the social and religious criticism at the heart of the first *Parable* books and in the Earthseed verses themselves view what we call "history" as an ever-unfinished project. Certainly, history would not end with refugees from a damaged Earth landing on a new world. In these early drafts of the next book, Butler planned

---

40. Ibid., 45.

to have these colonists—some of whom were Earthseed devotees—experience nearly debilitating hallucinations or blindness. In her drafts of what would be subsequent *Parables,* Butler sketched several characters who would be central to the narrative of colonizing a "ghastly, demon-ridden new world."[41] For example, Butler describes two characters, "The Christian Minister" and the "The witch or wizard." She describes the "witch" as being more "dangerous" than the minister, in that the witch promises that "if we can just follow the rituals properly, we need not bother to til [sic] the soil or maintain the various survival activities on the new world."[42] She goes on to note that according to the witch character, continuing any kind of survival activity "would be a distinct lack of faith," and that faith in magic would be paramount. Just these two characters—and the inevitable conflict that these characters might bring—are examples of the dangers of colonizing a new world, dangers that Butler had been writing brief sketches about dating back to 1989. In a document dated July 27, 1989, Butler wrote that stories "1" and "2" should focus on both surviving this new, inhospitable world, and surviving each other. Even then, she wanted to explore the conflicts that religion brings: "Give them real conflicts—religious v. Non-religious v. Individual religions that persist and are intolerant."[43] Again, this echoes her comments in interviews that religion would persist—even in a newly colonized extraterrestrial world.

The trickster here is the chaos of a new world. In Butler's notes, we see chaos in the form of the planet itself, with some unknown agent causing either mass hallucinations or mass blindness, or in the people themselves. An idea that Butler wrote down was to have "an absolute Stalanesque [sic] ruler [who] takes over in a colony."[44] This, of course, is a return to Butler's chief interests in exploring how human beings desire, acquire, and abuse power. Examination of a good number of pieces in the Octavia Butler Papers archive at the Huntington Library uncover the evolving work of a thinker who was informed by the intersections and collisions of race, class, gender, sexuality, and religion. Further, Butler examines and interrogates those intersections and collisions in light of what she saw was an emerging dystopian present in the United States.

Further, in the Huntington Library's archives is an unpublished monograph in which Butler collects all the published and unpublished verses that compose Earthseed. Butler describes this collection as intending to pro-

---

41. OEB 2036 "Two Novel" (Thursday, November 11, 1999).
42. Ibid.
43. OEB 480 (July 27, 1989).
44. OEB 480, "Ideas" (green paper).

voke thought. What kind of thought did Butler seek to provoke through this collection? She notes that is important to present these verses as Lauren Olamina's truth and for the reader to not perceive her as a charlatan or a fool. Further, these collected verses get at the practical goals of Earthseed of giving humankind something to strive toward. This, I think, helps us more clearly understand the *Parable* books not as dystopian nor utopian. Rather, as Canavan notes, we may read this as part of a ustopian (combination of utopia and dystopia) vision. For Butler, science fiction at its best provoked thought, and the Earthseed verses are part of prodding the human race to "take responsibility not only for our persona and group behavior, but for our future as a species."[45] Thus, Earthseed is about giving humankind something to strive toward. The preface to the monograph is illuminating. On their own and as part of the larger narrative, these verses do not refer to or rely upon a supernatural entity who rides into history to save humankind from its excesses. Here, I point to an undated note in which she briefly writes about Arthur C. Clarke's *Childhood's End*. That book explored the evolution of humanity after encountering a benevolent (if not wholly dictatorial) alien race who appear demonic. Butler notes that these aliens help evolve humankind beyond childhood. Part of that evolution beyond childhood requires humankind to abandon war, inflicting economic, social, and racial inequality, and general selfishness. Her note has the header "SF Classics and the ways they point."[46] Perhaps Clarke's book was a partial influence on her "ustopian" *Parable* series, for the *Parable of the Talents* ends in a similar way; however, there is no alien influence that pushes humanity to an evolved state. Rather, it is Earthseed, a religion created by a young Black girl living in a world nearly ruined by the selfishness of greedy, xenophobic white men, that drives humankind to the stars and "redirect[s] people away from the chaos and destructiveness into which they have fallen and toward a consuming, creative long-term goal."[47] Here, we may see in Butler not her pessimism, but rather her optimism (tempered, of course, by realism). With proper direction, humankind can work toward productive ends.

---

45. OEB 470, Butler, Octavia E. Earthseed: The Books of the Living: monograph: draft. Octavia E. Butler Papers, The Huntington Library, San Marino, California.

46. OEB 479. Butler, Octavia E. Earthseed: series: turquoise binder: notes. ca. 1995., Octavia E. Butler Papers, The Huntington Library, San Marino, California.

47. OEB 2392, "Questions and Answers Concerning Parable of the Sower and Parable of the Talents" (draft), Octavia E. Butler Papers, The Huntington Library, San Marino, California.

Conclusion

The goal of this chapter has been to provide a thicker description of Octavia Butler's *Parable* series as an example of intersectional Afrofuturism. Such a vision of Blackness via an intersectional Afrofuturism in Butler's works troubles rigid descriptions of Black identity and confronts the power dynamics within and outside Black communities. Returning to Butler's statement about how and why she began writing science fiction, her intersectional Afrofuturism is about giving voice to Blackness through the imagination.

The enduring power of Octavia Butler's pioneering intersectional Afrofuturism is found in the 2015 anthology *Octavia's Brood*. In the introduction to the volume, Walidah Imarisha notes that Butler said she never wanted to be the only Black woman writing science fiction:

> She wanted to be one of *many* Black female sci-fi writers. She wanted to be one of thousands of folks writing themselves into the present and into the future. We believe in that right Butler claimed for each of us—the right to dream as ourselves, individually and collectively. But we also think it is a responsibility she handed down: are we brave enough to imagine beyond the boundaries of "the real" and then do the hard work of sculpting reality from our dreams?[48]

Butler herself became the seed from which a critical discourse grew. In the case of the above quote and the text in which it appears, the editors and authors explicitly describe their work as political, using speculative fiction as a vehicle for political and social change. Indeed, now there are many Black women science fiction writers. Tananarive Due, N. K. Jemisin, and Nnedi Okorafor are just a few of the Black women writing Black people into the future.

Butler described her work as a positive obsession, a "furor scribendi."[49] This positive obsession, which led to so many influential short stories and novels, has informed Black scholars as they interpret her work and relate it to Black experiences. Recently, Monica Coleman and Tananarive Due have hosted a series of webinars responding to the COVID-19 pandemic called "Octavia Tried to Tell Us." Alicia A. Wallace reflected on Butler's *Parable* series as pointing to the power of Black women and girls to effect lasting

---

48. Imarisha, Brown, and Thomas, *Octavia's Brood*, 11.
49. Butler, *Bloodchild*, 195

change in turbulent times.[50] Wallace understands the *Parable* series as prescient and a warning and a call to action. Both she and Coleman and Due view Butler as a prophetic voice, speaking to Black women's realities and potential to pave the way for Black people to save ourselves.

---

50. Wallace, "You Should Have Been Listening to Octavia Butler."

CHAPTER 4

"It's Code"

Janelle Monáe, the ArchAndroid, and Queer Afrofuturistic Salvation

In the midst of ongoing tragedy of Black death at the hands of the agents of white supremacy, the depredations of rising authoritarianism in the United States, and emergent movements against sexual harassment, Janelle Monáe's work via her EP *Metropolis* and three full-length albums weaves narratives of racial, gender, and sexual freedom together with a sprawling science fiction saga. This chapter follows the pattern laid down in the previous chapter in that I positioned Octavia Butler as an architect of intersectional Afrofuturism, without which an Afrofuturistic religious thought would be impossible. Here, I contend that Monáe's music, the persona/alter ego of Cindi Mayweather, and the use of the android as representing "the other" is a signifying act that not only reads heterosexism, homophobia, and white supremacy but also functions subversively and as a revolutionary queerness. What Monáe performs is a liberated queerness that is constantly seeking deeper responses. Also, her performed queerness (as shown in her songs and "emotion pictures") is not subject to others' approval. This chapter will argue that Janelle Monáe is here to save us from our myopia via Afrofuturism. This chapter will trace the emergence of Janelle Monáe, her working-class roots as the impetus for the creation of Monáe, the creation of Cindi Mayweather and Monáe's use of the android as a signifier, and finally, her latest album *Dirty Computer* as the culmination of the work begun when she released the *Metropolis* EP as a queer Afrofuturistic manifesto.

To theorize Monáe's liberated and liberating queerness, this chapter will draw on Audre Lorde's foundational essay "Uses of the Erotic." Lorde's intersectional arguments from the perspective of a Black lesbian feminist concerning the power of the erotic as a liberating force give us the theoretical lens through which we may understand Monáe's sonic journey of self-discovery.

Who Is Janelle Monáe?

Janelle Monáe Robinson is a native of Kansas City, Kansas, and has often recounted the challenges that her mother faced as a janitor, challenges that led to Monáe's early adoption of the black and white tuxedo as a signifier of her mother's job. Her father was in and out of prison and struggled with drug addiction. As she notes in a *Rolling Stone* article, it was her extended family that provided her with a sense of home. Further, she notes that home was not without contradictions. It is, I think, those contradictions and contestations that enabled Monáe to forge a revised vision of herself. Again, her journey resembles that of so many Black people: She left Kansas City for New York City to study drama. In 2001, she moved to Atlanta, where she met Big Boi of OutKast and later formed the Wondaland Arts Society, a collective of like-minded artists. Big Boi introduced Monáe to Sean "Diddy" Combs, who signed her to his label, Bad Boy Records.

Monáe is not simply a singer from Kansas City. She is a singer, an actress, and a model. She is a spokesperson for Cover Girl cosmetics and Pepsi-Cola, has appeared on several fashion magazine covers, and has had groundbreaking movie roles in movies like *Moonlight* and *Hidden Figures*. Further, she has a starring role in a horror film called *Antebellum*, in which she plays a Black woman who time-travels back into American slavery.

Interestingly, the *Rolling Stone* piece makes a point of describing Monáe's devout Baptist family as a counterpoint to Monáe's assumedly more "liberal" self. While she does note that more than a few people in her family had made disparaging comments regarding LGBT people, it is more instructive that she says, "A lot of [*Dirty Computer*] is a reaction to the sting of what it means to hear people in my family say, 'All gay people are going to hell.'"[1]

Such descriptions of Monáe's family in the *Rolling Stone* article play to the assumption that "authentic" Black life is religiously fundamentalist and fairly unsophisticated. A related undercurrent in the piece is a remark that Monáe herself "returns" to a Midwestern drawl when she is around her

---

1. Spanos, "Janelle Monáe Frees Herself."

Kansas family members. What this piece ignores is the capacity of Black people to engage in "code-switching." Like Beyonce and other Black performers (especially Black women), Monáe has learned and perfected the art of code-switching.

The *Rolling Stone* piece notes the tensions that Monáe has concerning "the human behind the masks":

> Monáe does worry that the human behind her masks may not be enough. She has asked aloud, including in therapy, "What if people don't think I'm as interesting as Cindi Mayweather?" She'll miss the freedom of being the android. "I created her, so I got to make her be whatever I wanted her to be. I didn't have to talk about the Janelle Monáe who was in therapy. It's Cindi Mayweather. She is who I aspire to be."[2]

Like so many African Americans, "Janelle Monáe" is a reconstructed identity that is consistently going through reinventions, a self created in response to perceptions of other selves. Black performers often create alter egos and identities that reflect an ideal self. For example, Beyoncé named her third album after her alter ego, "Sasha Fierce." She described Sasha Fierce as her onstage persona, not the person she is behind closed doors.[3]

Nevertheless, it is Monáe's discography and its Afrofutristic imagery as well as the character of Cindi Mayweather that is of interest here, particularly how that Afrofuturistic imagery intersects with her gender and sexual orientation crossing. For some time, people speculated that Monáe was either bisexual or gay. In the past, she played with those questions in ways that both elided the question but also stood firmly on the side of LGBT expression and rights. In 2013, Monáe was a guest on the radio show *Sway in the Morning*. An initial attempt by the show's host to get her to "reveal" her sexuality was met with an unequivocal statement supporting love, regardless of sexual orientation or religious belief. However, Sway pressed the question further, and directly asked Monáe if she dated men or women, to which Monáe responded:

> You know what, I keep my personal life to myself. I think one of the things about that is that I want everyone to focus on my music and also I don't want to let anybody down. I want women to still be attracted to me—go get

---

2. Ibid.

3. "Beyoncé's Rise to Fame, Explained," edited by Alex Abed-Santos, Vox, https://www.vox.com/cards/beyonce-career-explained/who-is-sasha-fierce-beyonce.

my album! And I want men to still be attracted to me so I have to be political in this. I can't really tell y'all.[4]

This interview happened as Monáe was promoting her second studio album, *The Electric Lady*. Speculation regarding Monáe's sexual orientation likely stems from the manner in which she presents herself—or, rather, her alter ego Cindi Mayweather—as a nearly androgynous figure. At the same time, the android Cindi is quite sexual, but not in a gratuitous fashion that centers the male gaze. Additionally, it is interesting to note that Monáe's answer about who she dates shifts the focus. Instead of responding directly to the question, Monáe centers herself as an object of desire for both men and women.

What both the *Rolling Stone* piece and the *Sway in the Morning* interview point to is that both Monáe and Cindi Mayweather's android/androgynous science fictional personas throw "mainstream" popular culture into the classical estrangement associated with science fiction. To understand what I mean by describing Monáe's work and alter ego as estrangement, I turn to Darko Suvin's description of science fiction as cognitive estrangement. For Suvin, science fiction is subversive because it presents alternative realities that challenge the status quo.[5] In the case of Monáe/Mayweather, her presentation of self/other via the android challenges the heteropatriarchal status quo. Both the *Rolling Stone* article and the radio interview attempt to police Monáe's queer body into easily understood (read: heteronormative) boxes and identities. Why is Sway so invested in uncovering the nature of Janelle Monáe's sexual identity and who she dates? Why is the *Rolling Stone* writer seemingly so perplexed by her Kansas City relatives and Monáe's shift in accents?

The obvious response is that both of these media outlets function to maintain gendered, sexed, and racialized hierarchies and social relations, even as they appear to be open to gender, sexual, and racial difference. Monáe is able to engage these media outlets and simultaneously appear to conform to these mainstream expectations of Black womanhood and femininity and also explode them. As writers Daylanne English and Alvin Kim note, Monáe might be critical of the commodification of her androgyny and then-subtle queerness, but she is also keenly aware of its usefulness.[6] She is aware of how twenty-first-century visual cultures process Black women's bodies, and she uses that to confound our expectations. An example of this

---

4. Dayfloat, "Janelle Monáe Speaks."
5. Renault, "Science Fiction as Cognitive Estrangement," 114.
6. English and Kim, "Now We Want Our Funk Cut," 223.

is found in a 2015 Twitter exchange between her and a Twitter user named @mellowmac. In a since-deleted tweet, @mellowmac wrote, "girl stop being so soulful and be sexy . . . tired of those dumbass suits . . . you fine but u too damn soulful man." The user ended the tweet with two emojis, one of a "side-eye" face and the other with a tear drop face. Monáe responded, "sit down. I'm not for male consumption."[7] This particular exchange highlights Monáe's resistance to controlling narratives that assume Black women's bodies exist solely for (presumably) heterosexual male consumption. Drawing on English and Kim's analysis of Monáe's work, I might posit that Monáe's resistance to "male consumption" is not simultaneously resistance to capitalist consumption.

Theorizing Cindi Mayweather

While Monáe said that Cindi Mayweather is who she aspires to be, it may be that as a fictional alter ego to Janelle Monáe, Cindi Mayweather could engage in critiques of social and sexual transgressions that Monáe could not. In other words, Monáe uses science fiction and Afrofuturism as a vehicle to critique contemporary forms of oppression. Prior to Monáe's latest album, *Dirty Computer,* her works were characterized as suites: *Metropolis* was the first suite; her first full-length album, *The ArchAndroid,* was suites II and III; and the follow-up album *The Electric Lady* was suites IV and V. Cindi Mayweather is an android at the center of Monáe's Afrofuturistic saga that comprises the EP and the subsequent albums. She is an "Alpha Platinum 9000" android living in a sprawling megalopolis where androids perform the labor that the elite humans enjoy the fruit of. This dystopian society also has repressively strict rules that forbid human/robot sexual and romantic relations. At the beginning of first suite, "The March of the Wolfmasters" details the saga's central dilemma. Cindi has "fallen desperately in love" with a human being named Anthony Greendown. Such a violation is punishable by her termination and disassembly, which sends her into a frenzied attempt at escape from the repressive Droid Control. However, this unlikely love story is also the catalyst for Cindi becoming the equally unlikely figurehead of a robot underground and resistance movement.

As the website io9 notes, it is the videos for Monáe's songs, billed as "emotion pictures," that visually underscore the power of her Afrofutur-

---

7. Saltzman, "Janelle Monáe's Response to This Sexist Tweet Is Perfect."

istic visions.[8] For example, the "short film" for the song "Many Moons" has Cindi undergoing something akin to a transcendent experience: As she is performing for a group of humans engaged in a slave auction of her fellow Alpha Platinim 9000 androids, Cindi experiences what one might describe as an overload. As the song builds toward a frenetic conclusion, the video shows Cindi attempting to assimilate a vast amount of information. This information, broken down into words, phrases, and images from human history, appears to overwhelm her, and then she begins to levitate. As she ascends into the sky above the audience, she is shot through with some form of energy and then she terminates. The video ends with a quote from Cindi: "I imagined many moons in the sky, lighting the way to freedom." The visuals within the "Many Moons" video as well as others point to Monáe's science fiction influences and her positioning the android as a stand-in for oppressed minorities, both racial and sexual.

As Monáe moves into her first full-length album, *The ArchAndroid*, Cindi Mayweather evolves from lovestruck and persecuted android to potential savior figure. The song and video for "Tightrope" position the tuxedo-clad Monáe not as an outcast but as a rebel, flouting the repressive society's injunction against dancing. This calls to mind white supremacist consternation about and condemnation of Black expressive cultures. The video begins with a statement: "Dancing has long been forbidden for its subversive effects on the residents and its tendency to lead to illegal magical practices." Rather than conform to this society and its claims of android/Black inferiority, she and her compatriots (presumably other androids) who have been institutionalized at the Palace of the Dogs dance in secret—calling to mind the hush arbors that were the predecessors of the Black church—until they are discovered by a nurse at the institution. Incidentally, in a 2010 interview, Monáe claimed the Palace of the Dogs was an actual place. Again, Monáe uses a science fiction/mythological trope in order to make claims about otherness. In this interview, she says:

> I think we're gonna live in a world with androids and they'll be able to map out our feelings and our thoughts and you won't be able to differentiate. And so is the concept of the Arch Android, which is similar to the Arch Angel in the Bible and very similar to Neo in The Matrix, you know, the one, the mediator between the hands and the mind, the mediator between the haves and the have-nots, the oppressed and the oppressor.[9]

8. Pulliam-Moore, "Janelle Monáe Explains."
9. Forman, "Pop Sensation Janelle Monáe."

Her articulation of who Cindi Mayweather is is quite clear: She is not just an android; through her experience of love for the human Anthony Greendown, she is an android who has achieved sentience.

Monáe's 2010 claim that the ArchAndroid is like the archangel in the Bible is telling, as the archangel was of high rank and carried the word of God to human beings. Monáe fuses the archangel of Christian and Jewish lore with the mythic Neo of *The Matrix* to her android in order to signify that otherness may actually be divine. Not only may this android be a kind of divine figure, its divinity works to bring enlightenment to humankind.

The sentience of Cindi Mayweather as it is tied to love is Christian theology at work: We only become truly "alive" when we experience divine love through the revelation of Jesus Christ and, in turn, share that love with others. In this regard, Cindi is less Frankenstein's monster and more the incarnation of the divine in cybernetic form. The above quote appears to tie the climax of the "Many Moons" video with "Tightrope." If we view these videos as emotion pictures that tell a larger story, Cindi "comes back"—or is resurrected—in "Tightrope" to again be among her kind and to spread the gospel of love and dance.

Further, we may read Cindi as the Afrofuturistic version of freedom fighters like Harriet Tubman, Sojourner Truth, Rosa Parks, and Ella Baker. Throughout Monáe's Afrofuturistic saga, Cindi Mayweather's android self is the expression of Black women's hopes and dreams and their often unrewarded labor for Black people. As these hopes and dreams get recoded in the sci-fi epics called emotion pictures, Cindi as the Everywoman points to the prophetic and salvific powers of Black women. However, this Blackness, femininity, and queerness is not monolithic.

By the second full-length album, *The Electric Lady*, Mayweather has evolved even further. The emotion picture for "Q. U. E. E. N." (featuring Erykah Badu) continues the messianic science fiction of the ArchAndroid. In an unspecified time, the "Time Council" from Metropolis's Ministry of Droids claims to have stopped the rebel Janelle Monáe—not Cindi Mayweather—and her "dangerous accomplice, Badoula Oblongota," played by Badu. The Ministry of Droids has created a "Living Museum," where various "legendary rebels" throughout history have been put in suspended animation and placed on display. Two Black women enter the exhibit, subdue the exhibit's guards, and play the "Q. U. E. E. N.," which awakens Monáe, her band, and Oblongota from their suspended animation. Recalling the liberating power of song and dance from "Tightrope," the video ends with Monáe rapping that she cannot be categorized and "def[ies] every label" (a promise she later fulfills with *Dirty Computer*). The rap that concludes the song is a challenge to ostracized people to stand up and confront oppressive status quos. Indeed, the title of the song itself is an acronym that Monáe explains represents oppressed and outcast peoples. The "Q" stands for the queer community, the "U" for the untouchables, the "E" for emigrants, the second "E" for the excommunicated, and the "N" represents those who have been labeled as "negroid."[10]

The fourth and fifth suites of the Chase Saga show that others in the Neon Valley are beginning to stand up for and defend Cindi. One of the interludes on *The Electric Lady* is quite instructive. "Our Favorite Fugitive" is set in the radio station WDRD. DJ Crash Crash is taking calls from listeners; many of the calls are quite hostile to androids. The humans calling in express all manner of invective that we in the "real" world know signifies racist and homophobic sentiment. However, Josh, a student at Time University, asks if "the android community" believes that Cindi—now called "Electric Lady Number One"—is also the ArchAndroid. As Josh begins to further elaborate that "in the book of . . . ," the DJ hurriedly cuts him off.

This vignette points to the Messianic nature of Cindi Mayweather. It is clear that Monáe is following the mystery narratives within the Gospels and signified in science fiction movies like *The Matrix* to center this android as significantly different, even queer.

Monáe's Use of the Erotic

Monáe's third studio album, 2018's *Dirty Computer,* seems to move away from the messianic saga that preceded it. However, upon examination of the 45-minute emotion picture that accompanies the album's release, it might also appear that Monáe is willing to "kill" Cindi Mayweather so that Monáe herself can take center stage. That, however, is not the case, as shown in a recent interview with the website BuzzFeed that is quoted on the website io9.[11] Regarding *Dirty Computer*'s place in the Metropolis saga, Monáe notes that she had conceived of the *Dirty Computer* album before the ArchAndroid. The *Dirty Computer* emotion picture draws on such science fiction classics as *Blade Runner* to create its dystopian visuals and sound. It begins with a voiceover by Monáe that describes just how one could be considered "dirty": "They started calling us computers. People began vanishing and the cleaning began. You were dirty if you looked different. You were dirty

---

10. "Janelle Monáe Says 'Q. U. E. E. N.' Is for the 'Ostracized & Marginalized,'" Fuse, https://www.fuse.tv/videos/2013/09/janelle-monae-queen-interview.

11. Pulliam-Moore, "Janelle Monáe Explains."

if you refused to live the way they dictated. You were dirty if you showed any form of opposition at all. And if you were dirty, it was only a matter of time."[12]

The use of "dirty" and "clean"—especially as they are deployed against the romance between Jane 57821 and Zen (Tessa Thompson)—echoes the homophobic discourses of right-wing Christianity. In the dystopian society presented in this emotion picture, Jane and Zen's love is revolutionary. Their love is perhaps even more revolutionary than the love between Cindi May-weather and Anthony Greendown and is the embodiment of Audre Lorde's claims regarding the erotic. She describes the liberating power of the erotic in the following ways. First, the erotic provides power in and through shar-ing. Second, the erotic provides an "open and fearless underlining of [a] capacity for joy." Finally, the erotic places a demand upon the person that life "be lived within the knowledge that such satisfaction is possible, and does not have to be called marriage, nor god, nor an afterlife."[13]

Jane and Zen's love is not prurient, nor is it sanitized, as evidenced in the emotion picture's uses of the song and video "Pynk." Later, as the emotion picture uses part of the song "Django Jane," Monáe raps, "Arch-Android orchestrated . . . Black girl magic they can't stand it . . . we femme the future."[14] Also, in "I Got the Juice," Monáe sings:

> Got juice for all my lovers, got juice for all my wives (hey!)
> My juice is my religion, got juice between my thighs (hey!)
> Now, ask the angels, baby, my juice is so divine (hey!)
> Ain't no juice quite like yours, ain't no juice quite like mine (hey!)[15]

These and other lyrics in *Dirty Computer* center the joy that sexual liberation brings. To "femme the future" is to center the erotic in Black women's lives instead of marginalizing it. The sharing that the erotic prompts is evident in Monáe's call for collective action against misogyny and heteropatriar-chal structures. Monáe's liberated sexuality frames other forms of collective agitation against oppression. As Julia Sarantis notes in her essay on *Dirty Computer*, although this album and its visuals are set in a dystopian future,

12. Janelle Monáe, *Dirty Computer* video.

13. Lorde, *Sister Outsider*, 57.

14. Janelle Monáe, "Django Jane," recorded April 2018, track 6 on *Dirty Computer*, Wondaland Records, Bad Boy Entertainment, and Atlantic Records, digital.

15. Janelle Monáe, "I Got the Juice," recorded April 2018, track 9 on *Dirty Computer*, Wondaland Records, Bad Boy Entertainment and Atlantic Records, digital.

Monáe's Afrofuturism shows that "there is a lot of hope, joy, and critical work being performed."[16]

Returning to the song and video "Pynk," this celebration of the vagina does not dive into the pornographic. Rather, it follows Lorde's second use of the erotic. The video's description itself echoes Lorde:

> PYNK is a brash celebration of creation. self love. sexuality. and pussy power! PYNK is the color that unites us all, for pink is the color found in the deepest and darkest nooks and crannies of humans everywhere . . . PYNK is where the future is born. . . ."[17]

Monáe's Afrofuturism meets with Audre Lorde's description of the erotic in this "brash celebration" that will lead people into a better future. It is clear that this better future rejects economic and social structures that alienate us from ourselves and each other. The erotic is the way in which we connect not only to ourselves but also to and with and for others. This brash celebration then flows outward from the particular to the universal. PYNK is now an Afrofuturistic liberation centered in the erotic.

This leads to the third use of the erotic, the imperative to infuse it into every aspect of life as it compels us to live life fully and completely. Because *Dirty Computer* plays with time and space, resulting in a nonlinear narrative, this rejection of gendered and sexed binaries, and of the controlling narrative of linear time itself, means that the erotic in *Dirty Computer* takes dystopia and responds with a defiant "yes." This defiant "yes" is not limited to our sexual selves. Rather, it is the liberation of our sexual selves that can lead to liberation in our other selves. The memories that we see in the entire *Dirty Computer* emotion picture may be fragmented and placed in different temporal contexts, but they provide visual languages of liberation.

If *Dirty Computer* is a predecessor to the already established Metropolis Saga, Monáe once again draws on science fiction and takes an Afrofuturistic turn in order to confound our previously held expectations. She draws on the penchant within late twentieth- and early twenty-first-century science fiction sagas to construct the "prequel," the film or television series that does the work of explaining "how things came to be" and building the world(s) that were established in successive works. In this case, *Dirty Computer* sets the stage for the emergence and eventual persecution of androids like Cindi Mayweather. Returning to the statement that "They started calling us com-

16. Sarantis, "How Janelle Monáe's Visual Album."
17. Florio, "Janelle Monáe's 'PYNK' Video."

puters," Monáe echoes the dehumanizing ways in which racism, misogyny, classism, and homophobia work to render any perceived "other" in non-human terms. She warns us that the anti-android world of her prior (and yet subsequent) works begins with dehumanizing language.

Dirty Computer breaks down components of prior Afrofuturistic and queer productions, and reassembles them into a 45-minute mini-epic. This emotion picture is the Black woman's reformation, breakdown, and replication of Sun Ra's Arkestra. Monáe even remixes her own prior saga, deleting Anthony Greendown and Cindi Mayweather and the coy "around the edges" femme queerness that were part of her previous productions. Gone is the romance between an android and a human, replaced by two femme androids loving each other as part of a new, queer Afrofuturistic saga. Indeed, the aforementioned *Rolling Stone* interview opens with Monáe shedding Cindi (and the metaphor of the android) as her alter ego:

> "Being a queer black woman in America," she says, taking a breath as she comes out, "someone who has been in relationships with both men and women—I consider myself to be a free-ass motherfucker." She initially identified as bisexual, she clarifies, "but then later I read about pansexuality and was like, 'Oh, these are things that I identify with too.' I'm open to learning more about who I am."[18]

Dirty Computer—both the album and the emotion picture—serve as Monáe's statements about her and other Black women's sexualities. Her freedom to explore herself is not just a personal project; rather, her work serves as a template for other Black people to engage in the work of personal and communal liberation.

As a critique of "they," heteronormativity and white supremacy work to demand that "the other" deny and forget their feelings and histories. The "they" that *Dirty Computer* repeatedly references demand that those who have been labeled as "the other" endure a procedure that is called "cleaning." Here is where the emotion picture references the alliances between religion and cishetero white supremacy. As the "dirty" person is prepared to be cleansed, the person must recite a confession of uncleanness and their readiness to be cleaned. Indeed, a woman, clad in white and named Mother Victoria, strides through the halls of New Dawn as if she is the head of a religious order. It is implied that sufficiently "cleansed" people take their place

---

18. Spanos, "Janelle Monáe Frees Herself."

as "Torches," suggesting a convent-like order. Further, those who've been cleansed—meaning they have had the memories of their previous "dirty" life excised—are given new names. At the end of the film, Jane 57821 is no more; she is now known as "Mary Apple 54," and as a Torch, her existence is to extend the power of the faceless "they" and bring a "dirty" computer "from the darkness into the light," again signifying in religious language that presents the world in stark, dualistic terms.

Janelle Monáe as Queer Afrofuturistic Savior

As noted above, Janelle Monáe's latest album and emotion picture appears to have put the Cindi Mayweather alter ego aside in order to more fully live her truths. Through the lens of science fiction superheroes, this is the moment in which the hero fully reveals him- or herself to loved ones—for example, the scenes of *Superman II* when Clark Kent reveals to Lois Lane that he is Superman, or, as will be discussed in chapter 5, when King T'Challa reveals the existence of Wakanda to the world. These forms of revelation themselves follow closely religious narratives in which the savior figure reveals himself to a few followers or the world itself.

To return to Sun Ra, Prince, and her other musical touchstones, Monáe utilizes the cognitive estrangement of her androgynous, queer, pansexual selves in order to offer alternatives to rigid narratives of Black identity. As she works through her sexual identities, her gendered selves, and her musical representations of such, she sonically offers the Black listener and viewer a template for revision of their own selves. The "state of constant paradoxical tension" that English and Kim identify as part of Cindi Mayweather's presentation is itself a site of creative tension and creative possibilities for Black people. Such creative tensions and possibilities enable the Black listener and viewer to embrace the queer salvation she offers. English and Kim posit Monáe's Afrofuturism thusly:

> Indeed, it may be that Monáe and her compatriots are poised to "afford us some glimpse into a postmodern or technological sublime," a sublime that [Frederic] Jameson posits then immediately dismisses, given "the whole world system of present-day multinational capitalism." Janelle Monáe's and Wondaland's new, multivalent version of Afrofuturism, that is, neo-Afrofuturism—expressed via highly technologized music and vocals, dance, website manifestos and blogs, interviews, clothing, videos, extraor-

dinarily dynamic live performances, and even commercials—provides us
with a fresh, funky optimism that promises not so much to "remove" as to
move us, even in the context of contemporary capitalism.[19]

The queer Afrofuturistic savior that Monáe presents need not oppose capitalism; rather, she may take capitalism and turn its logics on itself in order to
effect change. Contemporary capitalism may not even be the enemy; Monáe
argues that the enemy is the disaffection engendered by racism, white
supremacy, heterosexism, and homophobia. While these forces use capitalism, they may not be the products of capitalism. Monáe's oeuvre shows us
that she too can exist fully within a capitalist structure.

Monáe's rejection of dualisms and description of herself as pansexual are
deft dismissals of sexual binaries that center heteronormativity and cisgender heteropatriarchal structures. To return to Lorde's "Uses of the Erotic,"
and as noted earlier in the chapter, Cindi Mayweather first functions as the
"other" who sees the possibility of embracing the erotic as a primary lens for
experience and existence. Cindi Mayweather and the other Alpha Platinum
androids implicitly and explicitly critique society's insistence on perpetuat-
ing heterosexism, racism, and homophobia. Monáe's first works all played
at the edges of the erotic, but it is *Dirty Computer* as a whole and a few select
songs that delve into Lorde's celebration of the erotic.

An example of the aforementioned is the first single from the album,
"Make Me Feel." Widely described as a "bisexual anthem," the song's funky
bass accompanied by a gender-fluid video and no gender pronouns in the
song itself is a celebration of the knowledge that the erotic reveals. Consider Lorde's statements concerning the functions of the erotic. First, the
erotic provides a powerful connection via joy ("whether physical, emotional,
psychic, or intellectual") with another person. Another function is the way
the erotic opens a person up to themselves. At this level, the erotic may
appear quite threatening. According to Lorde, once the erotic reveals deeper
selves, the individual begins to reevaluate every aspect of their lives. Such
reevaluation as it reveals newer selves then requires shifts in society itself.
For Lorde, the empowering nature of the erotic is a "grave responsibility,
projected from within each of us, not to settle for the convenient, the shoddy,
the conventionally expected, nor the merely safe."[20] In the case of "Make
Me Feel," Monáe combines the Afrofuturistic palette and model of her prior
works with frank sensuality, projecting a freedom—a dangerous, volatile

19. English and Kim, "Now We Want Our Funk Cut," 228–229.
20. Lorde, *Sister Outsider*, 57.

freedom—that can only be experience through the erotic. The line "it's like I'm powerful with a little bit of tender, an emotional sexual bender" conveys the ways in which the erotic fuels the construction of a new, liberated self. In an interview with *The Guardian*, Monáe described "Make Me Feel" as a "celebratory song." Further, she said,

> I hope that comes across. That people feel more free, no matter where they are in their lives, that they feel celebrated. Because I'm about women's empowerment. I'm about agency. I'm about being in control of your narrative and your body. That was personal for me to even talk about: to let people know you don't own or control me and you will not use my image to defame or denounce other women.[21]

The power of the erotic is the power to work on behalf of other people's sexual liberation. In the case of Monáe's song and video, she uses late twentieth-century capitalist logics to effect Afrofuturistic images of liberation for queer and nonbinary Black women. Liberation for Monáe is celebration, the ability to craft and disseminate celebratory narratives about Black women's bodies through the Afrofuturistic. "Make Me Feel" and the other songs and emotion pictures associated with *Dirty Computer* are Afrofuturistic visual forms of Black female liberation.

Conclusion

Janelle Monáe's queer femme Afrofuturism is a partial fulfillment of the kind of liberation that Octavia Butler's science fiction and Audre Lorde's revolutionary writing anticipated. As I describe her as a queer Afrofuturistic savior, it is evident that the imagery evoked in her songs, emotion pictures, interviews, and so forth draw on the kinds of messianic tropes that are familiar to Black audiences. However, her kind of messiah is not divorced from the erotic. Instead, Cindi Mayweather and Monáe herself embrace the erotic, put it front and center, and queer our messianic hopes and expectations.

While she certainly uses capitalism as a vehicle to disseminate her messages, she does not yet appear beholden to it in order to craft a denatured sexual and deracinated self. Indeed, Monáe has capitalized on her early success and parlayed it into roles that put Black women front and center. From her turn as Teresa, the maternal figure for Chiron in *Moonlight*, to her role in

---

21. Bengal, "You Don't Own or Control Me."

Hidden Figures as Mary Jackson, one of the quartet of unsung Black women who helped put humanity on the moon, Monáe has used her growing popularity to speak to Black women of all sexualities and classes past, present, and future. Like her predecessors Sun Ra and Prince, Janelle Monáe's queer Afrofuturism is as much interested in sonically smashing the patriarchy as it is about making us dance.

CHAPTER 5

Walking in the Path of the Prophets

Star Trek: Deep Space Nine, "Far Beyond the Stars,"
and Black Prophetic Visions

The previous chapters attended to real-world crafters of Afrofuturistic cultural productions. The respective works of Octavia Butler and Janelle Monáe expand the frontiers of Afrofuturistic thought as well as use Afrofuturism and the Black science fictional imagination to offer not only critiques of religion but other pathways of understanding and formulating Black religious lives. As real-world crafters of Afrofuturism, both Butler and Monáe expressed a love of science fiction that enabled them to craft their respective Afrofuturistic visions.

As Gene Roddenberry's creation, *Star Trek* (sometimes referred to as *The Original Series,* or *TOS* for short) represented a utopia in which humanity had finally overcome the major obstacles preventing it from flourishing: War, disease, famine, racism, and greed had eventually vanished from human experience. The United Federation of Planets and its exploratory/military wing Starfleet represented a utopian ideal in which humans will eventually explore "the final frontier" for exploration's sake rather than for expansion or conquest. In the *Original Series,* much of the conflict and drama derived from contact with "the alien of the week," or a sentient computer gone mad, or a human who had violated Starfleet's noninterference directive, popularly known as the Prime Directive. The *Original Series'* successor, *Star Trek: The Next Generation* (often referred to as *The Next Generation,* or *TNG* for short) continued the pattern laid down by the *Original Series,* eschewing story arcs in favor of mostly standalone episodes. However, *Star Trek: Deep Space Nine* (often referred to as *DS9*) was, at the time, a radical departure from its predecessors.

This particular chapter will focus on Captain Benjamin Sisko, his position in the *Star Trek* universe as the first Black lead of a *Star Trek* television series, his position as captain of "the most important space station in the Alpha Quadrant," his role as Emissary to the Prophets, and finally his role as one of the saviors of the Alpha Quadrant through the lens of an Afro-futuristic imagination. Sisko as prophet and savior of the fictional United Federation of Planets and the planet Bajor refigures the traditional Christocentric ideologies and gifts Black people with new religious possibilities. Specifically, this chapter will focus on the sixth-season episode "Far Beyond the Stars" as representative of Captain Sisko's prophetic Blackness. This episode departs from the mode of its predecessors in that it directly addresses white supremacy. Both the *Original Series* and *The Next Generation* addressed racism; however, they did so through analogy and metaphor. However, *Deep Space Nine*'s "Far Beyond the Stars" explicitly uses the captain's racial identity, heritage, and, through the intervention of extraterrestrial entities that exist outside of linear time, the experience of racism and white supremacy as the center of a narrative.

The figure of Benny Russell—the Black science fiction writer who creates *Deep Space Nine* and its residents in this episode—is a visionary prophet who sees the world as it could be. Russell is more like Octavia Butler instead of Samuel Delany in that Russell's creation includes the creation of the religion that leads to Sisko's encounters with the Prophets (or wormhole aliens, in Starfleet parlance). Both the actual Butler and fictional Russell have entered into a genre that ironically considers Black people as alien—so alien, in fact, that the science fictional imagination as constructed by white people cannot conceive of Black people in any future as real.

Star Trek Literature and *Deep Space Nine*

As I noted at the beginning of this book, I found myself watching rewatching "Far Beyond the Stars" and exploring it as a therapeutic intervention against blackpain after reading about the now near-daily occurrences of police brutality against Black bodies. Through the medium of science fiction television, this emergent personal ritual of watching this episode allowed me to achieve some form of catharsis, to scream, to rage, to cry. Of course, as a devout "Trekkie," I had seen the episode when it initially aired in February 1998, and multiple times after the series made its way to Netflix.[1] In constructing this essay, I sought out texts that attended to race, religion, and *Star Trek* in general and *Deep Space Nine* in particular. Certainly, the literature regarding *Star Trek* is continually growing; however, much of the work that explores *Star Trek* and religion focuses primarily on the *Original Series* and *The Next Generation*. However, there are essays and book chapters that attend to *Deep Space Nine* and religion. *Star Trek and Sacred Ground: Explorations of Star Trek, Religion, and American Culture* contains an essay that interrogates representations of religion in *Deep Space Nine*. Peter Linford's "Deeds of Power: Respect for Religion in Star Trek: Deep Space Nine" articulates the different approach this series took to religious belief. However, this essay is more of a critique of the series' approach to religious belief than an exploration of the effects of such presentations for the viewers. Further, essays that attend to religion in *Deep Space Nine* often elide the implications of the franchise's first African American lead also functioning as a savior/prophetic figure. Also, these essays do not explore the intersections of Afrofuturistic thought, religion, and *Star Trek* in general or *Deep Space Nine* in particular. For example, Murray Leeder's contribution to the edited volume *The Star Trek Universe: Franchising the Final Frontier* (2015) attends only to religion as presented and critiqued in *Star Trek: The Original Series* and *The Next Generation*. Jeffrey Lamp's essay "Sisko the Christ" in *Star Trek as Myth: Essays on Symbol and Archetype at the Final Frontier* explores Benjamin Sisko's role as the Emissary to the Prophets as analogous to a messianic figure, but the essay does not present any analysis of Sisko as a descendant of African American functioning as a savior figure. A promising treatment of the possibilities offered via *Deep Space Nine* in general and "Far Beyond the Stars" in particular is found in the fifth chapter of Roberta Pearson and Maire Messenger Davies's *Star Trek and American Television*. This chapter focuses on the world-building inherent in "Far Beyond the Stars," particularly the alternate world created by Benny Russell that the viewer knows as the *Star Trek* universe. The purpose of this chapter is to illustrate how *Star Trek* functions as a "narrative trendsetter"; in this case, "Far Beyond the Stars" functions as a narrative critique of racism and white supremacy.[2]

---

1. For a discussion of fan devotion to *Star Trek*, see Michael Jindra's essay "Star Trek to Me Is a Way of Life: Fan Expression of Star Trek Philosophy," in *Star Trek and Sacred Ground: Explorations of Star Trek, Religion, and American Culture*, edited by Jennifer E. Porter and Darcee L. McLaren (Albany: State University of New York Press, 1999). 217–30.

2. Pearson and Davies, Star Trek and American Television, 141.

Akin to this piece is Micheal Charles Pounds's exploration of the epi-sode "Explorers" in the third chapter of *The Black Imagination: Science Fiction, Futurism, and the Speculative.* Like the work that follows, Pounds's essay seeks to situate the episode "Explorers" as reversing Eurocentric narratives. According to Pounds, "After 'Explorers,' the Star Trek experience is revised and identification expanded by acknowledgment of its African origins as real and indispensable to appreciating the spirit of adventure and exploration that is the franchise touchstone and our shared legacy."[3] Of the essays and book chapters that have addressed *Deep Space Nine,* Pounds's essay is one of the few that explicitly connects the figure of Captain Benjamin Sisko to racial representation and interpretive strategies. Further, this essay appears in a volume specifically designed to address what the editors call "the Black imagination." The essay that follows builds upon that presentation of the Black imagination.

Star Trek: Deep Space Nine

When *Star Trek* was revived as a weekly television series in the late 1980s, Gene Roddenberry wanted the crew of this new *Enterprise* to be, for lack of a better word, perfect. Captain Jean-Luc Picard (played by Patrick Stewart) was as close to a perfect character as one might find in fiction. Picard's stern demeanor was coupled with a keen intellect and cultured interests in classical music, art, literature, and archaeology. His preferred beverage itself bespoke a character steeped in cultured tastes. Picard's standard order to the replicator was "Tea, Earl Grey, hot." *Star Trek: The Next Generation*'s replicator is itself an indicator of Roddenberry's utopian vision. In the series, and subsequent iterations of *Star Trek,* the food replicator virtually eliminates hunger, as it is a technology that can, upon command, produce virtually any food or beverage programmed into the computer. As with its groundbreaking predecessor, the voice of human reason and progress in *Star Trek* is in the form of a white, heterosexual male. It is those characters that provide the narrative thrust of the series, delivering the show's creed at the beginning of each episode. James T. Kirk (*TOS*) and Jean-Luc Picard (*TNG*) present the face of the putatively multicultural, 150-world United Federation of Planets. It is a formula that was turned on its head by the time *Deep Space Nine* made it to the airwaves.

---

3. Pounds, "'Explorers'—Star Trek: Deep Space Nine," 71.

Star Trek: Deep Space Nine was itself quite a departure from what had come to be understood as the traditional mold of *Star Trek* laid down by the *Original Series* and then continued with *The Next Generation*. Instead of a voyaging starship called *Enterprise* captained by a single, white-identified male and a supporting diverse crew of spotless morality, this particular iteration of *Trek* was led by an African American male captain who had a son, a female first officer (who was a former terrorist), and a host of culturally diverse and morally ambiguous people on a backwater space station. The series premiere titled "Emissary" begins with Commander Benjamin Sisko, then the first officer of the USS *Saratoga*, losing his wife in the Battle of Wolf 359, a catastrophic and apocalyptic battle between Starfleet and the implacable, cybernetic race called the Borg.[4] After the battle, Sisko, now a widower raising a son, is posted to the newly acquired space station Deep Space Nine. The Cardassians, who had occupied the nearby planet Bajor and brutally oppressed the planet's inhabitants for fifty years, had stripped and abandoned the station, leaving it for the Federation and Starfleet to take over.[5] It is at this posting that Sisko encounters aliens known as the Prophets.[6] The Prophets are noncorporeal entities that exist outside of normal space-time and live within a wormhole that connects the Alpha Quadrant (where much of the action in both *TOS* and *TNG* takes place) to the distant Gamma Quadrant. The Bajorans—a highly spiritual humanoid race—worship these Prophets. By the end of the series premiere, the Prophets have designated Sisko as their Emissary.[7] By extension, the Bajorans come to revere Sisko as the Emissary of the Prophets. This is a position that Sisko initially rejects, reflecting the secularized skepticism of Starfleet, the Federation, and, by extension, the larger *Star Trek* mythos.

One of *Star Trek*'s enduring problems has been its presentation of non-human cultures as being virtually monolithic. In this case, the problem has been the presentation of Bajorans as having one singular religion. Since the

---

4. The Borg were introduced in *Star Trek: The Next Generation* in the season 2 episode "Q Who" (airdate: May 8, 1989) and again in the classic season 3 cliffhanger and season 4 resolution "Best of Both Worlds, parts 1 and 2" (airdates: June 18, 1990, and September 24, 1990). Part 2 depicts the aftermath of Battle of Wolf 359, but not the battle itself.

5. In the first episode, it is clear that Deep Space Nine is decidedly not an ideal posting, which again distinguished this series from *The Original Series* and *Next Generation*, where being posted to the respective series' USS *Enterprise* held significant esteem. The course of the series saw the station change from an unimportant space station to a commercially important station, and then finally, to a vital station on the front lines of an intergalactic war.

6. *Star Trek: Deep Space Nine*, "Emissary," directed by David Carson, written by Michael Piller and Rick Berman, aired January 3, 1993, on Paramount Television.

7. Ibid.

introduction of the Bajorans in the *Next Generation* episode "Ensign Ro," the writers never introduced more than one religious orientation for Bajorans.[8]

While the *Original Series* and *The Next Generation* were inconsistent in their presentations of religious belief in the twenty-third and twenty-fourth centuries, *Deep Space Nine* was consistent in wrestling with questions that related to religious faith and belief. As mentioned above, the first episode of the series is a radical departure from the previous series in that the main character not only meets an alien entity that may be a deity, but he himself becomes known as a representative of those entities. While the series in its first few seasons takes pains to show that Sisko is not at all comfortable with the title and role of Emissary to the Prophets, over the course of the series— and definitely by the fifth and sixth seasons of the series—he embraces his identity as part of his destiny.[9] It is Sisko's relationship to the Prophets that functions as background to the sixth-season episode "Far Beyond the Stars."

In Mark Scott Zicree's proposed draft, this particular episode was supposed to focus on Jake Sisko, Benjamin's son. In the original proposal, Jake would have traveled through time to the past. However, Ira Steven Behr turned the script down, and then later suggested that the episode focus on the elder Sisko and deal with racism. Zicree, Behr, and Hans Beimler worked together to produce the final script. While it may appear problematic that the script was written by white men, the showrunners decided to ask Avery Brooks to direct the episode. As the production commentary on Memory Alpha notes, "Usually, when an actor directs, their character has a very small role." Instead, not only did Brooks direct the episode, his character played the prominent role in the episode. According to Behr, it would have been inappropriate to have a white director directing a narrative that centers on Black experiences of racism and white supremacy.[10]

In the episode, Captain Benjamin Sisko is feeling the weight of the Federation's two-year-old war with the Dominion, the militaristic, totalitarian power that is dominant in the Gamma Quadrant.[11] As he's talking to his

---

8. Later in the run of *DS9*, the writers introduced the cult of the Pah-wraiths; however, I would not characterize this as another religious orientation. Rather, this is a response by some Bajorans to a sentiment that the Prophets had abandoned them.

9. Several episodes, designated as "The Emissary Trilogy," demonstrate Sisko's evolution from actively resisting the title and role of Emissary to actively embracing it.

10. "Far Beyond the Stars (episode)," Memory Alpha, https://memory-alpha.fandom.com/wiki/Far_Beyond_the_Stars_(episode).

11. At this point in the series, the station Deep Space Nine has transitioned from being a "backwater space station" to one of the most important outposts in the Alpha Quadrant (the region of space that contains the species that populate the *Star Trek* universe). Further, this is the first *Star Trek* series to depict a sustained military conflict

father, who is visiting the station, Benjamin sees a man dressed in 1950s attire walk in front of his office. Soon, he begins not only seeing images *from* the '50s, he finds himself *in* the '50s. Further, he is no longer Captain Benjamin Sisko. Instead, he is Benny Russell, a science fiction writer living in New York City. From that point forward, the story takes place in 1950s New York as though that setting constitutes "the real world." Benny writes for a sci-fi magazine called *Incredible Tales*. The first scenes of Benny in the office set the episode's direct and unflinching tone concerning racism in the 1950s. The magazine's editor, Douglas Pabst, tells the assembled writers (all white with the exception of Benny and all male with the exception of Kay Hunter) that the readers want to know what the writers look like, so there will be a photo shoot. Pabst further tells Kay and Benny that they "can sleep late." Apparently, the public would not be able to deal with a Black or woman science fiction writer, a point that Pabst's foil Herbert Rossof makes in sarcastic fashion. We see from the outset the ordinary atrocities of white supremacy and how they wear down upon Black bodies, as dramatized when Benny argues that Black people like Langston Hughes have been writing, but is rebuffed by Pabst's dismissive "that is literature for Negroes and liberals." However, when the staff artist hands out conceptual art pieces that are used to frame stories, Benny becomes entranced by a drawing of a space station and takes it home. After an encounter with racist street cops, Benny goes uptown to Harlem and encounters a street preacher who points at him and tells him that "the Lord, God of the spirits of the Prophets, has sent his angel to show his servants what must soon take place. Praise the Lord. Open their eyes. Help them to see." The preacher calls Benny by name—an odd occurrence, since the preacher should not know Benny personally. The encounter ends with the preacher telling Benny, "Go now and write the truth that's in your heart. The truth that shall set them free!" This initial encounter with the preacher is not all unlike the Prophet Muhammad's encounter with the Archangel Gabriel or Moses's encounter with Yahweh in the burning bush. In a sense, this street preacher is exhorting Benny Russell to write an apocalypse, a revelation of that which is to come.

Eventually, Benny writes a story called "Deep Space Nine." Despite everyone in the office loving the story, Pabst refuses to publish it because the story's protagonist—named "Benjamin Sisko"—is a Black man who commands the station. To the editor's thinking, no one will accept a story in

---

between the utopian Federation and another galactic power. The Dominion was introduced in the season 2 episode "The Jem'Hadar" (airdate: June 12, 1994). War between the Federation and the Dominion broke out in the season five finale "Call to Arms" (airdate: June 16, 1997).

which the captain of a space station is a Black man. Pabst goes so far as to claim that such a story is not only "not believable," it might also cause a race riot. While this might appear absurd to viewers in the twentieth and twenty-first centuries, this claim is an example of the lengths to which white supremacy goes in order to thwart Black imaginaries. Although Rossof defends Benny's story—albeit, more from personal antipathy toward Pabst than from an actual desire for social justice—the rest of the office sits in sympathetic silence. It would appear that the editor is correct, as shown when Benny tells streetwise Jimmy that he's writing about Black people in space and Jimmy derisively dismisses him and the story—in fact, it is the only time the word "nigger" has ever been uttered in a *Star Trek* series. Benny's girlfriend, Cassie, is more concerned with the two of them settling into a quiet life in which she runs the restaurant where she works and Benny could write for *The Amsterdam News*, a Black-owned newspaper. Another encounter with the preacher spurs Benny to write six more stories about Deep Space Nine and Captain Sisko.[12] This encounter even more sharply underscores the religious parallels of this episode. Benny tells the preacher that he doesn't understand what the preacher wants of him. The preacher responds with, "To follow the path of the Prophets. Walk with the Prophets, Brother Benny. Show us the way." The episode shows us that science fiction has prophetic possibilities, that the words that Benny is exhorted to write can "lead us out of the darkness [and] onto the path of righteousness." Science fiction as prophetic imagination has the potential to show us better worlds—in this case, the preacher urges Benny to use that imagination to show humanity an existence free of the darkness of global white supremacy.

Further, he begins to see the people in his world as the characters he has created. For example, as his coworkers are reading his story, he sees Kay Hunter as Bajoran Major Kira Nerys, and the aforementioned racist street cops take the form of representatives from the authoritarian Cardassians and Dominion. Further, as Benny writes more stories, his realities begin to blur. He is becoming this Benjamin Sisko, and fears that he is losing his mind.

In order to get his first story published, Benny agrees to a compromise and makes the entire story a "dream." However, this compromise is not enough. Mr. Stone, the unseen owner of the magazine (who represents the intangible forces of oppression and structural iniquity and inequality) pulps the entire magazine's run and fires Benny. Benny has a nervous breakdown

---

12. It is possible that each new story that Russell wrote represents the six seasons of the television series. Such an inference is supported by the reappearance of Russell as a plot device in the season 7 episode "Shadows and Symbols," in which Russell's writing corresponds directly with events happening in Sisko's reality.

in the office. He tells those around him that they cannot destroy an idea and that those people in the story exist:

> You can pulp a story, but you cannot destroy an idea! Don't you understand, that's ancient knowledge. You cannot destroy an idea! That future, I created it, and it's real! Don't you understand? It is REAL! I created it and IT'S REAL![13]

When Benny wakes up in an ambulance, he realizes that he is wearing a Starfleet uniform. The preacher has appeared beside him, and tells him that he can now rest easy, and that he has walked in the path of the Prophets, for which "there is no greater glory." Benny asks, "Who am I?," to which the preacher responds, "Don't you know? You are the Dreamer, and the Dream." Benny looks out the windows of the ambulance and sees stars streaking by, the signature visual effect that represents to the viewer a starship at warp speed. It is at that point that the episode shifts permanently back to Captain Sisko and "our universe." Sisko awakes in Deep Space Nine's infirmary, and the doctor tells him that he has been unconscious for only a few minutes. Only a few minutes have passed during the period in which Sisko was living the life of Benny Russell, and in "our universe," Sisko had merely experienced some "unusual synaptic potentials."[14] In the episode's final scene, Sisko talks with his father and vows to continue fighting the Dominion, and his father surprisingly quotes the Bible:

> JOSEPH: . . . The question is, what are you going to do?
> SISKO: The only thing I can do. Stay here and finish the job I started.
> (a beat)
>   And if I fail . . .
> JOSEPH: "I have fought the good fight. I have finished the course. I have kept the faith."
> SISKO (looking at his father in surprise): I've never known you to quote the Bible.[15]

---

13. "Far Beyond the Stars."

14. Sisko's unusual brain activity and the attendant visions he experiences in "Far Beyond the Stars" is connected to a prior episode of the series. Season 5's "Rapture" saw Captain Sisko receiving visions from the Prophets as a result of a "plasma shock." The "synaptic potentials" mentioned in this episode are repeated in "Far Beyond the Stars" and work to connect Sisko's experiences in this episode with the Prophets.

15. "Far Beyond the Stars."

The episode ends with Sisko musing, "Somewhere, far beyond all those distant stars, Benny Russell is dreaming of us."[16] There is much to unpack here. Both Benny Russell and Ben Sisko are prophets who, through the realm and conventions of science fiction, inform and influence each other's prophetic visions.

The elder Sisko quoting from the Bible in the supposedly humanistic twenty-fourth century is itself instructive. It is the refutation of the assumption that religion would have no place in the Federation. We never saw Jean-Luc Picard quote from the Bible or espouse any form of religious faith or belief. Indeed, as noted above, he seems to labor under the assumption that humankind has "freed" itself from such beliefs. Benjamin does note that he has not known his father to quote from the Bible, to which Joseph replies, "I'm full of surprises." The surprise here is that the humanistic universe imagined by Gene Roddenberry, this universe that would have allegedly have no place for such things as the Bible, prophetic utterances, and religious faith, has now expanded. The Bajoran Prophets and their interaction with Benjamin Sisko is subversive in that a Black man is not just the commander of an important space station, he is the savior figure for a planet, and then for an entire quadrant of the galaxy. If science fiction readers in the 1950s could not imagine a Black man as a commander of a space station, then they certainly could not imagine a Black man as a conduit for entities that, for all intents and purposes, are gods.

Star Trek: Deep Space Nine and Blackpain

The scene in which Sisko/Russell "breaks down" is often criticized as being "overplayed" or, in the case of the A.V. Club review, "half-crazed poetry, the sort of broken heart madness that Brooks is so good at."[17] Another review on the website Jammer's Reviews describes Brooks's acting thusly:

> I'll admit that I think Avery Brooks may have overacted his payoff scene a tad more than he needed to. It seemed a little uneasy upon first viewing. But when I watched it again, it seemed to work better. If you think it through, Bennie is an example of one man who has reached his limits and can't take any more. Just when a lifetime of frustrations and fruitless patience finally seemed like it was going to pay off, he finds himself start-

---

16. Ibid.
17. Handlen, "Star Trek: Deep Space Nine."

ing all over again with nothing gained, and no progress made. He loses it. "Nervous breakdown" would probably be an applicable '90s term.[18]

These critiques are often subtle dismissals of the pain at the core of Black experiences in this nation. Further, while many of the reviews and analyses of this particular episode acknowledge the torturous history of race in this country, they do not adequately connect that pain, that *blackpain* to Brooks's reading of that scene. Simply put, critiques of Brooks's performance—particularly the breakdown—emanate from a white culture that cannot fathom blackpain. Avery Brooks's performance throughout the entire episode and the climactic breakdown in particular is a powerful dramatization of the blackpain that has framed Black life in America. This acting choice itself is a shout against the death-dealing and nihilistic forces of white supremacy. This is Black productive imagination in action as it speaks truths to power through dramatic acting. Once again, I read Brooks's performance as prophetic in itself. The breakdown at the climax of "Far Beyond the Stars" is prophetic in that it "calls out" the racism in a society that claims to be threatened by Black imagination and can only respond by inflicting pain upon Black bodies.

This particular scene in the episode characterizes what *Star Trek* in particular was able to do. This episode as a critique of racism is able to do so via the medium of science fiction. As a form of American mythology, *Star Trek* was able to critique and affirm the American experiment. It is Brooks's experience of directing and acting in the lead that frames this essay's argument about a Black imaginary. In discussing his directing and acting in this episode, Brooks said:

> If we had changed the people's clothes, this story could be about right now. What's insidious about racism is that it is unconscious. Even among these very bright and enlightened characters—a group that includes a woman writer who has to use a man's name to get her work published, and who is married to a brown man with a British accent in 1953—it's perfectly reasonable to coexist with someone like Pabst. It's in the culture, it's the way people think. So that was the approach we took. I never talked about racism. I just showed how these intelligent people think, and it all came out of them.[19]

---

18. Epsicokhan, "Star Trek: Deep Space Nine."
19. "Far Beyond the Stars (episode)," Memory Alpha, https://memory-alpha.fandom.com/wiki/Far_Beyond_the_Stars_(episode),

It is that unconscious expression of racism that could not imagine a future in which a Benjamin Sisko could be the captain of a space station. As Brooks notes, that unconscious racism is so deeply rooted that otherwise "intelligent" people will consider a Black man crazy if he can "see" a future in which Black and white people aren't ruled by racism. In the episode, after Benny has come back with six sequels to the initial Deep Space Nine story, the editor Douglas Pabst asks him, "Have you lost your mind?!?" Benny replies, "Lately, I've been asking myself the same question."[20] Black imagination as disruptive imagination may likely be "crazy," but it is crazy insofar as it works against a status quo that serves a white supremacist imaginary.

Benjamin Sisko and Benny Russell as Prophets

To characterize Benjamin Sisko and Benny Russell both as prophets, we must jump back and forth through time. The Prophets that Sisko met in the series premiere and urged Russell to "write the words" do not exist in linear time. In "Emissary," Sisko has to explain the human experience of linear time and its unpredictability to them. It is established that the Prophets have the ability to interact with the corporeal universe outside of time. Benjamin Sisko's journey in this episode obviously mirrors Benny Russell's journey. However, I contend that, as Sisko notes at the end of the episode, Benny Russell is dreaming of us. Further, we may understand the "vision" that Sisko experienced as being every bit as real as the lifetime that Captain Picard experienced in the acclaimed "The Inner Light." If we take Sisko's vision as real, then the temporal and physical distance between Sisko and Russell collapses. Indeed, had showrunner Ira Steven Behr gotten his way regarding the series finale, the viewer would have seen this collapse of space and time. At the 2018 Star Trek Las Vegas convention, Behr revealed how he wanted to end the series. On the panel dedicated to "Far Beyond the Stars," Behr said that he wanted to end the series with Benny Russell walking around a soundstage at Paramount Studios where his creation, "Deep Space Nine," was being filmed. Rick Berman, the other showrunner for *DS9*, rejected the idea. According to Behr, Berman asked, "Does this mean The Original Series was in Benny's head?"[21]

---

20. "Far Beyond the Stars."

21. Heather Ferris, "Deep Space 9 Far Beyond the Stars at the 2018 Star Trek Convention in Las Vegas," YouTube, August 8, 2018, https://www.youtube.com/watch?v=jxvpSSAapco&t=728s.

Benny Russell writing the words that will lead the people out of darkness are akin to proclaiming the word of the Lord to the Egyptian pharaoh. In this case, however, this proclamation is to the subjects of oppression, not the oppressors themselves. The subversive nature within this story of "Far Beyond the Stars" lies in that the prophetic word is not to white people or directly about them. Certainly, white supremacy frames the narrative—and is presented as an analogue to the rapacious nature of the Dominion—but white supremacy is not supreme. White supremacy and the Dominion may exist in linear time, but they frame their quests for dominance in time—and such quests can be thwarted. They may be able to destroy ships, and they may be able to destroy stories, but they cannot destroy the idea of freedom that built those ships and wrote those stories.

By the time "Far Beyond the Stars" aired, Sisko had fully embraced his role as Emissary to the Prophets, largely out of a growing affection for the planet Bajor and its inhabitants. As the Prophets repeatedly told him, "You are of Bajor." However, the war between the Federation and the totalitarian Dominion was clearly a test of his resolve to remain in that role. As noted above, the episode begins with Sisko apparently ready to quit not just the war, but also his role as Emissary. The Prophets then may have thrust him into memory/vision/reality in which his ancestor dreamed this world called the United Federation of Planets.

Russell's inspiration to take a drawing of a space station and build an entire galactic Federation that emphasizes mutual understanding and cooperation and is free from racism, hatred, and so forth is constitutive of Black science fiction writing. Black science fiction writers have long used the medium as a way of critiquing the oppressive structures that deal death and misery to Black peoples. It would not be surprising that a Black science fiction writer in the 1950s might create a future world in which racism no longer immediately governs the lives of Black people. In the case of Benny Russell, he reframes the implacable, insatiable desire for domination that composes white supremacy in the form of the Dominion. The racist cops who harass him outside of his office are, in their *DS9* roles, agents of the Dominion and its ally, Cardassia. If we think of Black imagination as active resistance to the death-dealing forces of white supremacy, then I read Russell's creation of Deep Space Nine as defiance—we Black people will not only survive and flourish well into the twenty-fourth century, but we will also rise to command the most important outpost in the Federation as well as one of the most powerful ships in the quadrant. Like Afrofuturists in "our" world, Russell uses the medium of science fiction to reframe the lives of Black people in his world. For example, instead of a being a struggling restaurant waitress, Cassie is now Kasidy Yates, a fearless freighter captain. Jimmy, the wayward youth cut down by the soulless minions of white supremacy, is now Sisko's son Jake, who, in the world created by Russell, is a successful writer in his own right.

Further, this episode follows in a vein of *Star Trek* episodes in which the captain leads a wholly different life. For example, the *Original Series* third-season episode "The Paradise Syndrome" featured Captain Kirk losing his memory and essentially being adopted into a tribe of humanoids that parallel Earth's Native Americans. While the Enterprise is attempting to divert a planet-killing asteroid from striking the planet, Kirk (now called "Kirok") has become accepted as the tribe's god, and assumes a fairly carefree life with Miramanee, the tribe's priestess. As would become a standard trope in these kinds of episodes, the tribe turns on Kirk and Miramanee once it is proven that Kirk is not a god and stone both of them, killing Miramanee, who was also pregnant with Kirk's child. This kind of tragedy was part of *Star Trek: The Next Generation*'s fifth-season episode "The Inner Light." In this episode, the *Enterprise* encounters an alien probe, which projects some kind of energy beam onto Captain Picard, knocking him unconscious. In just twenty-five minutes, Picard experiences forty years in the life of a man named Karmin, a scientist who discovers that his planet is slowly dying as a result of increased radiation from the planet's sun. The planet's elders placed the memories of the culture into the probe and sent it into space in order to somehow preserve the memory of their civilization. The episode ends with Picard playing a Ressikan flute that had been placed in the probe—the same flute he learned to play in the alternate lifetime. This particular episode garnered high praise, winning the 1993 Hugo Award for Best Dramatic Presentation. It has been routinely considered as one of the best episodes of the franchise.

However, "Far Beyond the Stars" departs from the tragedy that ends *TOS*'s "The Paradise Syndrome" and *TNG*'s "The Inner Light." Sisko does not suffer loss; rather, Sisko's experience of Benny Russell's life gives him the strength and inspiration to continue leading the fight against the Dominion. The experience gives him the determination to continue fighting for a world that Benny Russell had envisioned.

For Black people to write themselves into a future is to adopt and adapt an eschatological hope that does not rely on an otherworldly afterlife. While the future of which Benny Russell dreams is neither a religious heaven nor an unblemished utopia, Russell nevertheless functions as St. John the Divine, receiving and relating a revelation of the end of oppression. As such, when the "spirit" in the form of the preacher urges Benny to "write the words that will lead us out of darkness," Benny is, like St. John, outlining a vision of the future in which the descendants of the oppressed receive vindication. Here, the "new Heaven and new Earth" are humans of all races pushing out into the stars and transforming Earth into a virtual paradise. I read Russell as presenting Deep Space Nine as a gospel of liberation that stands as fulfillment of James Cone's theological project. When the Prophet speaks to Benny and urges him to "write the words . . . that will lead us out of darkness," I see the Prophet as the indwelling, inspiring spirit that empowers the oppressed person to engage in prophetic utterances. Further, when the Prophet (who in the "real" world of the Federation is Benjamin Sisko's father) tells Russell first that hope and despair are often hand in hand and then that there is no greater glory than to walk in the path of the Prophets, I read these statements as science fictional representations of divine wisdom. This is the prophetic imagination in action. The dreamer understands that their work is itself part of the dream. As Walter Bruggemann noted in the introduction to *The Prophetic Imagination,* "I suspect that whatever is 'prophetic' must be more cunning and more nuanced and perhaps more ironic."[22] Here, Bruggemann is talking about the work of the prophetic in an increasingly secularized world. It cannot take on a thoroughly oppositional approach to the "world"; rather, the prophetic must approach the world imaginatively. I would add that the prophetic must also approach the world with passion. The representation of divine wisdom through human voices must be driven by a kind of passion that allows for cunning, ironic approaches to the world. The work of the dreamer is cunning in that it is subversive. Benny Russell uses the medium of science fiction to subvert white supremacy, to throw its racist imaginary into turmoil. The United Federation of Planets, Deep Space Nine, and the multiracial, multicultural crew are the indictments against the white supremacist imaginary and show an eschatology in which the white supremacist imaginary has finally been rendered inert.

The story that Benny Russell wrote involved characters set in a universe that we "know" to have been created by Gene Roddenberry in the 1960s. However, for Benny Russell's characters and story to work, he would have had to create and outline for the reader the underlying political structures and history of the United Federation of Planets. By the internal logic of the episode, it was not Gene Roddenberry who created *Star Trek*; rather, it was Benny Russell, who, in Sisko's words during the episode's coda, "was dreaming of us." Once again, returning to the prophetic imagination, the writers and actors may be asking, "What if Star Trek had been created by a

---

22. Bruggemann, *The Prophetic Imagination,* loc. 85 of 4382, Kindle.

black person?"²³ This science fictional imagination acts as a meta-narrative, daring the viewer to see a fictional universe that we "know" to have been created by a white male through a different lens. This is a return to Womack's articulation of Afrofuturism in which a cultural worker sees Black experiences either absent or misrepresented, and "set[s] out to do something about it." Thus, Afrofuturism as we see it in "Far Beyond the Stars" functions as a deep corrective of the overwhelming whiteness at work even in the supposedly multicultural *Star Trek* fictional universe.

The episode itself is a metanarrative critique of racism in American popular culture. In terms of fan rankings of the various *Star Trek* series, *Deep Space Nine* usually occupies a position lower than that of the *Original Series* and *The Next Generation,* but higher than *Voyager* and the much-maligned prequel series, *Star Trek: Enterprise.* As I noted earlier, the "mold" that the *Original Series* set and *The Next Generation* followed privileged white heterosexual male experience. Indeed, Captains Kirk and Picard are held as paragons of Starfleet captains. When *DS9* began, Sisko was not even a captain; this would be the first *Star Trek* series in which we would see the lead earn the rank. While *Star Trek* has been critical of racism among humans, the franchise itself has not wholly been free of it. This, of course, is part and parcel of the problem with science fiction. While we may indeed dream worlds and existences beyond our own, those imaginations are not completely free from hegemonic narratives. The androcentric problem at the heart of the *Star Trek* franchise is the androcentric problem at the heart of science fiction, namely, the conceit that white heterosexual male experience and narratives are the narratives that matter. Black lives may have mattered, but they did so only insofar as they supported white heteropatriarchies.

It is here that I return to Afrofuturism. I will quote part of a piece about Afrofuturism that appeared in the *Nassau Weekly,* a Princeton University student-run publication:

> Afrofuturism wants you to step back and see the slave ships as space ships. As author Nalo Hopkinson said, African people were snatched up from their homes by invaders, forced to cross an entire ocean, and deposited in a foreign place where their abductors tried to take away their culture, language, and history. That kind of thing sounds more like science fiction than reality. And of that culture, language, and history, Hopkinson says, "We remade them. Where we could not remake them we conjured them.

23. Steven Barnes's novelization of "Far Beyond the Stars" explicitly describes Benny Russell as having created *Star Trek,* albeit in several unconnected short stories. In the novelization, Benny's creation of "Deep Space Nine" brought the previous short stories into focus.

We rebuilt ourselves as people anew." Thus, the African American story is rewritten as one of supreme victory—and one that is ongoing.[24]

What we need to be able to contribute to Black theological and religious conversation is more dreaming. When I say that we need more dreaming, I am thinking of those of us who find ourselves drawn to science fiction and find ourselves referring to those worlds envisioned in the works of Octavia Butler, Janelle Monáe, George Clinton, and the like. I think that a narrative such as the one found in "Far Beyond the Stars" casts dreaming as a subversion of what we call reality. To dream, as Benny Russell does, of Deep Space Nine and Captain Benjamin Sisko, and to write down, draw, record, sing, and film those dreams is to follow the voice of the Prophets and present narratives that lead us out of the darkness of the white supremacist imaginary.

Further, the Black imaginary at work in this episode draws on the role of the Prophet as a reimagining of deities. As mentioned above, the series features noncorporeal entities that exist outside of linear time, yet interact in time with Captain Sisko. In this particular episode, the Prophets are represented by the figure of the Black street preacher who appears at several points to exhort Benny to continue writing the words. I contend here that this episode may yield a reimagining of "God" in which the motivating spirit or noncorporeal entity urges humanity toward shaping change. As mentioned in the synopsis of the episode, Captain Sisko is close to despair, wondering if he should leave Starfleet. His experience as Benny Russell, as a vision given to him by the Prophets, gives him the strength to continue his role in the war against the Dominion and himself function as an agent of change.

An interesting and important note here is Avery Brooks's own understanding of Benjamin Sisko as Emissary to the Prophets. A feature on the 2007 *Star Trek Fan Collective: Captain's Log* DVD contains interviews with each of the actors who were captains in the franchise. The interview is broken up into smaller segments. Of interest here is the "Sisko as Emissary" segment. At first, Brooks describes Sisko's ambivalence with being identified by the Bajorans and the Prophets as Emissary. However, he then notes, "As I talked about this character, and what his lineage is and everywhere African people are there is a relationship to the spiritual and the divine . . . I'm sure that he had some sense of what [the Bajorans], their spirituality was about."[25] Brooks connects African-descended peoples' practices and views to

---

24. Mar-Abe, "Ferguson Is the Future."

25. ManticoreEscapee, "Avery Brooks Interview (2007)," YouTube, September 6, 2017, https://www.youtube.com/watch?v=8OV4JG2U2RY.

Sisko. This connection is reinforced throughout the series in general, and in "Far Beyond the Stars" in particular. For example, in the third-season opener "The Search, Part 1," we see that Sisko owns a 2,000-year-old Yoruba mask. In "Far Beyond the Stars," Benny Russell's apartment has a Dogon door, among other West African artifacts. For Brooks, Sisko's African heritage is connected to instead of divorced from a larger view of the spiritual and the divine. As such, the viewer receives visual cues in the form of the masks and carvings that both Sisko and Russell have in their respective personal spaces. As director of this particular episode and the central figure of the series, Brooks understands *Star Trek* in general as presenting a vision of the future and describes himself as wanting to be part of the solutions that bring about a brighter future for humankind.[26]

Conclusion

Black imagination as shaping God and God shaping Black imagination is that prophetic moment in which we, like Benny Russell, tell the world that what is created is real, and white supremacy cannot destroy that. Black imaginations, like the Blackness from whence they come, are as disruptive as they are prophetic. The futures we create participate in the life of God-as-world. We live and we develop our Blackness in community. We do not submit to terror. Rather, we create these futures, "far beyond all those distant stars," these futures in which Black lives not only matter, but they rise, and they are real.

---

26. Ibid.

CHAPTER 6

"Wakanda Forever!"

Black Panther, the Divine Feminine, and the
Subversion of Toxic Masculinity in the
Western Superhero Monomyth

Movies based upon comic book superheroes have entered the mainstream as not only profitable but also culturally relevant entities. Of course, movies like *Superman: The Movie* (1978) and several iterations of *Batman* in the 1990s and early 2000s set the tone for comic book movies. The inaugural issue of any comic book introduces the hero's origin. Usually, heroes emerge as the result of a tragedy, their origins becoming iconic and prototypical: Superman is rocketed to Earth to survive the destruction of his home planet Krypton. Batman begins his life of nighttime crime-fighting after witnessing his parents' murder. Spider-Man receives his powers after being bitten by a radioactive spider, but then learns that "with great power comes great responsibility" after he fails to use his abilities to stop a thief—who later shoots and kills his uncle.

As such, the source material coupled with quantum leaps in special effects led to another wave of blockbuster superhero movies. After years of failed to mediocre films, Marvel Studios spearheaded what we might call the Modern Age of superhero films, introducing tightly plotted movies with near-perfect casting (including reviving Robert Downey Jr.'s career) and engaging and entertaining plots, and fully leaning into the fantastic and science fiction conventions of the source material. Marvel Studios went a step further and ensured that each entry into the Marvel Cinematic universe was connected to and would introduce other aspects of the "Marvelverse." Indeed, DC Comics, Marvel's longtime competitor and the company that ushered in the comic book superhero, has not been nearly as successful as Marvel has been in creating an equally interwoven and engaging cinematic universe. With the exception of 2016's *Wonder Woman* and 2018's *Aquaman*, the DC cinematic universe has not experienced the same box office success nor the same critical acclaim, primarily because the executives at Warner Brothers and the directors of the early DC universe movies sought to ground their characters in far grimmer settings and circumstances.

While movies like *Superman: The Movie* might have "made you believe a man can fly," with the exception of the *Blade* trilogy of movies in the 1990s, superhero movies have had difficulty making one believe that Black superheroes exist. Simply put, both DC and Marvel superhero movies have been overwhelmingly white, heterosexual, and male. These movies reflect the overwhelming whiteness of the source materials. As Jonathan Gayles, producer of the documentary *White Scripts and Black Supermen: Black Masculinities in Comic Books* notes, superhero comic books are a "white male power fantasy."[1] Further, Gayles notes that the few Black male superheroes in comic books are often either extremely limited in their powers or directly in service to white characters.[2] Aside from Blade, the other Black superhero movies in the 1990s were somewhat less than stellar. 1997's *Spawn* featured a Black male lead and was a serious take on the comic book source material; however, like the comic book character, the actor spent most of the movie in a costume that masked his face. The movie itself was largely forgotten. *The Meteor Man* of 1993 and *Blankman* of 1994 were more comedic than serious. Again, these movies have fallen into obscurity.

Marvel Studios' *Black Panther* is the latest in a wave of superhero comic books adapted to the silver screen. As of the writing of this essay, the movie has crossed the $1 billion mark at the box office and has already cemented its status as one of the highest-grossing superhero movies of the decade. Further, this movie has garnered an impressive array of awards, including three Academy Awards, two of which were firsts for Black women in technical categories that have been overwhelmingly white. It was also nominated for Best Picture, making it the first superhero movie to ever be nominated for that award. The anticipation and buzz surrounding the movie largely focused on the nearly all-Black cast and its setting in the technologically advanced African nation of Wakanda. The importance of seeing a Black

---

1. Screening of "White Scripts and Black Supermen: Black Masculinities in Comic Books" at 2012 DragonCon, Atlanta, GA, with Damien Williams as moderator.
2. John Hope Franklin Center at Duke University.

superhero not supporting a white superhero or otherwise framed by whiteness is inestimable and has already been the subject of several essays and thinkpieces. However, what is also fascinating is the movie's presentation of religion and attempts at addressing its deep cultural impact among African Americans.

In the aftermath of *Black Panther*'s success, a few African American preachers and congregations (namely, Jamal Bryant, pastor of Empowerment Temple in Baltimore) used the movie's visual palette and thematic elements to set up Bible studies and sermon series. However, these efforts not only appeared to capitalize on the movie's popularity but also functioned to bolster the relevance of Black Christian practices and experiences. In other words, Black preachers began reading and interpreting Wakanda through Western Christianity, even though there is nothing inherently "Christian" in it. According to an article on the website The Grio, Bryant and his church planned to use the month of March to "wear African themed attire all the way up to Easter." An advertisement for the sermon series titled "The Gospel from Wakanda: Building a Black Nation from the Bible" features Bryant's face awkwardly photoshopped onto an image of T'Challa sitting on the Wakandan throne. The symbolism of such an image in conjunction with the title of the series is fairly overt: Bryant appears to set himself up as the potential head of a utopian Black nation based upon the Bible instead of based on vibranium.

This impulse to impose Christian theological parallels and narratives were not restricted to churches. In academic discourses, calls for papers sought to connect the movie to Black theological frameworks. The website PopCultureAndTheology.com published a March 19, 2018, blog post titled "Liberation Theology in Black Panther." In this post, Corey Patterson attempts to connect the movie to James Cone's foundational theological arguments. The same site later presented a call for papers as part of a potential volume on *Black Panther* and Black liberation theology. As of the writing of this chapter, at least two program units within the American Academy of Religion have, as part of their annual call for papers, asked for submissions related to Afrofuturism in general and *Black Panther* in particular. However, such calls once again position *Black Panther* in potentially Christian theological contexts.

This chapter contends that *Black Panther*'s Afrofuturism presents an African/Black religion that, like Wakanda itself, is not informed by white supremacy. Further, as Wakanda's spirituality/religion is informed by African religious traditions, the religion we see in *Black Panther* offers the viewer (especially African American viewers) creative alternatives to "Western" monotheisms. *Black Panther* plays upon religious tropes found through-out comic book/superhero movies and revises them via Afrofuturism. The intersection of Afrofuturism and Black religious thought provides the Black viewer with an Afrofuturistic religion not tied to resisting white supremacy via heroic Blackness.

Another argument this chapter advances is that *Black Panther* subverts the typical masculine savior figure trope. While the viewer may focus on the dichotomy between T'Challa and Killmonger, Okoye, Nakia, and Shuri subvert that dichotomy; further, they function as an antidote to the toxic masculinity that is the invisible enemy within this movie. Additionally, the movie itself subverts the hero's origin story that so often serves as the intro-duction to the character. It is Killmonger's origin that we see unfold, and it is his origin that ties into all the elements of the Western monomyth. As such, *Black Panther* presents a rather subtle critique of the nature of the Western monomyth.

Movie Synopsis

The movie begins by a son asking his father to tell him the story of home. Home here is Wakanda, so the viewer sees the mythic beginning of Wakanda, from the vibranium meteor that strikes the African continent to the uniting of the four tribes to Wakanda's eventual isolationism in order to protect this vital resource from being exploited by the colonizing powers. The movie shifts to Oakland in 1992 to present even more backstory: Wakan-dan prince N'Jobu is planning some kind of operation with a friend (later revealed to be another embedded Wakandan spy, Zuri), only to have his plot foiled by his brother, King T'Chaka. N'Jobu pulls a gun on Zuri, but T'Chaka intervenes, killing N'Jobu. This sets up the major conflict of the movie, as N'Jobu's son Erik not only watches the Royal Talon depart but also finds his father's dead body.

The movie shifts to the African continent, where Nakia and T'Challa are returning to Wakanda following T'Chaka's death. The ritual ceremony in which T'Challa would assume the throne and the mantle of Black Panther is interrupted by M'Baku, leader of the Jabari tribe, who challenges T'Challa to ritual combat. T'Challa defeats M'Baku and assumes the throne. Mean-while, Erik Killmonger steals a vibranium artifact from a London museum and, along with his accomplice Ulisses Klaw, plans to sell it. This sets up the movie's first big action scene, as T'Challa, Nakia, and General Okoye of the Dora Milaje travel to South Korea to intercept this sale and capture Klaw.

Killmonger foils T'Challa's plans and makes his way to Wakanda to reveal himself to his royal relatives and challenge T'Challa for the throne. After defeating (and presumably killing) T'Challa, Killmonger takes the throne; takes the Heart-Shaped Herb, thereby gaining the powers of Black Panther; and plans to use Wakanda's advanced technology to wage a genocidal war against the rest of the world. Nakia, T'Challa's sister Shuri, and his mother Queen Ramonda flee to Jabariland with the last of the Heart-Shaped Herb and ask for M'Baku's help to retake the throne. There, they find T'Challa in a coma. Shuri, Nakia, and Queen Ramonda administer the Heart-Shaped Herb and beseech the ancestors to restore T'Challa. In the movie's final act, T'Challa and Killmonger battle once again. This time, T'Challa is victorious, returns to the throne, and establishes a Wakandan Outreach center in Oakland at the site of his uncle's death.

What Is the Significance of Wakanda?

At the end of the movie, one of the most important scenes occurs mid-credits. As moviegoers now know, the Marvel movies are known for inserting additional scenes in the middle and at the very end of the end credits. The general function of these scenes is to serve as a bridge to future Marvel movies. In this case, the mid-credit scene in *Black Panther* takes place at the United Nations. T'Challa, flanked by Okoye and Nakia, addresses the General Assembly, telling the body that the nation of Wakanda is ready to end its policy of isolation and stands ready to share its resources with the world. After a stirring speech in which T'Challa asserts that the world is a single tribe, and "the foolish build barriers while the wise build bridges," a white representative asks, "What can a nation of farmers offer the world?" T'Challa gives a knowing smirk, and the end credits resume.

In this one scene, the movie's Afrofuturistic vision of religion is laid bare, as it calls to mind the passage from the Gospel of John:

> The next day Jesus decided to go to Galilee. He found Philip and said to him "Follow me." Now Philip was from Bethsaida, the city of Andrew and Peter. Philip found Nathanael and said to him, "We have found him about whom Moses in the law and also the prophets wrote, Jesus son of Joseph from Nazareth." Nathanael said to him, "Can anything good come out of Nazareth?" Philip said to him, "Come and see."[3]

---

3. John 1.43–46 (New Revised Standard Version).

For those who were skeptical that a Black-centered superhero movie that highlighted a futuristic African society could be wildly successful, the first week's astounding box office as well as its critical acclaim is Philip's response to Nathanael: Come and see. Further, the French representative's query is both a rebuttal to skeptics and also a not-so-subtle critique of global white supremacy as it is a question that reinforces the salvific power contained in an African nation that avoided the crushing effects of colonialism. What this (technologically advanced) nation of farmers can offer the world is a view of the world and a relationship to technology not bound by avarice. The movie itself stands as a cinematic and mythological response to the white man's burden and the implicit question, "Can anything good come out of Africa?"

What does Wakanda signify for Black people? It and its citizens as represented by T'Challa, Nakia, Shuri, Queen Mother Ramonda, and General Okoye signify a place of belonging, a realm of possibilities not framed or overdetermined by white supremacy. The outside world that Wakanda has isolated itself from is a world dominated by colonialism and global white supremacy. As outlined in the opening narrative, Wakandans recognized the powerful potential of vibranium and decided that it could not fall into the hands of outsiders. Wishing to keep their technologically advanced society a secret from a world that "descended into chaos," Wakanda decided to "hide in plain sight," and present their country as a poor, resource-deprived society. Of course, this is itself a play upon the white supremacist presentation of African societies as uniformly impoverished and "backward."

Over many years, Black peoples have speculated about advanced African societies, lamenting the loss of those societies to invasions and so forth. At the edge and center of those speculations was the hope of recovering a glorious African past. Such a recovery would serve as the counterpoint to white supremacist assertions that Black peoples around the world had nothing to contribute to the advancement of civilization. Such speculations are not necessarily the province of conspiracy theorists and YouTube video bloggers. We can turn to W. E. B. Du Bois's *Souls of Black Folk* and find an early twentieth-century assertion that Africa had a mighty past:

> The shadow of a mighty Negro past flits through the tale of Ethiopia the Shadowy and of Egypt the Sphinx. Through history, the powers of single black men flash here and there like falling stars, and die sometimes before the world has rightly gauged their brightness.[4]

---

4. Du Bois, *Souls of Black Folk*, 9.

This quest for a mighty African past is a balm against the pervasive claims throughout European and American history and philosophy that Africa was and is some blighted hellscape that requires the guiding hand of the civilized white man. Historically, the white man's burden had been the philosophical justification of global white supremacy. Arguing from the position of technological supremacy, European and American historians, politicians, philosophers, and theologians claimed that it was the "burden" of the white race to "civilize" nonwhite peoples in general, and African peoples in particular. However "noble" the stated burden was, it was actually an excuse to justify the brutal subjugation, enslavement, and near-extinction of indigenous peoples.

When the viewer is treated to the first glimpses of Wakanda, it is not the technologically advanced Golden City. Rather, we see a virtually unspoiled country, indeed, a nation of farmers and shepherds. The animals run free through a land not spoiled by deforestation and strip-mining. When the Royal Talon approaches what appears to be a mountain of dense trees, T'Challa says, "This never gets old"—just then, the craft passes *through* the trees, now revealed as a gigantic holographic screen that hides the Golden City. The music swells, and we see the Golden City spread out before us, a technological and architectural jewel. The city's various towers are lush with foliage and trees, signifying a balance with and respect for nature that is virtually absent in Western cities—such a view is reinforced when the action shifts to London. Whereas Wakanda is rendered in vibrant colors, London is virtually monochromatic.

A second view of the Golden City shows us how technology can coexist with nature. After T'Challa's coronation and experience in the Ancestral Plane, we see him walking through the streets with Nakia. If we pay attention to this tiny slice of life in the Golden City, most everyone walks. We do not see streets clogged with fossil fuel–burning cars and trucks. Also, there is an extensive public transportation network in the form of magnetic levitation enabled trains that zip through the city and smaller trams that run unobtrusively at the ground level. Amidst these advanced forms of transportation, people walk, eat at open-air cafés, and patronize shops. There are no signs of "big box" stores or chain coffee shops, or any other imprint of Western multinational corporatism.

Even more, we see Black women and men walking, eating, and going about their daily business. While that might seem of little note, it is helpful to examine these scenes a bit further. Something that also may have gone unnoticed is the absence of any police presence. While we do at one point see the Dora Milaje following King T'Challa, they are there to protect the king and in no way harass or interact with the citizenry of the Golden City. While there is no other visible police presence, women appear to walk freely without being catcalled or subjected to other forms of harassment. Men do not appear to have antagonistic relationships with each other, nor do they appear to harass other people. From what the viewer can grasp in these brief glimpses of daily life in Wakanda, Black men, women, and children appear to enjoy their lives unfettered by the scourges of white supremacy, colonialism, and heterosexism.

Thus, it is clear that Ryan Coogler endeavored to show Black audiences the possibilities of all-Black spaces. The presentation of Wakanda is itself a defiant shout against the pop-cultural presentation of all-Black spaces as deficient and dysfunctional. We might view the Wakanda of the present as juxtaposed with Oakland of 1992 and again in the present as subtly emphasizing the depth of the depredations of white supremacy and its effects upon colonized peoples. Note that in both versions of Oakland, there are virtually no Black women present. Further, although Oakland is decidedly urban, compared to Wakanda's cityscapes, it, like London, is stark and bleak. In contrast, Wakanda's vibrant, ecologically friendly cities and lush but not marginalized rural landscapes appear paradisiacal.

Perusing *The Art of* Black Panther as well as reading interviews with the movie's production designer, Hannah Beachler, reveals even more tantalizing tidbits about Wakanda. For example, Beachler notes that she modeled the Royal Talon off of a Dogon mask. She also noted that she treated Wakanda as a character itself. In the case of *Black Panther*, Wakanda was not only an imagination of Beachler's, but it was also important to director Ryan Coogler. For both Beachler and Coogler, "getting Wakanda right" was vitally important:

> You know, we had to create all of this history—just like you'd know about any city, or your own hometown. That's how much we had to go in on Wakanda, because Ryan said to me one day: "What are the names of the streets? What do they do in that building? What is it about this park that makes it unique? What's the history of that area? What different parts of town are there? Who lives there?" . . . So we just started from the beginning. We started with a timeline and made a timeline of, like, 10,000 years ago. We started 10,000 years ago, and we worked our way up to 2018. . . .
>
> I always say the production designer is the believer. I have to believe in this world; I had to believe that I was a Wakandan architect to create Wakanda, and I had to be there 24–7 for a year. That was my mindset. So it

was all about that, always. And for each film, you do that in the different world you're telling the story of.[5]

The costuming was equally detailed. Ruth Carter's work participated in creating, as a piece on CNN calls it, "a new vision of Africa through Wakanda." For Carter, the creation of the various looks that the characters would wear was part of constructing an Afrofuturistic aesthetic:

> "I knew Marvel comic books and that this super fandom was big, so I was enthusiastic. I was curious," Carter said. "I thought this has got to be an important film, and it had to be something that was Afrofuturist. . . . I would have to represent images of beauty, forms of beauty, from the African tribal traditions so that African-Americans could understand it; so that (non-black) Americans could understand African-Americans better; so we could start erasing a homogenized version of Africa.[6]

As with the creation of Wakanda's futuristic cityscapes as well as its rural harmony, Carter's costuming uses Afrofuturism in order to center Black beauty. The various African tribal inspirations, from the metal next rings of the Dora Milaje to Queen Ramonda's crown, to the use of vibrant color to represent the characters, all are reflective of a desire to subvert the "often-negative images of Africa that have been used to shame Black people across the diaspora for centuries."[7]

Creating Wakanda was not an abstract exercise. For Beachler and Coogler, Wakanda had to feel real. Creating Wakanda was part of creating the mythology that is the movie's background. Consider the great locations of ancient and contemporary mythologies. Valhalla, Mt. Olympus, Gotham City, Krypton, and even descriptions of Heaven and Hell in Christian thought are all places that, for fans and adherents, are ultimately real. These celestial and extraterrestrial places function as the axis upon which those religious and fictional worlds turn. It is not surprising that when we see various versions of the planet Krypton in the Superman mythos, it is presented as a virtual paradise. It should not also be surprising that, in the Marvel Studios movies, we see places like Asgard and, to a lesser extent, Avengers Tower as aspirational locations. What we saw in Wakanda was not just someone's imagination; rather, it was the hope and dream of Black

---

5. Kai, "Whose World Is This?"
6. Alleyne, "How 'Black Panther' Costume Designer."
7. Ibid.

peoples who had not seen themselves so gloriously reflected onscreen. The past, present, and future did not "collide"; it merged into the vision that was Wakanda. We, the viewers, could imagine ourselves as part of this Wakandan life. In the foreword to *The Art of* Black Panther, Coogler articulates the importance of creating Wakanda and *Black Panther* and ushering this vision to the screen:

> As for the question of what it means to be African, I found the answer in this project. During my trip to the continent, I traveled and met with other African people my age, and I discovered that they were so much like me and my family back in the States that I felt completely at home. I recognized several of their rituals as things that we would do back home. I realized that for African Americans, our African culture wasn't lost: somehow, after all the horrible things we went through, we still found a way to hold on to it.[8]

Wakanda is the stark rejection and inversion of the white man's burden. Wakanda's burden, as shown in the movie's philosophical debate between Nakia and N'Jadaka/Killmonger, is about how to bring Wakanda's technological advancements to a decidedly dystopian world. The burden here is to alleviate the suffering that white supremacy and colonialism have caused. Having avoided that suffering by closing themselves off to the outside world, Wakandans like Nakia, W'Kabi, and T'Challa (as well as, of course, Killmonger/N'Jadaka) have distinctly different views regarding engaging the outside world. On one hand, W'Kabi, leader of the Merchant Tribe and close confidante to King T'Challa, and Erik Killmonger/N'Jadaka take a traditionally imperialist approach. At an early point in the movie and prior to Killmonger's invasion, W'Kabi advises T'Challa to "clean up" the outside world, presumably through the use of force. Here, the use of superior technology against lesser powers in the name of civilizing them appears, but this time, it is Africans who would propose using superior technology against Europeans/Americans.

However, the movie clearly rejects such a notion. As such, *Black Panther* eschews functioning as a revenge fantasy. Indeed, the movie could have taken a revenge fantasy path and set T'Challa and Wakanda up against a white enemy. Instead, the movie reframes the ongoing debate within African American and diasporic communities regarding appropriate responses to global white supremacy. Killmonger/N'Jadaka's desire to violently overthrow white supremacy is informed by and suffused with the same cultural chauvinisms of Western societies. As he notes after he assumes the throne

---

8. Roussos, *The Art of Marvel Studios*, 9.

after having appeared to kill T'Challa, "The sun will never set on the Wakandan Empire." His desire is apparent: He seeks to remake Wakanda in the image of his oppressors.

The Tragedy of Erik Killmonger's Toxic Masculinity

If there is an underlying moral within Black Panther, it is that might does not make right. Erik Killmonger's desire to use Wakandan technology in order to enact a genocidal campaign against white people is, as mentioned above, chauvinistic. It is myopic, and, ultimately, quite tragic. Indeed, the tragedy of N'Jadaka/Killmonger is framed by his origins, in which he discovers his dead father's body in the nation of his oppression. In a sense, he has been betrayed by both homes. His uncle kills his father and abandons him, while the country of his birth has imprisoned his mother, who died in prison.[9] Further, he does not get to live to see the beginnings of Wakandan efforts to redeem the country of his birth.

Such a tragedy is underscored throughout the movie. N'Jadaka's tragedy reaches its climax after T'Challa defeats him and retakes the Wakandan throne. After T'Challa stabs Killmonger, it appears that he has had some kind of awakening. He looks around and says that his father said that Wakanda was the most beautiful thing he'd ever seen and that he would show it to him. Killmonger says, "Do you believe that? A kid from Oakland running around believing in fairy tales." Feeling sympathy for Killmonger, T'Challa takes him to a precipice to see the beautiful Wakandan sunset and offers to heal him. The mask of toxic masculinity descends upon Killmonger again as he says, "Why? So you can just lock me up? Nah. Just bury me in the ocean with my ancestors that jumped from the ships, because they knew that death was better than bondage." In a final act of defiance, Killmonger pulls the spear out of his chest, and dies. The tragedy inherent in this final moment is that Killmonger's myopia and his chauvinism prevent him from truly apprehending the beauty of Wakanda and the mercy that T'Challa offered him. He assumes that T'Challa offers to heal him in order to imprison him— this one line is also an oblique reference to the prison-industrial complex in the United States, one that is punitive instead of rehabilitative. Killmonger cannot imagine any other system of correction or punishment, and chooses death, believing it to be more "honorable."

Further, Killmonger's tragedy is that he became that which he beheld. If we take seriously Toni Morrison's assertion that white supremacy's func-

---

9. Parker, "'Black Panther': Ryan Coogler Reveals."

tion is to distract us from our work, we see that Killmonger fell victim to the very worst impulses of that distraction. The movie makes it clear that he has no respect for any of the women in his orbit. He coldly shoots his female accomplice; is immediately disrespectful to his aunt, Queen Ramonda; disregards General Okoye's admonition to use Wakanda's technology only for defense; and very nearly kills his cousin Shuri. His notion of racial uplift is distorted via an imperialist revenge fantasy in which Black peoples around the world embark upon a genocidal war against their former oppressors.

Religious Themes in *Black Panther*

Black Panther's Afrofuturism is not limited to presentations of the technological utopia that is Wakanda. We see Afrofuturism merged with Black religion in the religious and spiritual life of Wakandans. Ancestor veneration is facilitated by technology, showing that Wakanda is neither a secular society nor a theocracy. It is implied that the vibranium meteor that struck Wakanda altered the plant life around it and that alteration facilitates entrance into the Ancestral Plane. As such technology is wed with spiritual/religious experience, the movie implicitly rejects the mind-body dualism prevalent in the West.

Divinities in *Black Panther*

The Afrofuturism of *Black Panther* does not appeal to a singular deity as found in Western societies. The only appeals to a deity in the movie are primarily to the Panther Goddess Bast and, to a much lesser extent, to Hanuman. In the prelude to the movie, the first Black Panther was led to the Heart-Shaped Herb in a vision given to him by Bast. Aside from repeated invocations of her name, we know little if anything else about Bast.

Despite the lack of information about Bast, it is clear that Wakandan society at least acknowledges the existence of this goddess, and Wakandans invoke her more than occasionally. Further, Wakandan society engages in ancestor veneration, and invokes them in times of extreme duress. Most importantly, the panther goddess presents a theological counterpoint to Western monotheisms. If Wakandan society's spirituality led to a unifying figure like the Black Panther, this may be an implicit critique of the Western concept of divine right of kings, as well as a critique of Western monotheism and the alleged divine approval of regional and global conquest. Certainly, had T'Challa had the same imperialist impulses of both Killmonger and W'Kabi, he could have cited the mythology of Bast leading the first Black Panther to the Heart-Shaped Herb and the unification of the three Wakandan tribes as the impetus for uniting Africans worldwide—just as Killmonger claimed.

Nevertheless, the figure of Bast as the primary Wakandan deity raises some compelling critiques of Western monotheism and Black peoples' relationship to gods that are not theirs. Indeed, perhaps this movie engages in a subtle assertion that real liberation may be found in an Afrofuturistic rejection of the Western gods and a reimagination of African deities. Certainly, we see in Wakanda an absence of the kinds of misogyny (and heterosexism and homophobia, as in Marvel comics lore, two of the Dora Milaje are in a relationship with each other) that permeate the West and are justified through appeals to the god of Christianity.

Intersectional Humanity in *Black Panther*: Centering Nakia and Okoye

Kinitra Brooks's presentation of conjure feminism is helpful in understanding the intersections of Nakia and Okoye in the movie. Brooks's work in recovering conjure is a recovery of her grandmother's practice of conjure, from which she gleans from a submerged past and points us toward new possibilities. For Brooks, the holistic practices of not only her grandmother but other Black women ancestors is part of a network of knowledge that brings a different kind of liberation. Instead of reading liberation as a system of inverted or revised power relations, Brooks's conjure feminism is rooted in Black women's communal system and practices.[10] In the case of *Black Panther,* it is a subtle move to show Black women taking care of the garden of the Heart-Shaped Herb, as it foreshadows Queen Ramonda and Nakia using the herb to restore T'Challa. As I read *Black Panther* as a subversively Black feminist text, I also read it as subverting Western monotheisms that position toxic masculinities at the center. The Panther Goddess Bast, along with the Dora Milaje and General Okoye, Nakia, Shuri, and Queen Ramonda, signify on the superhero genre's eliding of women of color's spiritualities. By centering these Black women at nearly every pivotal point in *Black Panther,* Coogler deftly shows the possibilities that diverse Black spiritualities offer. This movie mirrors Black women's efforts to reclaim goddess traditions and

10. Brooks, "Myrtle's Medicine."

African spiritualities as vehicles by which Black women's experiences are not only centered, but understood as instructive for Black peoples seeking to construct new Black communities and communal experiences beyond white supremacy.

Humankind as presented in this movie is a far richer source of religious discussion. As humans are the center of the movie's narrative, *Black Panther* shows humans in general and Wakandans in particular as part of a much larger mythological tapestry. On the one hand, we have Killmonger, who has sacrificed his humanity in service to a misguided desire for empire. At several points in the film, other characters explicitly note that he has allowed hatred to consume him and press him to become like his oppressors. Throughout, we see Killmonger as a misogynistic chauvinist who uses Black people as a prop for his quest for power.

While the obvious counterpoint to Killmonger's toxic masculinity is T'Challa's more thoughtful, introspective approach to Wakanda and the Black women in his life, it is Nakia and Okoye who represent the movie's humanistic soul. Early in the film, we see Nakia imploring T'Challa to take a more engaged stance and end Wakandan isolationism. Nakia's exhortation is borne of a deep concern for the rest of the world, apparently irrespective of race, religion, class, and gender. When we first see her, she is on a mission to rescue African women and a boy who have been kidnapped by a group of men who are an analogue to the real-life Boko Haram. After returning to Wakanda, Nakia tells T'Challa that she cannot enjoy the splendor that Wakanda offers while knowing that there are so many people in the world who are suffering. If Wakanda is a utopia, Nakia argues that it is Wakanda's moral obligation to share the fruits of that utopia with the rest of the world.

Like Killmonger, Nakia has seen the suffering that global white supremacy has caused. Like Killmonger and W'Kabi, she wants to do something about that suffering. She tells T'Challa that she has found her calling, and she cannot ignore the suffering in the world. However, she proposes using Wakanda's resources to provide assistance to the rest of the world. She tells T'Challa that Wakanda can provide assistance and refuge to others and do it better than other nations. Her prediction is fulfilled at the end of the movie when T'Challa establishes a Wakandan Outreach Center in Oakland, California, and in the place where his uncle N'Jobu was killed by King T'Chaka.

In effect, we may view Nakia as the prophet who is a herald to T'Challa's savior figure, the spirit that animates T'Challa's action. As Andrea Hairston points out, it is the women of Wakanda who are able to imagine different possibilities that T'Challa nor Killmonger cannot.[11] Because they are able to imagine different possibilities, their actions preserve the nation and afford it the opportunity to extend its gifts to the rest of the world.

Further, we see Nakia directly rejecting any attempt to minimize her voice and identity. Early in the film, we see Nakia and T'Challa walking through the streets of the Golden City. She implores him to open up Wakanda and use its considerable resources and technology to help improve the world by sharing with less developed nations (presumably including nations in the G8) as well as serving as a refuge for the world's outcasts and refugees. After this, T'Challa responds by saying, "If you weren't so stubborn, you would be a great queen." Nakia sharply replies, "It is *because* I am so stubborn that I would be a great queen." Sensing that T'Challa is trying to create an opening for a rekindled romantic relationship, Nakia quickly adds, "*If* that's what I wanted." In reflecting on that scene, T'Challa attempts to describe Nakia's persistence and her argument as "stubborn"—a term often derisively applied to Black women who refuse to be subordinate to Black male directives and dictates. In a sense, T'Challa attempts to "neg" Nakia. "Negging" is a backhanded compliment that functions as emotional manipulation. By holding out an "incentive" of being queen, it appears that T'Challa wants Nakia to subordinate her talents to his status. However, such attempts are fully negated by the movie's end. In a final scene that mirrors the earlier scene with T'Challa and Nakia, they once again walk through the Golden City. Gone is T'Challa's regal arrogance and assumption that Nakia would want or need to be queen. This time, he is far more contrite. He thanks her for saving him, his family, and Wakanda. Nakia responds that it was her duty to fight for what she loves—including T'Challa.

Here, it is instructive to examine another particular scene and connect the activity of Black women with Afrofuturistic spirituality that suffuses the movie. After Killmonger appears to have killed T'Challa and has assumed both the Wakandan throne and the mantle of the Black Panther, Nakia wisely spirits Shuri and Queen Ramonda to safety, for it is nearly certain that he would have killed them both. Then, Nakia goes to the Garden of the Heart-Shaped Herb and secrets away a plant just as N'Jadaka commands the garden's burning. Later, as the women attend to T'Challa's recovered body and administer the herb to him, they invoke the ancestors. It is Nakia who says, "Wake up, T'Challa," and the scene shifts to T'Challa on the Ancestral Plane.

---

11. Hairston, "It's Our Time."

Nakia's dream-like "Wake up" is the voice that brings him back to life, the breath of the spirit that brings him back from the bliss of the Ancestral Plane, back to himself, and back to his mission as Black Panther. On the surface, Nakia is presented as T'Challa's love interest. However, we can also read Nakia as the voice of wisdom, bringing life to the nation. Nakia's voice moves the nation, since it moves T'Challa to reject Wakandan isolationism shift toward global cooperation.

General Okoye, as Hairston points out, also devotes herself to the nation, not an individual—not even her own husband, W'Kabi. If Nakia is the voice of wisdom that animates T'Challa back to life and alters his trajectory, then Okoye is the active power that animates the nation. W'Kabi ignores her wisdom when she tells Killmonger that Wakanda has only used its advanced weaponry for defense. He sides with Killmonger at his own peril, for when the Wakandan civil war reaches its conclusion and she commands him to drop his weapon, he asks Okoye, "Would you kill me, my love?" To which she responds, "For Wakanda? Without question!" She is the warrior goddess whose martial prowess is tempered by a fierce love for the nation that supersedes the love for her husband. That love for Wakanda forces her to initially pledge her and the Dora Milaje's loyalty to Killmonger, since he challenged T'Challa and won the throne in lawful combat. However, it is clear that she wanted to back T'Challa; when he reappears, she says, "He lives!" If Nakia's is the voice that brings life to T'Challa, Okoye's is the voice that proclaims T'Challa's resurrection to the believers.

While it may be problematic to read Black Panther through savior-figure tropes, it is instructive to note how this movie reframes those tropes through intersectional Afrofuturism. Like Janell Monáe, Ryan Coogler, Hannah Beachler, and costume designer Ruth Carter remix those prior tropes and filter them through an intersectional Afrofuturistic lens. The women of *Black Panther* are the embodiment of the Golden City. Its utopian allure does not and cannot exist absent Nakia and Okoye—as well as Shuri and Queen Ramonda.

The humanist utopia of *Black Panther* requires its people to be in touch with and conversant about their feelings. This is what intersectional Afrofuturism has repeatedly told us. This is what Lauren Olamina's hyperempathy as it leads to the establishment of Earthseed told us. This is what Janelle Monáe's discography and emotion pictures have told us. Even the critiques of utopia as found in *Star Trek: Deep Space Nine* centered balancing logic with feeling. In *Black Panther,* we see the centering of feeling and intuition aligned with tradition over brute force. Killmonger's utopia was, in the final analysis, a dystopian vision, as he could only imagine the world through the lenses of cisheteropatriarchy that he inherited as an American. T'Challa could only imagine Wakanda as it had always been: isolated and stagnant. But it is the women of Wakanda who show them—and the viewer—the potential of the glorious vision of the Golden City.

Black Panther as Eschatological Hope

In a later chapter, I turn to Christophe Ringer's examination of *District 9* and Afrofuturism and his use of eschatology in order to situate the near-futurity of the South African setting of the movie. He draws on Victor Westhelle's centering of "geography and place as an integral part of understanding historical change."[12] This is a productive way of reframing eschatology and is useful for understanding Wakanda as a place of hope for African Americans. As the movie itself became a global phenomenon, many people of African descent began performing the Wakandan salute and repeating "Wakanda Forever."[13] Further, as a form of mimesis, Black people began dressing up as characters from the movie for Halloween and sci-fi/comic conventions. As an interpretive frame for Afrofuturism, this view of eschatology can help us understand Black people's desire to actualize Wakanda in some shape or form.

Taken together, these themes provide an Afrofuturistic response to the repeated question, "Who are you?" This movie gifts the Black viewer a science fictional response to the existential questions of identity and identification that have plagued Black peoples since the beginning of the transatlantic slave trade and the subsequent plundering and destruction of African societies as well as the homes and societies that the descendants of the enslaved attempted to build in the West. For example, in the aftermath of the movie, a new convention sprang up in Chicago called Wakandacon. As the centerpiece of this particular fan convention, Wakanda functions as the place in which Blackness can be experienced and expressed in its fullness. The website for the convention describes it as "an inclusive place where you can be a nerd about anything—pop culture, gaming, tech, womanhood, politics, or your own beautiful Blackness."[14] The "About" section goes further:

---

12. Ringer, "Afrofuturism and the DNA of Biopolitics," 57.

13. The salute itself became so pervasive that a few of the actors in the movie asked that people stop greeting them with the Wakandan salute. Nick Evans, "Michael B. Jordan Asks Black Panther Fans to Stop Saying Wakanda Forever," *Cinema Blend*, June 20, 2018, https://www.cinemablend.com/news/2438459/michael-b-jordan-asks-black-panther-fans-to-stop-saying-wakanda-forever.

14. https://wakandaconforever.com/philosophy/.

We wanted to figure out how to recreate Wakanda in real life.

We imagined a place free and unshackled from the ravages of racism; of exploitation; of discrimination; of emotional, physical, and sexual violence. With that in mind, we hope to create a space for people of all types to come together, educate each other, and celebrate all of our passions. It's an event where we can dress up, dance, connect, support each other, and celebrate the entire diaspora looking past the present and into our future.[15]

This is a direct counterpoint to the scholar who, in Andrea Hariston's piece, denigrated Black people dressing up like Wakandans. The unnamed scholar described such mimicry as "adolescent"—once again, reinscribing the narrative that superhero comic books and movies are juvenile pursuits and unworthy of sustained analysis and engagement. In the absence of a physical Wakanda, the mimesis of cosplay (costume play) helps us mentally create Wakanda. The Wakanda that is envisioned vis-à-vis cosplay helps Black people envision a reality in which all Black bodies matter and are valued. To quote Hairston at length:

I am still an adolescent, a child, a young adult, a middle-aged lady, and a post-menopausal fairy god-bitch. I went to *Black Panther* three times, and I bought the DVD. I will dress up like Okoye or M'Baku or Ramonda or any other character if I feel the spirit. Costumes help me perform who I mean to be; performance is the moment you make meaning of your experience! Theater is not "real" or a "mature" political engagement with reality. Theater is a transcendent, out-of-time, out-of-space, out-of-skin engagement with the cosmos, a shape-shifting, time traveling SHAKE-UP of your mind/body/spirit. Theater makes reality, not the other way around. That's the Magic of performance, of story. From random atoms, swaths of light and sound, performers and storytellers create the worlds that we all live in.[16]

The meaning-making that Hairston emphasizes in describing her mimesis is focused on transforming the "make-believe" of a movie like *Black Panther* into a reality. In this case, Wakanda does not exist as an escapist fantasy. Rather, it exists as the blueprint for a Black future not bound by white supremacy. To refer to the prior chapter, Wakanda as a creation of the Black minds of Ryan Coogler and Hannah Beachler exists, and it is real.

---

15. Ibid.
16. Hairston, "It's Our Time."

PART III

Afrofuturistic
Thought Experiments

CHAPTER 7

Space Is the Place

Sun Ra, the Nation of Islam, Afrofuturism, Eschatology, and Utopia

Black Theology and (a Lack of an) Eschatology

In *A Black Theology of Liberation*, James Cone appears to dispense with a detailed eschatological vision for Black people. Unlike Sun Ra's vision of Black pasts, presents, and futures, Cone's systematic theology in *A Black Theology of Liberation* seems to contradict his own claim that "without a meaningful analysis of the future, all is despair" when he says

> The future is still the future. This means that black theology rejects elaborate speculation about the end. It is just this kind of speculation that led blacks to stake their whole existence on heaven—the scene of the whole company of the faithful with their long white robes. Too much of this talk is not good for the revolution. (142)

Here, Cone argues that a singular focus on heaven (or, as he derisively called it, a "pie-in-the-sky theology") detracts from seeking and achieving liberation from white supremacy in the here and now. The above was his attempt at reconciling Martin Luther King Jr.'s Christian theology and eschatological hope with Malcolm X's strident critique of Christianity. Malcolm critiqued Christianity as being far too preoccupied with a "pie in the sky" view of

God and humans to be useful for Black peoples' liberation. King, on the other hand, argued that the beatific visions in Christianity could be useful for Black people (even as he also rejected "pie in the sky" theologies). As such, Cone's attempt at merging both Malcolm's and Martin's eschatologies focuses on making Christian hope a reality. Since Cone's theology of liberation is grounded in orthodox Christian theology—which he could not reject—any liberated future must occur in and through Christ's resurrection.[1] With that, Cone dispenses with any talk of what the future for Black people might look like. Even the possibility of describing life after liberation remains forestalled, since Black liberation theology is grounded in describing Black life as framed by and resisting white supremacy. Perhaps this is part and parcel of the thrust of Afropessimism as it claims that Black life can only be described as a response to white supremacy. Barbara Holmes notes that "liberation rhetoric" within Black liberation theologies "seemed visionary, and yet it could only describe what members of marginalized communities were not and what they would no longer put up with. Very little was said about the big picture."[2] If too much talk about the future was "bad for the revolution," it is so because revolutionaries saw such speculation as a distraction.

How could too much talk about the future be bad for the revolution? Is not the revolution that liberates Black minds and bodies all about the future? Perhaps it is because Black theology as rooted in Western Christian thought can only view eschatology on two coordinates: time and space. Perhaps, then, for Cone, "too much talk about the future" loses all coherence, as Black liberation from white supremacy exists on a linear temporal coordinate aligned with the second coming of Jesus Christ. An event like this—along with the subsequent destruction of the unjust order of global white supremacy—exists in the not-yet, an ever-receding point at the "end" of history.

Indeed, Cone may have had a point in not engaging in detailed discussions about "the future." While Cone saw the future as the elimination of white supremacy, how could he have described a Black future in detail without setting readers up for a failure? Black people in the United States have constantly seen hopes for self-sufficient Black communities violently dashed. Take, for example, my hometown of Tulsa, Oklahoma. I need not recount the details of the Tulsa Race Massacre; rather, I will briefly focus on what drew Black people to Tulsa in the early twentieth century. In the late nineteenth

---

1. Cone, *A Black Theology of Liberation*, 141.
2. Holmes, *Race and the Cosmos*, 38.

and early twentieth centuries, what would become the state of Oklahoma experienced an oil boom. Along with the false rumors that the former Indian Territory would be founded as an all-Black state, the promise of prosperity and a measure of independence held out hope for Black people, many of whom were fleeing the racial tyranny of the post–Civil War South.

Black people who relocated to Oklahoma in general and to Tulsa in particular called it "the promised land."[3] Scott Ellsworth's *Death in a Promised Land* briefly recounts how Black people who moved to Tulsa were able to carve out spaces of self-determination and some measure of economic advancement. Despite being hemmed in by the legal and cultural structures of white supremacy, "Black Wall Street" or "Little Africa," as Black Tulsa came to be known, flourished. However, the devastation wrought by whites during the Tulsa Race Massacre put a brutally violent halt to such flourishing. While the Greenwood district did rebound after the massacre, it experienced a steep decline in the 1970s and '80s, a victim of "urban renewal" and the general financial starvation of North Tulsa.

This is an experience not limited to Tulsa. Black people who sought better lives by fleeing the South and moving to the West or the urban North experienced all manner of setbacks and obstacles. In response to these setbacks and obstacles, new religious, cultural, and political movements arose, offering Black people tangible forms of relief from the crushing effects of white supremacy.

This chapter will explicitly link eschatology with utopia and reconfigure a discussion of eschatology by drawing on Vitor Westhelle's arguments in *Eschatology and Space*. Westhelle contends that, as it has been inextricably tied to Western Christianity and philosophical thought, eschatology considers only linear time (past, present, and future) and fails to account for another dimension: space. I use this as a starting point for a discussion concerning Afrofuturism, eschatology, and utopia and refer back to the prior chapters' focus on particular locations as representative of an Afrofuturistic ideal. Also, as this chapter will examine the Nation of Islam's use of Ezekiel's Wheel as a powerful UFO that will destroy the armies of white supremacy, the foregoing discussion will draw on Stephen Finley's work on Africana esotericism. This chapter will first examine Sun Ra's eschatology and will then move to a discussion of the Nation of Islam's use of Ezekiel's Wheel as well as science fiction themes as part of its cosmology and eschatology.

---

3. Ellsworth, *Death in a Promised Land*, 1.

Sun Ra, Architect of Afrofuturistic Eschatology

Born Sonny Blount, Sun Ra, like hundreds of thousands of fellow Black people (including Elijah Poole), fled the South and relocated in the urban North. After a brief stint in prison for evading the draft, Blount moved to Chicago, where he met and became friends with Alton Abraham, who would also be his business partner, and, according to Paul Youngquist, "fellow architect of better worlds."[4]

Sonny and Abraham created a secret society named Thmei Research. Its goals were to collect and disseminate scholarly research in aid to Black radicalism. As Youngquist notes, "[Thmei] resembles similar initiatives undertaken to better the lives of blacks in Chicago and elsewhere. Thmei's agenda chimes with that of an emerging black nationalism."[5] Youngquist also notes that Thmei emerged alongside the Nation of Islam, and that both orders prospered in the Black communities of Chicago.[6] Such flourishing may be attributed to the promises of a better future that they held out to impoverished and disenfranchised Black peoples. Both Thmei and the Nation of Islam emerged in an urban context in which the convergence of worldviews could percolate without the auspices of traditional Black religious structures. These organizations recognized that for Black people to flourish, they needed a collective mythology, one that Black Christianity could not provide. However, unlike the Nation of Islam, Thmei and Sun Ra rejected organized forms of Black religion, arguing that they "failed to promote black life."[7]

For Sun Ra, music promotes Black life. Music that was socially and culturally progressive would be transformative, leading Black people to be open to substantive change. Sun Ra describes music as a "universal language." Further, he describes music as a "spiritual language."[8] This spiritual and universal language is used to communicate universal truths to a society riven by white supremacy. When Sun Ra describes himself as "another kind of sunrise," and says that every song tells a story that humanity needs to know about, he is arguing that music conveys ancient knowledge—a knowledge to which Black people have access.[9] According to Youngquist, Sun Ra

---

4. Youngquist, *A Pure Solar World*, 31.

5. Ibid., 35.

6. Ibid.

7. Ibid., 55.

8. ProjectDystopia, "Sun Ra Documentary," YouTube, March 9, 2011, https://www.youtube.com/watch?v=7Esmjx8eVcE&t=565s.

9. Youngquist, *A Pure Solar World*, 55.

thought that "music might achieve what politics and religion could not: a wholesale change in the way people live that opens reality to wisdom and beauty."[10] It is clear that Sun Ra's Afrofuturistic eschatology was based on an aesthetic, an approach to music that centered it as the basis for "wisdom and beauty." Such wisdom and beauty emanates from music that is in tune with the cosmos.

Outer space and the technologies spawned by the space race became an indelible part of Sun Ra's music and philosophies. According to Sun Ra's biographers, he was the first jazz musician to embrace electronic instruments, using the Minimoog synthesizer and the Outer Space Visual communicator to create his futuristic sounds.[11] Both Paivi Vaatanen and Youngquist note that human ventures into space functioned as a point of hope for Sun Ra. If the powers that were beginning to take steps into space saw it as a new area of colonization and conquest, Sun Ra would see space as the place where Black people could finally achieve transcendence. While he would reject the eschatological philosophies of Christianity, he would draw on those eschatological hopes and reframe religious conceptions of heaven via the quite real possibilities of life-bearing worlds.

Not only did Sun Ra incorporate outer space into his futuristic visions, he consistently made references to Egypt as part of a Black utopia. While it might appear that Sun Ra's invocation of Egypt is about retrieving a glorious Black past, Graham Lock notes that the Egypt of an "Astro Black Mythology" in inextricably tied to outer space. Further, Sun Ra's rejection of Christianity is tied to his embrace of a mythological Egypt as the source for a Black past and future. An interview with Graham Lock illustrates Sun Ra's critique of Christianity:

> GL: I've read that from an early age you rejected Christianity and were opposed to gospel music, the spirituals?
> SR: I wasn't really opposed to it. I looked at the condition of black people in America and I judged the tree by the fruit. *I knew that [inaudible word or words] good for them couldn't possibly be good for me because they don't deal with progress. They back there in the past, a past that somebody manufactured for 'em. It's not their past, it's not their history.* They don't know nothin' about their history . . . and all that enslavement and all that ignorance and whatever they got, they was forced to have it and it became a habit. They got a habit of being ignorant.[12]

---

10. Ibid., 64.
11. Vaatanen, "Sun Ra: Myth, Science, and Science Fiction," 40.
12. Lock, *Blutopia: Visions of the Future,* 20; my emphasis.

His innovative use of electronic instruments was part of a tradition in Black life of repurposing things and re-presenting them as part of Black creativity. This forward-thinking appropriation of electronic instruments as part of the production of Black futures may have been part of an explicit critique of Black Christianity and gospel music. Essentially, Ra is asking, "How could a form of music tied to a religion of enslavement liberate Black people?" How could it provide Black people with a liberating vision when it is tied to an enslaved past? In a way, perhaps we may read Sun Ra's criticism of Black Christianity as being thematically connected to James Cone's apparent rejection of a detailed eschatology. If Black liberation theology is the theology of Black Christianity and Black Christianity is inextricably tied to the past, then how could either Black Christianity or the liberation theology that emanates from it say anything substantive regarding Black futures? In Sun Ra's estimation, Christianity as adopted by African Americans does not promote progress. Lock goes on to articulate that Sun Ra's critique of Christianity is also based on assertion that it "trapped [African Americans] in a false history and, in doing so, cut them off from their true historical legacy."[13]

Space Is the Place

In 1974, Sun Ra released an eighty-five-minute science fiction jazz film, *Space Is the Place*. From the beginning of the film, eschatology and music combine to form a uniquely Afrofuturistic experience, one that would be referenced in Janelle Monáe's music and videos and Ryan Coogler's *Black Panther*.[14] At the beginning of the film, a ship hurtles through interstellar space while a chorus chants, "Don't you know yet? After the end of the world!" The scene then shifts to the protagonist Sun Ra entering an uninhabited planet and describing it as a destination and hope for African Americans. As Sun Ra walks through this alien garden, calling the viewer's mind back to the mythological Eden, he notes that this planet's sounds are different. These sounds are framed by music, which, unlike the sounds of Earth, is beauty. Sun Ra says that on Earth, the sounds are "guns, anger, frustration." He muses that this new planet can be a utopia for Black people. Free of the negative vibrations of white supremacy, this unnamed planet can serve as an eschatologi-

---

13. Ibid.

14. Eschatology is the examination and discussion of "last things," or, in Christian thought, the end of linear time and the emergence of the "kingdom of God" and "a new heaven and a new earth."

cal hope, an actual place that can serve as a new beginning for Black people to voluntarily emigrate to. As Paul Youngquist puts it, "Only a Black planet can ameliorate ills wrought by racism and segregation."[15] Justice for Black people cannot be achieved on a planet so thoroughly consumed by violence, anger, and racist hatred. Such a vision of a planet that can be a home for Black people has to be free of environmental degradation and white supremacist exploitation.

Space Is the Place functions as a sonic and visual blueprint for an emergent, post–civil rights movement Afrofuturism. Sun Ra's magnum opus lays out a sonic and visual blueprint for what comes to be known as Afrofuturism. As others have pointed out, it is possible to read *Space Is the Place* as a rejection of both the concept of the "person" promoted by Western philosophical thought—and routinely denied to Black bodies—and the antiessentialism of Black Atlantic thought.[16] Rather, Sun Ra's movie points to a third path, one in which Black people move toward the "post-human." Leaving Earth and charting a path to a new world, one in which its harmonies are in line with Black subjectivity, is part of what J. Griffith Rollefson calls "the strategic anti anti-essentialism of Afrofuturism."[17]

This strategic anti antiessentialism is part of the cognitive estrangement within the plot of *Space Is the Place*. As mentioned above, the opening chorus and Sun Ra's introduction set up the otherworldliness, the "strangeness" of the journey the viewer is to take. At the beginning of the movie, Sun Ra declares that time has "officially ended." I read this as a declaration that time no longer exists as the exclusive province of white Western interests. This early proclamation sets up the time-shifting within the movie itself. The past and the present play out virtually simultaneously, stripping the viewer of the conceit inherent in Western essentialism that time and history are a grand march toward some gloriously white future. Rather, the narrative in the movie shifts abruptly from what we perceive to be the future to 1940s Chicago. Here, we are thrown into a speakeasy and introduced to the antagonist, a satanic figure known only as the Overseer. In the two linear time periods that we see, the Overseer occupies the role of pimp; his unsavory and distasteful character and opposition to Black liberation are firmly ensconced in one of the most predatory figures within Black communities.

It is clear that *Space Is the Place* is crafting an Afrofuturistic mythology in which the exodus of Black people from a corrupt and dying world is itself part of a larger mythological narrative. It is also clear that the movie is

---

15. Youngquist, *A Pure Solar World*, 212.

16. Matiluko, "Sun Ra's Space Is the Place."

17. Rollefson, "The 'Robot Voodoo Power' Thesis," 91.

building upon Black reception of the Exodus narrative and motif and divine intervention (in the movie, transformed into a science fictional intervention) as a template for an extraterrestrial construction of new worlds. At the end of the film, the Overseer is defeated—primarily as a result of his own arrogance, which is itself a signification on white supremacy—and those who have received Sun Ra's message relocate to the new world, the promised planet for Black people. The Earth, source of disharmony, oppression, and corruption is destroyed, and the Overseer along with it.

I Go to Prepare a Place for You: Space Is the Eschatology

At this point, it is necessary to return to Westhelle's examination of eschatology and centering space as an eschatological coordinate. Westhelle's eschatology is a critique of modern theology's lack of engagement with space as an element of eschatological hope. He notes that Christian theology devalues space, severing it from time.[18] How does space function as an eschatological coordinate for Sun Ra? Space—and the world that Sun Ra creates for Black people—is an eschatological hope for Black people. Space being *the* place means that it is a location, expansive and engulfing, that supersedes the hatreds on Earth. If space is the place, it is so because it offers Black people greater hope than can be found on this terrestrial plane. Indeed, the claim that space is the place is to implicitly point out that Earth is *not* the place.

Even though we only see this new world briefly, the hope of this harmonious world dominates Sun Ra's mission on Earth. The world that Sun Ra's music evokes calls out and destabilizes the wretchedness that dominates Earth. Sun Ra's world, with its vibrations and harmonies, is a virtual Eden, one that is completely absent of white people. This discovery and colonization of this planet effectively ends linear time. This world supplants—but also walks in Christian narratives of a new heaven and a new Earth. While Sun Ra may reject Christian theologies, this new world evokes Christian imagery and Jesus telling the disciples, "If I go and prepare a place for you, I will come again and will take you to myself, so that where I am, there you may be also."[19] Sun Ra's planet echoes liberation theology's message of the coming kingdom of God.[20] In this case, it is not the kingdom of God breaking into history. It is a Black man from outer space offering Black people

---

18. Westhelle, *Eschatology and Space*, 16.
19. John 14:3 (New Revised Standard Version).
20. Westhelle, *Eschatology and Space*, 77.

a place that is prepared to accept and nurture the creativity and energy of Black lives.

As Sun Ra has been described as an architect of Afrofuturism, I want to take a further step and describe him as perhaps one of the architects of Afrofuturistic eschatology.[21] Merging apocalyptic visions most at home in monotheistic religions, mystery cult imagery and language, and science fiction tropes, Sun Ra might offer a response to James Cone's claim that too much talk about the future might be bad for the revolution: Talk about the future is *necessary* for the revolution. Sun Ra's fusion of funk, soul, jazz, and Afrofuturism provides a template for successive Afrofuturists to talk, write, sing, and paint Black futures. Sun Ra's Afrofuturistic eschatology *is* the revolution. It is the revolution in that Sun Ra wants to shift the frame of reference away from a past that centers white oppression and toward a future that centers Black freedom and creativity.

The Nation of Islam, the Myth of Yakub, and the Mother Plane

Much has been written about the Nation of Islam's origins, from C. Eric Lincoln's landmark study to more focused essays dealing with the Nation's approaches to gender, race, and health. However, few of those treatments have contextualized the Nation of Islam (NOI) as part of the Black speculative or as a part of Afrofuturism. Sun Ra's Arkestra and the Nation of Islam's Mother Plane are twentieth-century Afrofuturistic eschatologies. While more attention has been paid to Sun Ra as an "obvious" forerunner to Afrofuturism, Black religious thought can also pay closer attention to the NOI's incorporation of science fiction tropes and themes in framing both the origins of Black people (and, by extension, the Nation of Islam) and the eschatological hope of Black redemption from white supremacy. Both Sun Ra and the NOI emerged in the context of twentieth-century urban centers and would have encountered each other; however, it is clear that while Sun Ra's eschatology pointed toward a redeemed Blackness as part of the cosmos and emphasized a desire for a pure, untainted world where Black people could peacefully flourish, the Nation's eschatology was more apocalyptic. This section will center the NOI's use of Ezekiel's Wheel (dubbed by the NOI as the Mother Plane) and its eschatological worldview as part of an Afrofuturistic cosmology.

---

21. Rollefson, "The 'Robot Voodoo Power' Thesis," 84.

Founded in the midst of the Great Depression, the Lost-Found Nation of Islam offered an alternative to Black Christianity. It did so by articulating an origin for Black people not rooted in enslavement and degradation. Beginning with NOI founder Wallace Fard Muhammad and continuing with successor Elijah Muhammad, the Nation's teachings took on a decidedly science fictional bent. In describing the origins of white people, both Wallace Fard and Elijah Muhammad clearly borrowed from the science fiction tropes prevalent in the early twentieth century. Mixing themes from the Bible (with which most of his followers would have been familiar) and the Q'uran, Wallace Fard Muhammad introduced a narrative of a glorious Black past that would have been a comfort to disillusioned Black people who had been part of the Great Migration from the South to the North, but found no paradise in those northern cities.

This glorious Black past begins some 66 trillion years ago, when the Earth was populated by Black people. Even in this mythological past, a scientist exists as the cause of a great disaster. In this cosmology,

> a black "scientist" (the black God of the moon) became dissatisfied because he was unable to make all the people speak the same language. So, he decided to destroy the people by causing a great explosion on the moon. A planetary body was blasted out from what was then the moon and traveled twelve thousand miles in to space. What is now the earth, in turn, traveled thirty-six thousand miles into the atmosphere . . . the part that was called the moon capsized, and its remaining life was destroyed.[22]

This narrative of the Black origins of the Earth might appear familiar to comic book and science fiction fans, as it bears similarities to Superman's origins and the emergent theme of the "evil scientist" in science fiction. The evil scientist is almost always motivated by a twisted desire to "improve" humanity, paradoxically, through means that usually put humankind in great jeopardy.

The Myth of Yakub begins with describing an idyllic Mecca in which the majority of Black people (dubbed the Original People) were satisfied. However, this dissatisfied genius scientist named Yakub decided to create his own race. Merging biblical locations with the specter of selective breeding, both Wallace Fard and later Elijah Muhammad taught that Yakub took 59,999 followers to the isle of Patmos. There, he established a totalitarian regime with strict policies regarding reproduction. The goal of these extreme

22. Lieb, *Children of Ezekiel*, 139.

restrictions regarding human reproduction was to create what would come to be known as the white race. This near-apocalyptic narrative sets the stage for Moses and other events in the Old Testament with which Black people would have been familiar. Clearly, such a creation mythology was created in order to refute racist mythologies regarding the "origins" of Black peoples. However, unlike the myth of the Hamitic curse, the Myth of Yakub drew on science fictional tropes of a mad scientist and his goal of destroying an idyllic paradise. By appropriating the emerging field of genetics as the basis for this racial mythology, the narrative gains a veneer of truth.

Of even greater interest here is the apocalyptic eschatology that bookends Muhammad's science fictional creation myth. Drawing on a passage from the Book of Ezekiel, Muhammad claimed that Black people—or, at least, those Black faithful who subscribed to the teachings of the Nation— would be taken up and away from this corrupt, racist world. Of particular focus for the Nation of Islam is the vision of a vehicle as described in the first chapter of Ezekiel:

> [15]As I looked at the living creatures, I saw a wheel on the earth beside the living creatures, one for each of the four of them,[16] As for the appearance of the wheels and their construction: their appearance was like the gleaming of beryl; and the four had the same form, their construction being something like a wheel within a wheel.[17] When they moved, they moved in any of the four directions without veering as they moved.[18] Their rims were tall and awesome, for the rims of all four were full of eyes all around.[19] When the living creatures moved, the wheels moved beside them; and when the living creatures rose from the earth, the wheels rose.[20] Wherever the spirit would go, they went, and the wheels rose along with them; for the spirit of the living creatures was in the wheels.[21] When they moved, the others moved; when they stopped, the others stopped; and when they rose from the earth, the wheels rose along with them; for the spirit of the living creatures was in the wheels.[23]

The wheel imagery has some significance within African American religious experiences. The wheel takes center stage in the Negro spiritual "Zekiel Saw the Wheel," and may have occupied a deeper role in African American spirituality. In 2016, archaeologists from the University of Maryland discovered artifacts that indicated a syncretic merging of Christian and African cosmologies. According to a *New York Times* report, Dr. Mark P. Leone and

---

23. Ezekiel 1:15–19 (New Revised Standard Version).

126 • CHAPTER 7

his graduate students discovered "an intact set of objects that they interpret as religious symbols—traditional ones from Africa, mixed with what they believe to be a biblical image: a representation of Ezekiel's Wheel."[24] While the *Times* article does not specify what time period these artifacts were from, a report on the University of Maryland's College of Behavioral and Sciences dates the excavation between 1865 and 1880.[25] Also, in the post that appears on the college's site, Leone cites African Methodist Episcopal church members who say that Ezekiel's Wheel represents the presence and power of God.[26]

Elijah Muhammad repurposes the Wheel in the Sky and describes it as a powerful UFO that will defeat the forces of white supremacy and usher in a more just world order. The Wheel in the Sky as not only a UFO, but a "Mother Plane" that will defeat the wickedness of white supremacy, is clearly a response to the crises engendered by white supremacist sentiments and actions against Black people. Michael Lieb calls the Nation of Islam "the children of Ezekiel":

> With the matrix of my investigation in a "sacred" text, the Book of Ezekiel, I call those who seek to harness the power that gives rise to technology the children of Ezekiel. Inventors, scientists, technologists, evangelicals, and poets, they are visionaries all. For them Ezekiel's visio Dei represents the wellspring of the impulse to fashion a technology out of the ineffable, the inexpressible, the unknowable. Drawing on the forces within the vision, they reinvent it, re-create it, "technologize" it in their own terms.[27]

Unlike Black Christianity, which the Nation of Islam both borrows from and also critiques, the Nation of Islam reads Ezekiel through the lens of Western technological advancement. The wheel that Ezekiel saw exists in and through time and emerges to destroy the haughty, arrogant technologies possessed by the United States. Elijah Muhammad's description of the "Mother of Planes" plainly views this advanced technological marvel as the means by which white supremacy will finally be destroyed. Muhammad describes the Mother of Planes as being "one half mile by a half mile and . . . the largest mechanical man-made object in the sky. It is a small human planet made for the purpose of destroying the present world of the ene-

---

24. Wilford, "Ezekiel's Wheel."
25. University of Maryland College of Behavioral and Social Sciences, "Ezekiel's Wheel."
26. Ibid.
27. Lieb, *Children of Ezekiel*, 3.

mies of Allah."[28] This engine of destruction is the "mother" of the smaller unidentified flying objects that are more powerful than the air forces of the Western powers. This Mother Wheel is the answer to the space race that had begun after World War II. As Elijah Muhmmad put it, Western white powers had attempted to dominate the Earth, and had set their sights on space.[29] However, their assumed greatness was irrelevant when put against the power of the Mother Wheel. Further, this engine, this Mother of Planes, is distinctly Black in origins. According to Muhammad, this vehicle was also part of Ezekiel's vision, but it was so unlike anything Ezekiel (or anyone else of that period) had seen that they described it using imagery that they could comprehend.[30] Again, such a merging of technology, science fiction, and religion is not new. As Lieb points out, Ezekiel's Wheel has been appropriated as a celestial vision before. Lieb points to John Milton's use of the wheel in Paradise Lost as a vehicle of divine retribution and justice. Calling it the "technology of the ineffable," Lieb notes that the chariot or wheel functions polemically.[31] If Ezekiel's wheel functions polemically for Milton, it is so doubly for the Nation of Islam, as the wheel becomes a centerpiece of the Nation's apocalyptic eschatology.

More importantly, Stephen Finley's work in Africana esotericism and his examination of the Nation of Islam is vital to understanding the Afrofuturistic eschatology of the Nation. As Finley, Margarita Simon Guillory, and Hugh Page note in *Esotericism in African American Religious Experience*, Africana esoteric studies

is a poetics of discovery rather than strictly a field or discipline. Those involved in it are makers (poets) and in some instances devotees rather than mere scholars (those with the leisure to study). They are comfortable in the discourses of the arts, humanities, sciences, and theological disciplines. Many are also fluent in the languages of several uninvited guests to the academic banquet (e.g., Africana Studies, Ethnic Studies, Womanist Studies, Cultural Studies, and Queer Studies). More than a few are also at home in the esoteric idioms of the Black Atlantic. As for the questions that animate this project—they are as varied as the initiates who cross the threshold beyond which are the warp and weft of the Communitas Africana. Such an enterprise defies strict disciplinarity.[32]

28. Muhammad, *Message to the Blackman*, 291.
29. Muhammad, *The Mother Plane*, loc. 118, Kindle.
30. Ibid., loc. 366.
31. Lieb, *Children of Ezekiel*, 27.
32. Finley, *Esotericism in African American Religious Experience*, 13.

Africana esoteric studies takes the NOI's Mother Wheel seriously, as it is part of a religious experience that is uniquely Black. Further, the Mother Wheel is part of a religious language that exists outside of "normal" time and rationality. Stephen Finley examines the Mother Wheel from a history of religions and integrative psychoanalysis to uncover the meaning of "Mother" in the Wheel. For Finley, the Mother Wheel as a UFO signifies a "complex subjectivity" within the Nation. This complex subjectivity vis-à-vis the language about the Mother Wheel constitutes a "meaning making" grounded in African American esotericism. Indeed, Louis Farrakhan's language about his encounter with this Mother Wheel is intentionally confusing. Those who are within the Nation can understand what Farrakhan is saying, primarily because he is not only taking a narrative handed down to him from Elijah Muhammad; he also situates Elijah Muhammad as a truth-telling prophetic voice.

Further, Farrakhan's two experiences with the Mother Wheel combine with his experience in Tepotzlan, Mexico, to produce a religious narrative of transcendence. This narrative is firmly grounded in UFO abduction narratives but combined with a narrative of a transmission of knowledge consistent with religious narratives of enlightenment. Finley describes Farrakhan's visions of the Mother Wheel as part of Black genius, a genius that Black people have as a spiritual and cultural inheritance. Finley also presents four propositions for understanding the Mother Wheel in the Nation's cosmology as they are tied to understanding the Nation's approaches to race, gender, and sexuality.[33] First, the "Mother" in Mother Wheel might "signify abstract conceptions such as truth, freedom, and purity that are often represented in the feminine—ideas such as wisdom."[34] At this level of analysis, the abstract nature of the Mother Wheel lends itself to idealized feminine interpretations. As noted above, the second interpretation of the Mother Wheel has to do with Black genius—specifically, Elijah Muhammad's description of the Mother Wheel as "the Mother of All Wheels." Its technical superiority far surpasses any of the destructive technologies that the white Western powers might possess. A third interpretation of the Mother Wheel suggests that the term "Mother" serves as a deflection away from any homoerotic impulses.[35] The fourth and final interpretation of the Mother Wheel situates it as an analogical Mother.

While Finley articulates a psychoanalytic reading of the Mother Wheel that helps us understand the NOI's approach to gender and sexuality within

33. Finley, "The Meaning of Mother," 448.
34. Ibid.
35. Ibid., 452.

its cosmology, I think that within this cosmology is an eschatological component. I will quote Finley at length:

> Mother, therefore, signifies all black bodies. It is a metaphor for them. *It offers an ideal to which all black bodies can and should aspire.* Though colonized, lynched, enslaved, and oppressed, they are heirs to the mother of all technologies and have only to live their possibilities and realize them in the material world. Subsequently, as the mother of all planes, the Wheel means that black bodies have the potential to survive death ostensibly, since Farrakhan encountered Elijah Muhammad and Master Fard Muhammad in the womb of Mother (Farrakhan 1986; Finley 2009: 369–71). *Hence, the Wheel discloses the secret knowledge of life and death and the afterlife of which Mother has the power to give and to take* (Jonte-Pace 1996).[36]

The eschatological dimension of the Mother Wheel is that it offers Black people a technological past, present, and future. This secret knowledge, revealed to both Elijah Muhammad and then Louis Farrakhan, provides Black people a hope for the present as well as the future. The Mother Wheel redirects Black eschatological hope away from the devices and technologies of the corrupted Earth. The Mother Wheel's eschatological dimension is not oriented toward reconciliation with this present world. Indeed, its existence and function are decidedly apocalyptic.

Black to the Future: Synthesizing Sun Ra and the Nation of Islam's Apocalyptic Eschatologies

Taken together, both Sun Ra's and the Nation of Islam's apocalyptic eschatologies are compelling in that they offer Black people prophetic visions of the future. Simply put, they both say that the current white supremacist order cannot and will not endure and that Black people can imagine better places. Further, they offer Black people a visual and sonic eschatological vocabulary. This eschatological vocabulary is also as compelling as it is mysterious. It is tied to the kinds of religious languages that Black people in the urban metropolis would have been familiar with. Nevertheless, their respective eschatologies improvise upon received Black Christian eschatologies, mixing with them other forms of "secret knowledge." Both Sun Ra and the Nation of Islam envision some form of ship coming with an apocalyptic

---

36. Ibid., 457; my emphasis.

mission. Sun Ra's ship in *Space Is the Place* and the NOI's Mother Wheel both bear some kind of special knowledge that will be revealed. Both vehicles of Black liberation portend the destruction of the "old" white supremacist order and herald a new world to come.

Both Sun Ra and the Nation see a "new world" as a world of justice and righteousness. Where Sun Ra focuses on this new world as a world revealed by harmonious music, the Nation focuses on this new world's robust physicality literally destroying the old world. Indeed, as I read Elijah Muhammad's description of the function of the Mother Wheel, it appears to have a terraforming function:

> Allah (God) Who came in the Person of Master Fard Muhammad, to Whom praises are due forever, is wiser than any god before Him as the Bible and the Holy Qur'an teach us. He taught me that this plane will be used to raise mountains on this planet (earth). The mountains that He will put on this earth will not be very high. He will raise these mountains to height of one (1) mile over the United States of America.[37]

The terraforming function of this Mother Wheel was apparently used before in the creation of this world.[38] Therefore, it will be used in the remaking of this world. Specifically, this terraforming will essentially destroy the former United States. Again, Elijah Muhammad points to the Bible as both the historical source of this narrative and a prophetic source for understanding the Mother Wheel. The end of the book *The Mother Plane* cites Isaiah 24:20 and positions the Mother Wheel as the work of God that effects divine justice.

I see a synthesis of Sun Ra's and the Nation's apocalyptic eschatologies in *Black Panther* in that the revelation of the Royal Talon in Oakland not only echoes Sun Ra's spaceship's appearance in *Space Is the Place*, it also functions as the NOI's Mother Wheel, signifying an end to an old order. I do not think it an accident that Ryan Coogler situates the beginning and end of the movie in Oakland. Coogler is engaging in a synthesis of these disparate eschatologies, harmonizing them via the Afrofuturistic eschatology in *Black Panther*. The visuals and locations in *Space Is the Place* jump from a future in which humanity has annihilated itself to 1943 and then again to Oakland, 1972. The Oakland of 1972 where Sun Ra and his Arkestra return becomes the Oakland of 1992 as well as of 2018 in *Black Panther*, where, at

---

37. Muhammad, *Mother Plane*, loc. 536, Kindle.
38. Ibid., loc. 547.

the movie's conclusion, T'Challa reveals the Royal Talon, which Black boys playing basketball call "a Bugatti Spaceship." It is possible to read all of these versions of Oakland as existing in the same space-time continuum as Wakanda. The Sun Ra who disembarks a spaceship in 1972 and reveals himself at an Oakland community center prefigures King T'Challa's brief but revealing encounter with a young Black boy who, upon seeing the Royal Talon, asks, "Who are you?" as the film then cuts to Sza's "All The Stars." The world that opens up to this young man is far different from the world that has been framed by white supremacy. In both Sun Ra's *Space Is the Place* and in Coogler's *Black Panther,* revelation and liberation are not forestalled into some unreachable future. Further, the eschatological revelation that can transport us away from oppression is not dependent upon a remote deity. Even if Black people cannot immediately relocate to a Black planet, through music, Black people can transform this world. The music of the stars and the cosmos resonates in Black people. The worlds that both Sun Ra's and Ryan Coogler's respective Afrofuturistic epics open up are visions of what could be for Black people. "Who are you?" as repeated throughout *Black Panther* serves as a reflective meditation on Black identities and the possibilities that Afrofuturism offers.

However, it is also possible that this climactic scene is also a resignification on the Mother Wheel eschatology within the Nation of Islam. Throughout the movie, the viewer is reminded that Wakanda possesses technologies that could destroy every white supremacist power on Earth. Indeed, we see that vibranium-infused vehicles are able to shrug off high-powered weapons fire, vibranium clothing is able to project shields and redirect kinetic energy, and that one vibranium handheld sonic cannon can destroy a tank. Clearly, the Royal Talon and other vessels constructed in Wakanda have the power to function like the Mother Wheel and utterly destroy the forces of white supremacy. Instead of appearing as a harbinger of violent doom to the forces of white supremacy, the Royal Talon's appearance in Oakland simultaneously fulfills and inverts the Nation of Islam's use of the Mother Wheel as an apocalyptic prophecy. Further, the terraforming function that Elijah Muhammad refers to in *The Mother Plane* is transformed in *Black Panther*. In this case, the Royal Talon's appearance is a revelation to one young Black boy, "terraforming" his possibilities. The Royal Talon's decloaking and this young man's question, along with T'Challa's statement that the buildings that were once sites of death and deprivation would be transformed into sites of hope and advancement, are a symbolic destruction of the "old" world and the creation of a new one.

Conclusion

Afrofuturistic views are deeply connected to the eschatological in all its dimensions. The Afrofuturist who engages Black religious thought is not necessarily beholden to Christian discussions of "end things"—indeed, the Afrofuturist might reject such a notion. If we take the Black speculative seriously, we might assert that there is no end. Eschatology, then, is academic shorthand for discussing the future and those things that may come. For the Afrofuturist, the act of writing, producing films, making music, and so forth are actions that call forth the future, and that tease out of the blackness new visions of Blackness.

This chapter has endeavored to position Sun Ra, the Nation of Islam—and, by extension, *Black Panther*—as framing a vision of a Black future that is not predicated on Christianity. Such a Black future can be envisioned as a place. Sun Ra's Afrofuturism takes Oakland as an anchor that can bridge the Black viewer's imagination to a possible future. Ryan Coogler draws on that imagery as well as Black visions of the metropolis and crafts a twenty-first-century Afrofuturism for Black audiences. Even if such a place is not "real" in that it cannot be immediately realized—after all, neither vibranium nor Wakanda "actually" exists—that does not mean that we cannot endeavor to create imagery that inspires Black peoples to construct real-world analogues as well as reconfiguring Black religious identities. The next and final chapter will address Afrofuturism as a source for redefining Black religious lives.

CHAPTER 8

"Who Am I? Who Are You?"

Afrofuturism and Black Religious Identity

I began this book with a brief autobiography. In initial visions of this book, I had titled it *The Autobiography of an Ex-Religious Nerd,* signifying on James Weldon Johnson's *The Autobiography of an Ex-Colored Man.* However, that seemed to be in tension with how I described myself to first-year students eager to know if I myself was religious. In response to that question, I have often replied, "Does *Star Trek* count?" What is in the background of this book is a response that yes, Afrofuturism does count as a way of reimagining the self. If this chapter takes seriously Anthony Pinn's views regarding the use of popular culture as a theological tool, it should be noted that this book does not seek to reduce Afrofuturism as a religious resource to simple fandom.[1] It is my assertion that Afrofuturism provides the emergent or existent Black nerd the resources to navigate attempts at reducing Black life and religious experience to either the church or a vacuous spirituality and simultaneously opens Black nerds up to various forms of religious experience.

This chapter contends that Afrofuturism in all its diversity can provide to Black people narrative frameworks that can give deep or thicker descriptions to experiences of estrangement. For example, as mentioned in the autobiographical sketch, I modeled myself off *Star Trek*'s Mr. Spock as a way

---

1. Pinn, *Why Lord?,* 117.

of coping with being picked on. Further, I became enamored with Vulcan detachment and devotion to logic. Collecting comic books and diving deep into both comic lore and *Star Trek* minutiae helped make sense of a chaotic childhood and adolescence, as well as helping to make my ostracized self seem "special." To extend this to a larger discussion of the potential of Afrofuturism and the development of a Black religious identity, a person may find in the works of Octavia Butler resources for re-visioning God and thinking differently about Black orientations to the world. A Black person may find in Janelle Monáe's inventive use of Afrofuturism the resources to understand their queer selves.

From Octavia Butler's collected works to Janelle Monáe's Afrofuturistic saga to *Deep Space Nine* and Wakanda, we see that Afrofuturism is intimately connected to critiques and revisions of Black religious experience. Throughout each chapter, I have argued that Afrofuturism can be part of Black people's approach to religion and spiritual lives. Clearly, Octavia Butler's Earthseed emanates from a Black woman's interrogation of the nature of God in light of rampant and unanswered suffering. Further, Janelle Monáe's Cindi Mayweather as the opening for Monáe's own eventual revelation of herself as a Black queer pansexual highlights the constructive ways in which Black queers can and do use science fiction and Afrofuturism to come out and flourish. Fictional worlds as depicted in *Star Trek: Deep Space Nine* and *Black Panther* offer a range of Black identity formations and possibilities. In the case of the aforementioned, questions of identity emerge to the foreground. Throughout *Black Panther*, T'Challa is confronted with the question "Who are you?" The question is at times accusatory, and at other times triumphant. However, at the end of the movie, it is the opening to liberation. As I noted in looking at "Far Beyond the Stars," the question that bookends the episode is "Who am I?" Benny Russell and Benjamin Sisko's dilemma is framed by this existential question. The answer itself is powerful, as the preacher discloses to Benny that he is both the dreamer and the dream. This revelation shows us the power of the Black imaginary, the power of Afrofuturism to aid in the construction of Black identities.

Perhaps a weakness in theorizing Afrofuturism is the lack of focus on the Afrofuturist. Going back to Dery's coinage of the term, he never explained what, exactly, would describe the Afrofuturist. His conversation partners at the time did not move the conversation toward discussions of what would constitute an Afrofuturist. Rather, we as workers within and consumers of Afrofuturism merely assumed, as Womack does, that any Black geek or nerd who has wondered about the absence of Black people in science fiction and then set about to "do something about it" could "arguably" qualify as an

Afrofuturist. As I am returning to this description as presented in chapter 1, I am contending that such a presentation is fairly thin. This is not to say that Ytasha Womack's description is "wrong." Nor is this to say that Dery et al. were derelict in their duty. Afrofuturism as an identified discourse was in its infancy. If we are to arrive at a robust model of Afrofuturism, we need thicker descriptions of not just Afrofuturism, but also the Afrofuturist.

This chapter builds upon the question of Black identity and argues that Afrofuturism addresses the Black subject as its own religious identity. This chapter proposes that we may describe this as humanistic Afrofuturism. This chapter stakes a claim that aligns with Anthony Pinn's African American humanistic project. As part of this project, this book situates Afrofuturism as the productive site in which Black subjects claim their identities beyond the often-suffocating strictures of the Black church and Christian identity formations. This chapter's argument is fairly straightforward. As Black religious scholars understand new religious movements in the Black metropolis as leading to the creation of new Black religious identities, so too might Afrofuturism lead to the creation of newer Black religious identities. Afrofuturism also arose in the Black metropolis, fueled by the same kinds of cultural interactions and exchanges that led to the emergence of Black religions like the Nation of Islam and Father Divine's movement.

Black Religious Identity Formation

Theoretically, this chapter owes a debt to the historical work laid out by Judith Weisenfeld's *New World A-Coming* and the theological work done by Anthony Pinn across several of his works. Their work informs this chapter's thesis that contemporary Afrofuturism as presented in mass culture performs the function the new religions in America's urban centers once did in helping Black people construct new racial identities. Additionally, Carolyn Moxley Rouse, John L Jackson Jr., and Marla Frederick's *Televised Redemption* and its analysis of Black religious media serve as a means of "transform[ing] Black subjectivity . . . by providing black Americans with new conceptual and practical tools of how to be in the world and by changing how black people are made intelligible and recognizable as moral citizens."[2] While Rouse and others look at Black religious media as a vehicle by which Black people constructed new religious identities, this chapter adapts this to explore Afrofuturism's role in shaping newer Black religio-cultural iden-

---

2. Rouse, Jackson, and Frederick, *Televised Redemption*, 10.

tities. The pervasiveness of Wakanda as a shorthand for a utopian Black vision, the previously mentioned "rise" of the Black nerd, and the growing interest in African traditional religious practices may be read as part of a desire to craft new Black identities not shaped and framed by traditional Black Protestantism. This chapter seeks to bring together the arguments of the preceding chapters and point to science fiction in general and Afrofuturism in particular as resources for reshaping Black religious identities.

Weisenfeld examines the emergence of Black religious identities that eschew Black identities as framed by white supremacy. Her work begins with a story of a Black man registering for the draft and rejecting the government's classification of "Negro." This particular story was not an isolated one and, according to Weisenfeld, signified a trend in which Black people reimagined their racial identities via new religious movements in the urban centers of the United States. What is key for this study is that those Black people who reimagined their Black identities "endowed it with meaning derived from histories other than those of enslavement and oppression."[3] While Weisenfeld begins with the new religions that emerged as a result of the Great Migration, we may go back just a bit further and take a brief look at Marcus Garvey's Universal Negro Improvement Association (UNIA). The UNIA may even be understood as an early attempt at creating a Black utopia. Garvey's "Up, up you mighty race! You can accomplish what you will!" was a call for Black peoples to reclaim their rightful and forgotten glory, to create a Black nation that would rival the European powers that had enslaved and colonized them. Pinn describes the change in African American identity formation thusly:

> Following the tracks of the Great Migration and other historic developments after the socioeconomic and political reckoning called the Civil War and Reconstruction, the psychosocial posture of African Americans changed radically, particularly after the first decade or so of the twentieth century. That is, the emergence of the twentieth century is marked by a change in perspective—a movement of both bodies and ideas—expressed in significant ways through the increasingly unapologetic language of cultural production.[4]

Drawing on Alain Locke, Pinn traces the emergence of an unapologetically Black series of cultural productions. The Harlem Renaissance is a sign-

---

3. Weisenfeld, *New World A-Coming*, 6.
4. Pinn and Valentin, *Creating Ourselves*, 14.

post of such an unapologetic presentation of cultural productions designed to showcase "The New Negro," whose identity is emancipated and who produces emancipating works. The Black religious identity from "The New Negro" on through the tumultuous years of the civil rights movement and into the emergence of a Black Power aesthetic may tend toward either oppositional frameworks such as those found in the Nation of Islam, or conciliatory and reconciliatory frameworks such as typified in the thought of Martin Luther King Jr. Likewise, Black cultural productions may reflect such frameworks.

According to Weisenfeld, the new religions of the emerging Black metropolis emphasized Black religious and cultural identities that stood in stark contrast to the white world around them. As such, these new Black religious identities were extremely strict, focusing on clothing and food as markers of a distinct Black religious identity.[5] The new religions of the metropolis like the Nation of Islam and Father Divine's movement sought to give to Black people new identities that were not constrained by whiteness.[6] Indeed, Divine's movement explicitly rejected race as a real category. As explored in a previous chapter, the Nation of Islam constructed an entire racial mythology and cosmology that centered Black people as "the original people," and urged Black people to reclaim their rightful place as an advanced and independent nation. Thus, the Nation and Father Divine, for example, sought to liberate Black people from the suffocating grip of white supremacy. However, in contradistinction to the new Black religions of the metropolis, Sun Ra's embryonic Afrofuturism sought a Black identity free of the kinds of doctrinal rigidity that characterized the Nation of Islam and Father Divine's movement.

It is clear that the new Black meccas that attracted Black people like Sun Ra held out the promise of new opportunities and the possibility of constructing new Black identities. For example, it is possible to read the creation of Sun Ra and the Arkestra as the explicit rejection of "terrestrial" Blackness, as it is a Blackness that is still in thrall to white supremacy. It is not sufficient to merely invoke some form of a glorious Black past; rather, it is incumbent upon the "new" Black person to fashion a new identity that transcends the temporal and physical constraints of white supremacy. Further, such a reconstituted Black identity in and through "astro blackness" and even Afrofuturism is itself a signification on the dehumanizing attempts of white supremacy to strip Black people of their ancestral names.

---

5. Weisenfeld, *New World A-Coming*, 78–79.
6. Ibid., 3.

While the emergence of the Black nerd does not have quite the solid historical background as does the emergence of the Nation of Islam or Sun Ra's Arkestra and his Astro-blackness, it is not a stretch to say that there has been a shift in Black popular culture such that it is now possible to define or describe oneself as a Black nerd or "Blerd" without it appearing as a contradiction or caricature. Entertainers like Donald Glover (who had at one time been rumored to play Spider-Man—a rumor that set the internet ablaze) and Janelle Monáe speak openly about their love of nerd culture, comic books, and science fiction. It is their openness about their love of nerd culture that makes it possible for other Black people to declare their love of and identification with nerd culture.

Further, it is not uncommon for Black artists to draw on science fictional or fantastical motifs and imagery. Missy Elliott is a primary example of contemporary uses of science fictional imagery and motifs. Her groundbreaking music videos like "The Rain," "Get Your Freak On," and "Beep Me 911" as well as her recent MTV Video Music Awards performance push the boundaries of technology in reconfiguring Blackness using science fictional images and motifs. In reference to her MTV Video Music Awards performance, at one point a CGI spaceship appears over the audience and begins "snatching" dancers out of the audience. Missy's hip-hop futurism is also sex-positive and Black woman-affirming.

Wakandacon and Blerdcon as Case Studies

In prior chapters, I mentioned Wakandacon, a Black-themed and Black-owned convention with the intent of creating Wakanda in the real world. Dave Barthwell, his brothers Ali and Matt, and his friends Taylor Witten and Lisa Beasley organized this Black fan convention. According to an article on The Verge.com, Wakandacon was intended to tap into something:

> But one large group of fans is still hungry for what those Trekkies finally found in 1972. Geek culture, like everything else, has still been historically dominated by cishet white men, even though it's a marginally more accepting corner of society. And as fandom has grown more commercialized, thus becoming more accessible and socially acceptable than ever, that inequality has been reinforced and even validated.[7]

---

7. Maloney, "How the First Wakandacon,"

What the above quote references is the first *Star Trek* fan convention, held in 1972. It was a gathering—small by today's fan convention standards— of *Star Trek* fans (soon to be derisively dubbed "Trekkies") who wanted to gather and share their love of the canceled television series. Indeed, the cast members in attendance spoke about how surprised they were that so many fans wanted to keep the show alive. As fan conventions grew in popularity, frequency, and attendance, Black people found that they were not well represented in these conventions either on panels or in general attendance. As a brief aside, the last sentence of the above-quoted paragraph appears to have been validated, as shown in the World Fantasy Convention's response to a letter asking for more people of color to be represented as Guest of Honor at the 2019 convention.

Indeed, the Verge article also details the failure of a similarly themed convention prior to Wakandacon, which jeopardized the success of the fledgling enterprise. It should be noted here that the fan convention—or "con" for short—functions as a primary site in which sci-fi fans claim and perform their identity and identification as devotees. In the case of Wakandacon, the organizers intended for it to exist as a space for all Black people, to give them a place "where our histories are no longer narrowly delineated, we are no longer weighed down by what has been done to us."[8] The con's philosophy goes on to articulate a vision of Black identity in which Black people have the space to take control of their own destinies, behaviors, and expectations. The Barthwell siblings and the other people who helped organize Wakandacon do not wish to erase Blackness or claim some form of "post-racial" Blackness; rather, they seek to center the worlds that *Black Panther* posits as a starting point for reframing Black identities. This, as the next chapter will argue, is an Afrofuturistic eschatology at work. It is also an Afrofuturistic vision of the Black self released from the strictures of cisheteropatriarchal white supremacist structures. In simpler language, Black folks can go to Wakandacon and experience—however briefly—the freedom of Blackness as envisioned in the movie. Also, while this Black freedom may reference previous iterations of Black freedom (the Black consciousness movement of the 1970s, Afrocentricity of the late 1980s and '90s), it functions more inclusively than those prior iterations.

A similar convention predates Wakandacon by a couple of years. Blerdcon began in 2017 in Arlington, Virginia. According to the Blerdcon homepage,

---

8. Wakandacon, "Philosophy," https://wakandaconforever.com/philosophy/.

Blerdcon is an event that highlights and celebrates Blerd culture and creates a marketplace of ideas where sharing that culture can take place with
proper context, attribution and positivity in an inclusive environment.
    Blerdcon celebrates our connection with LGBTQ, the disabled, POCs
and the international community! All are welcome to partake in the experience as we are an open community who love all the same nerddom.[9]

Like Wakandacon, Blerdcon's organizers seek to create a space for Black
people in general and for Blerds in particular to enjoy their particular fandoms and feel represented and safe. While Blerdcon may appear to focus
more on cosplay than Wakandacon, both conventions are clear about centering Blerd identities as a site of joy and celebration. Looking at both Blerdcon's and Wakandacon's schedules of events, both spaces offer a wide array
of activities and panels that appear to embrace the spectrum of Black cultural identities. It also might appear that both Blerdcon and Wakandacon
ignore any form of religious/spiritual practices that would intersect with
Blerd identities. However, upon a closer examination of the 2019 Blerdcon
schedule, there was one Sunday morning session that stood out. At 11:00
a.m., Blerdcon scheduled the "Anime Sunday Worship Experience." Here is
how the experience was described:

Welcome to the Church of Anime. Here, higher beings use animated works
to give us messages about perseverance, hope, relationships, and righteousness. This is not your typical church, for the Church of Anime does not
subscribe to any one religion. It is open to those of all faiths (or none) to
explore the ways anime can give us a holy message. This Sunday Service
will commence with a song, a ritual, and a sermon to get you on your way.
This is an alternate opportunity to worship in a geeky way.[10]

To see such an event on the Blerdcon schedule might at first appear as a form
of mockery, an attempt at denigrating the sacred by fusing traditional Christian worship with anime. However, what if we were to look at this from the
perspective of the Blerdcon attendee? They may have lived a life steeped in
the traditional Black church or some other form of Protestant Christianity,
may yet love religious expression and belief, and also love anime. This event
is not mockery; rather, it honors the fusion of the secular and sacred. Perhaps it troubles such attempts at neat divisions. Drawing on the themes of

---

    9. Blerdcon, "About Blerdcon," https://blerdcon.com/about-blerdcon/.
    10. Blerdcon, "Anime Sunday Worship Experience," https://blerdcon.com/event/
anime-sunday-worship-experience/.

religious cultures, this event positions anime as a gift from "higher beings" and serves a moral function. In this event, anime—and its fandom—is not merely a nerdy pastime.

Digital Spaces as Reshaping the Blerd and Black Religious Identity

Out of a love for both Black and nerd cultures, Black nerds found ways to gather and share that love. Pointing to the early days of the internet as presaging groupings like Wakandacon and Blerdcon, we can look at Alondra Nelson's 1998 founding an online community called Afrofuturism. In 1998, online communities were not nearly as ubiquitous as they are today, and bulletin board systems and chat rooms relied on the fickle nature of some internet service providers; further, if a person was not part of an institution of higher learning, they likely would not have had access to high-speed internet. Nelson's Afrofuturism listserv "began as a project of the arts collective apogee with the goal of initiating dialogue that would culminate in a symposium called Afrofuturism/Forum."[11] As Nelson notes, this listserv emerged in a time in which most discussions of African diasporic communities were preoccupied with "the digital divide."[12]

Despite this foundational digital space, the nature of the Black nerd was far from settled, largely because of the overwhelming whiteness of geek culture in the 1990s. Black connectivity via the internet predicted the rise of Black Twitter, meme creation and sharing, and viral narratives. This book emerges during a period in which social media is under a great deal of scrutiny for aiding in the proliferation of white supremacist ideologies. Social media giants like Facebook and Twitter have been identified as allowing for all manner of hate speech directed toward Muslims, Blacks, women, LGBTIQ communities, and so forth.[13] However, I look at these spaces as simultaneously functioning as spaces that allow for the flourishing of Blerd communities as well as serving as internet cities in which Black nerds virtually engage in the same sort of mixing and remixing that our ancestors did when they moved to the urban centers of the North. It is these same Blerd communities that, in turn, make it possible for Blerd gatherings such as Wakandacon and Blerdcon. For example, an entry on Reddit's r/Blerds subthread "blerdlifeandculture" has an entry by a user with the handle

---

11. Nelson, "Introduction," 9.
12. Ibid.
13. Moon, "Facebook Accused."

"stufstuf." The user notes that "Everyday I thank God for the internet" and knowing that their "obsession with comic books, with video games and technology is totally normal and good."[14] "An Open Love Letter to Every Blerd" on BlackNerdProblems.com echoes the precarious nature of finding community with other Blerds and situates internet Blerd communities as models of intraracial diversity:

> You are nurses, artists, teachers, and computer programmers, yet are still subculture enough to build an armor of confidence sexier than any costumed hero you admire. You enjoy your alone time and maybe call yourself an introvert, which is Latin for "I'm not going out tonight; I just got my pull list." You drop obscure references in casual conversation with such surety that others feel excluded if they don't understand, and it's well and good because you've never been exclusive—you want people to join. Not a week goes by a Blerd doesn't make a joke and think to themselves, "if y'all were caught up on Walking Dead you'd get it," and then book mark the joke in their mind to Tweet it among family.[15]

To draw on the emergent literature on new media and religion, Blerds are carving out new identities via these digital spaces. Logging onto social media, finding tweets and posts by other Blerds and then retweeting, commenting, and posting in exclusive threads as well as creating side-chats are ways in which Blerds can digitally connect with each other. The interaction via these spaces functions as one might expect from religious communities; the dissection of movies like Jordan Peele's *Us* and *Black Panther* as well as other forms of speculative fiction that does not necessarily center Black people are in themselves rituals that demand the Blerd display a significant knowledge of the media being discussed. For example, recent episodes of the final season of *Game of Thrones* have garnered Black Twitter's collective imagination. The website Shadow and Act recently compiled tweets from Black Twitter users that simultaneously mocked season 8's second episode and also showed how committed Black viewers (who may or may not identify themselves as Blerds) are to the fantasy series. Under the hashtag #DemThrones, thousands of Black Twitter users parsed and more than occasionally eviscerated episodes and characters.

For example, Twitter user @yngfalafel took a scene in which two Black characters ride into Winterfell and receive hostile glares from the white den-

---

14. Reddit, https://www.reddit.com/r/Blerds/comments/nerdy_black.
15. Calhoun, "An Open Love Letter to Every Blerd."

izens and overlaid Lil Nas X's hit "Old Town Road." The user said that they "spent 10 minutes on this edit and it was worth every second."[16] Since this was posted on April 14, the tweet has had 835 thousand views, 10.3 thousand retweets, and 33.7 thousand likes. Even celebrated director Ava duVernay joined in Black Twitter revelry regarding "demthrones." As Zaron Burnett put it in an essay titled "Why Black 'Game of Thrones' Fans Need #DemThrones," "Many high profile fandoms have long been predominantly male and pale, which skews the conversation . . . [the hashtag #DemThrones] offers Black Twitter a unique way to enjoy Game of Thrones as part of a parallel fandom. One that's for us, by us."[17]

However, Blerd communities are also welcoming for those who are new or perhaps recent "converts" to nerd culture.[18] Further, Blerds use social media to critique the representations of gender and race via the show (as well as through other television shows and movies). Such collections of critiques themselves may become the foundation for scholarly work. A related area might be the emergent work on Beyoncé's recent Coachella performance and subsequent Netflix documentary, *Homecoming*. In a recent Facebook post, I queried if Black scholars might consider "Beychella"—as her Coachella performance has been dubbed—and the Netflix documentary as a form of Afrofuturism. Several acquaintances and colleagues affirmed my question. Additionally, I posed questions via Facebook that asked Black people who might consider themselves as nerds about the intersections of their nerd interests and their religious/spiritual lives. This admittedly nonscientific series of questions yielded a diversity of responses and perspectives. Some people held their sci-fi and fantasy fandom as wholly separate from their religious and spiritual lives, while others described their fandom as intimately intertwined with their religious and spiritual lives. I posed several questions to Black members of the group. I also posed the following questions on my own Facebook page:

1. Do you consider yourself a sci-fi/fantasy nerd?
2. How do you see being a nerd or Blerd as part of your Black identity/ Blackness?
3. Do you see your sci-fi/fantasy fandom as part of a religious/spiritual life? If so, how?
4. How do you see the internet (and sites like Facebook/Twitter) as creating and holding space for Black nerds?

16. Burnett, "Why Black 'Game of Thrones' Fans Need #DemThrones."
17. Ibid.
18. Stout, *Media and Religion*, 74–75.

The responses were interesting. In response to the third question, a person noted, "I think my love of speculative fiction and Afrofuturism have made me more willing to explore my Christian upbringing from a less traditional point of view." Another person noted that their identity as a nerd was "woven into [his] blackness." He went on to say,

> I'm a black nerd. Black before nerd from a time when the nerd community at large didn't have too many black folk welcome. Same lack of representation, same microaggressions. My nerdness was never a problem for me in black circles the way my blackness was a problem for others in nerd circles.[19]

Another example is a Black woman on Twitter with the handle @auntileshea who reflected on what *Star Trek* means to her. She wrote:

> I remember the day Leonard Nimoy died, I lived with someone who was confused as to why I was so upset. Star Trek has been my escape out of this world that judges me for existing. It brings me so much peace. Gene [Roddenberry] was so ahead of his time and I hope to meet him in the afterlife.[20]

This tweet was in response to a Star Trek on CBS All AccessTwitter campaign that supported the Black Lives Matter movement after protests erupted across the United States in response to George Floyd's murder. These digital spaces that Blerds carve out via Facebook, Twitter, and so forth give Blerds the kinds of freedom and community building that might have been impossible two decades ago. Indeed, a 2015 Buzzfeed "listicle" by Aaron Barksdale described the experiences common to the Blerd—the tenth and final one was "Eventually finding 'your' people on the Internet."[21] Prior to the rise of the Blerd and digital spaces on the internet, Black nerds had very little if any agency in how they were portrayed. The image of the Black nerd calls to mind sitcom characters like Steven Urkel, whose oversized glasses, highwater pants, mismatched clothing, suspenders, and nasal voice functioned to separate him from the other "normal" Black characters. Even currently, a popular Netflix series like *Stranger Things* situates the Black nerd character as an oddity within his own family, which itself seems to be isolated

19. Facebook conversation, May 14, 2019.
20. https://twitter.com/auntieleshea/status/1273669246711717889.
21. Barksdale, "10 Experiences."

away from the rest of the white denizens of the fictional town of Hawkins, Indiana.

Who Are You? Afrofuturism as Prophetic Black Identity

This chapter does not argue that Afrofuturism offers a neatly laid out blueprint for constructing or reconstructing Black religious identity. To reduce Afrofuturism and Blerd life to a series of proscribed identities, creeds, and rituals would rob it of the vitality that makes Blerd life so fascinating and variant. Nor does this mean that Afrofuturism and an Afrofuturistic approach to religion offers superior resources; rather, I contend that, as Pinn points out, popular culture in general and Afrofuturism in this case offer substantive resources for Black people to make their way into fuller and thicker descriptions of religious life. Afrofuturism is a site of imaginative construction for the Black individual, not the only site of imaginative constructions. Tensions, of course, may remain.

Drawing on Black speculative works that have been categorized as Afrofuturism, we see that Black religious identities may be understood as dwelling in the prophetic. It should be noted here that such a claim leaves open a temptation to regard Black religious identities as heroic identities. Such a temptation would then fold an Afrofuturistic approach to religion into a heroic project and would constrain the imaginative possibilities of Blackness. Instead, what this chapter proposes is that Afrofuturism as it lends itself to the construction of prophetic Black identities recognizes that Black identities are not fixed identities, but are always open to and pointing toward the more.

As Victor Anderson would put it in his lectures on ethics, we are open to the more by way of our experience. This "more" of which Anderson speaks may be described as a unity of experiences and our capacities to interpret those experiences as part of a larger unity. Again, Butler's Earthseed and formulations of God as change are instructive here, as these verses do not offer doctrinal statements oriented toward an organized and institutionalized collective. Rather, prophetic Black identities formed through engagements with Afrofuturism see the more, the God-as-Change, as a liberating activity to which we devote our imaginative powers.

The question "Who are you" has appeared in and through the gospels, and again in popular science fiction. As mentioned before, *Black Panther* and other forms of Afrofuturism take the question and turn it back upon the

Black viewer. It should not be a surprise that "Wakanda forever" and the Wakandan salute made their way into Black cultural expression, for they became signifiers for an Afrofuturistic Black identity.[22] The question operates thematically throughout the movie and points back toward the viewer. Indeed, the Black boy who asks the question at the end of *Black Panther* may be doing so because he has never seen a Black person like T'Challa before. Thematically, it ties back to the earliest part of the movie, in which Queen Ramonda admonishes T'Challa to "Show him who you are!" during M'Baku's challenge.

Taken together, these questions point toward the "religious" in an Afrofuturistic Black identity, in that they are eschatological, they are moral, they are personal. Ultimately the "God" that our religions create is a reflection of our positions in relation to our personal and collective mythologies. The God-as-change concept takes us as Black people into a divine life and activity that we ourselves create and nourish.

Daniel Spiro notes,

> Perhaps it is best to say that we should have two senses of self, one of which is deeper than the other, but neither of which is dispensable. We are unique beings, and we absolutely must nurture our uniqueness. And yet because we are also integral parts of the divine fabric and emanate from the divine source, we can legitimately think of ourselves as divine beings. The more we reflect on these two senses of self, the more we will see that rather than being inconsistent, they are quite complementary.[23]

I take this as a starting point for Black people constructing an Afrofuturistic religious identity. The uniqueness of Blackness coupled with science fiction/Afrofuturism is part of carving and claiming spaces that had previously been denied to us. To claim the self as part of the divine (if not divine itself) takes us back to Butler's Earthseed verses. Not only are they not tied to grand claims regarding an otherworldly entity who constantly requires human praise, fealty, and obeisance, they do not diminish the importance of the self, in this case, the Black self. An Afrofuturistic religious identity may be one that is oriented toward describing ourselves as part of the divine activity.

Afrofuturism gives us a new sense of who we are in that we are able to construct and reconstruct Black identities vis-à-vis the possibilities presented

22. Mohdin, "The 'Wakanda Forever' Salute."
23. Spiro, *Liberating the Holy Name,* 167.

in Black speculative fictions. The digital metropolis gives Black people new spaces through which we can construct new Black religious lives and identities. For all the attention that Facebook has rightly received for not policing white supremacist groups, it has also become a space that has seen the emergence and flourishing of Black groups that advocate for the celebration of forms of Black difference. For example, a group called "PLANETJOBN: The Extraordinary Journey of a Black Nerd Group" boasts a membership of over 200,000 Facebook users and a very active comment section. However, the group rules describe the group as "neutral territory" and forbid posts that engage politics or religion. We might read this as demanding a purely "secularized" space, one "free" from religion as defined via organized religious traditions. However, I might read this as seeking to liberate a Black nerd space from the doctrinal and credal rigors attached to organized religious traditions. What such a group might do is attempt to actualize the perceived secularity of, say the twenty-fourth century as depicted in *Star Trek*.

Conclusion

This chapter has sought a link between Afrofuturism and Black religious identity. Drawing on growing disaffection with organized and institutional Black religious structures, we see that some Black people have embraced religious and cultural alternatives instead of altogether abandoning religious thinking. Blerds have not described their fandoms as religion per se, so this chapter has taken a risk in interpreting such fandoms and groupings as potentially religious. This chapter has been a thought experiment, asking, "What if we looked at Blerd culture as a form of religion?" What if Wakandacon and Blerdcon are the kinds of gatherings that, as offshoots of the initial Afrofuturism listserv, give Blerds forms of devotional expression that are new and evolving? What if, during Blerdcon, the Church of Anime grows into an alternate form of religious expression for Blerds? What if Afrofuturism blossoms into a fully fledged form of intellectual and cultural inquiry, so that a Black person may declare themselves an Afrofuturist without need of defining the term or the identity?

"The Shape of Things to Come"

Future Directions in the Intersection of Afrofuturism and Black Religious Thought

Throughout this book, I have endeavored to draw robust connections between Afrofuturism and Black religious thought. The goal of this work is to enlarge Black religious thought vis-à-vis the Afrofuturistic imagination. We have seen initial attempts at connecting Afrofuturism to Black religious thought, but those efforts have been preliminary and not well sustained. There have been book chapters and essays. Further, they have occasionally been so closely linked to Black liberation theology and its conception of God, the effort could not necessarily move beyond the Christian God. Thus, this project has opted to engage Black religious thought instead of Black liberation theology.

While this project has not engaged Black liberation theology consistently, I would like to think that Afrofuturistic religious thought can draw upon Black liberation theologies as James Cone and other Black and womanist theologians open up radical interventions within Christianity. These theologies also open up the use of Black cultural productions as sources for liberation and transgressive practices. Afrofuturistic religious thinking might drive us to look at Black liberation theology as a base upon which to build visions of Black futures.

I have only pointed to one direction in the engagement between Afrofuturism and Black religious thought. Obviously, this exploration does not assume that this is the only direction in which Afrofuturistic engagement with Black religious thought can go. I propose that Afrofuturism as a new lens within Black religious thought can and should engage in explorations of the Black subject, the notion(s) of spirit, and reconfiguring/reimagining community. To that end, I will call this new lens Afrofuturistic religious thought. However, before I delve into this new lens, I think it is important to note that this project has also been tacitly concerned with theorizing Afrofuturism. Each of the preceding chapters has been concerned with outlining not only the connections between Afrofuturism and Black religious thought but also the contours of Afrofuturism itself, and moving beyond description and toward situating Afrofuturism as a theory.

To begin, I turn to N. K. Jemisin's foundational essay, "How Long 'til Black Future Month?" What began as a celebration of Janelle Monáe's *The Electric Lady* I think forms a foundation for a theory of Afrofuturism. In this essay, Jemisin juxtaposes the white utopian fantasy of *The Jetsons* with Monáe's ultratechnological, intersectional, and yet, not wholly utopian Black future.

In this essay, a draft of which appears on her web page, Jemisin wrestles with the toxic nature of speculative fiction not only in terms of its propensity to exclude Black people, but also in its creators' penchant for degrading Black bodies. She begins the essay by charting her own path into science fiction, which sounds similar to Octavia Butler's path and the autobiographical sketch I positioned at the beginning of this book. What is common to all of these is the realization that Black bodies, thoughts, and ideas are routinely marginalized within the genre, and that Black enjoyment of science fiction is equally marginalized. I note that what is common in these three descriptions of encountering science fiction is a kind of estrangement *within* Black communities. Further, both Butler and Jemisin articulate that they do not wish to reproduce "mainstream" science fiction's monochromatic cultures. Jemisin notes that she does not desire to create all-Black futures— she "just wanted fantasies of exploration and enchantment that didn't slap [her] in the face with you don't belong here messages. [She] just wanted to be able to relax and dream."[1] This, I think, may be a foundational characteristic of Afrofuturism, the decidedly intentional rejection of constructing monocultural worlds that Black characters inhabit. The unalloyed "optimism" of the monochromatic utopian vision of something as supposedly innocuous as *The Jetsons* presents its own form of cognitive estrangement. As Jemisin notes, as an adult, she watched this cartoon and asked where the world's other peoples went. She noted, "It's creeping me right the fuck out." Afrofuturism's rejection of such a monocultural presentation then

---

1. Jemisin, "How Long 'til Black Future Month?"

begins in cognitive estrangement, and is paradoxical, as those who produce and consume Afrofuturism and its productions may quickly identify with the worlds reproduced therein. For example, Wakanda in *Black Panther* is simultaneously foreign and yet familiar to the Black viewer and the Black nerd (Blerd). It is a place that we yearn for, but we know it does not exist; as such, it compels us to attempt to (re)create it. Cognitive estrangement is at the heart of "Far Beyond the Stars"; instead of a futuristic world, Captain Benjamin Sisko (again) experiences being transported through time and occupying a liminal position in a hostile world. In this case, we see a radical dislocation from a world that we desire to a world that is all too familiar. Octavia Butler's work lives in the realm of estrangement—neat resolutions almost never occur, yet the reader is able to find within her work Blackness that is severed from white supremacy and, for good or for ill, through self or through the intervention by nonhuman others, able to construct new selves. It intentionally speaks to Black readers who understand the "nuances" and functions as a way for us to create alternate worlds (even if they're not wholly positive).

A second feature that is part of Jemisin's juxtaposition of science fiction and Afrofuturism is that Afrofuturism is not an escape from Blackness. It is not utopia—nor is it wholly dystopia. As seen in Butler's work, and as can be glimpsed in Monáe's oeuvre, Afrofuturism rejects these binaries as they do not serve an expansive narrative of Blackness. Such binaries as "utopia" and "dystopia" do not serve Black futures as they are notions of society based upon linear conceptions of time and history. Afrofuturism plays with "ustopia"—neither singularly dystopia nor utopia, but playing upon both. As such, Afrofuturism plays the trickster role, confounding our expectations of such narratives. Afrofuturism runs headlong into Blackness, embraces Blackness, and notes that Blackness is indeed worthy of cherishing and fostering so that it can experience some form of futurity. It runs to Blackness and embraces it with the kind of love that can only come from seeing a future for it. Afrofuturism runs to Blackness and embraces its contestations, contradictions, and conundrums.

A third feature of Afrofuturism is related to the second in that Afrofuturism refuses to be an apologia for Blackness. Those who work within and shape Afrofuturism do not do so in order to secure white approval. To do so would be to center whiteness in such a way as to invalidate the "futurism" at work. Afrofuturism is the speculative fictional distillation of Toni Morrison's brilliant critique of racism and white supremacy:

> The function, the very serious function of racism is distraction. It keeps you from doing your work. It keeps you explaining, over and over again, your

reason for being. Somebody says you have no language and you spend twenty years proving that you do. Somebody says your head isn't shaped properly so you have scientists working on the fact that it is. Somebody says you have no art, so you dredge that up. Somebody says you have no kingdoms, so you dredge that up. None of this is necessary. There will always be one more thing."[2]

When I say that Afrofuturism is the distillation of the above, I mean that Afrofuturism is not at all concerned with presenting Black subjects, characters, settings, and so forth for white approval. Afrofuturism may explore racism, but racism is not necessarily Afrofuturism's central concern. It may be the vehicle through which compelling stories and vistas are imagined; however, the Black subjects therein are not positioned in a titanic struggle solely against racism. Afrofuturism appears to simultaneously acknowledge and overturn Mark Dery's assumption that Black people do not read science fiction and center Morrison's pronouncement of racism as a distraction. So, Afrofuturism does not have to "explain" the Blackness of its subjects—or its consumers.

Thus, we come to the third feature in theorizing Afrofuturism: It is the theory of the Black nerd, or the Blerd. Afrofuturism is not a cosmetic alteration of an existing superhero or android—as in the case with the comic industry's propensity for temporarily sidelining a "legacy" (read: white) character (usually through some form of "death," though almost every comic fan knows that death in superhero comics is almost always temporary), and replacing them with a person of color. Rather, it is the unique propensity within Black creativity to take the familiar within speculative fiction, to invert it, or remix it. The Blerd is a complex amalgamation of both commonly understood and unconventionally constructed forms of Blackness, traditional sci-fi and fantasy fandom, fantastic occupations of these fandoms, and the creation of new science fiction, horror, or fantasy.

Afrofuturistic Religious Thought and the Black Subject

It is obvious that Afrofuturistic productions center Black people throughout the African diaspora. However, I think future directions in Afrofuturistic religious thought might take a cue from systematic theologies and theologi-

2. Portland State, "Black Studies Center Public Dialogue, Pt. 2," May 30, 1975, Sound-Cloud, https://soundcloud.com/portland-state-library/portland-state-black-studies-1?mc_cid=7a27cfd978&mc_eid=e2efbcffa9.

cal anthropologies and explore more fully who the human being is in Afrofuturism and what Black religious thought can learn from Afrofuturism. Here I will offer some brief suggestions.

First, the human being in general and the Black subject in particular are contested sites and entities. This is an academic way of saying that Black people in the diaspora have complicated histories and ways of constructing identity. The Black subject is a site of radical hope and transformation. Here, let us consider Nnedi Okorafor's novella series *Binti*. Binti, a young girl from the Himba ethnic group, runs away from her home to attend Oomza Uni, a prestigious intergalactic university. En route to the university, the transport ship is attacked by the Meduse, an alien race at war with a group of humans called the Khoush. Binti is the sole survivor of the attack, and after showing the healing properties of the mixed clay from her homeland called otijze and allying with a young member of the Meduse named Okwu, she is able to foster a peace between the humans and the Meduse. In the case of Okorafor's Binti, the hero of the story is so because of her capacity to overcome fear and share the gifts of her native land with others.

While Binti is part Meduse as a result of the Meduse attack on her transport, she describes herself as human. Aside from the gifts of her being in some part Meduse, the abilities of her astrolabe, and the otijze, the power that Binti possess is her connection to her fear and her fearlessness. The willingness to transcend the limitations set upon her by the fearful is part of how we can view the Black subject in Afrofuturistic religious thought. Seeing—with our limited senses—the possibilities that lie before us is seeing and feeling the ways we can be better than what came before while building upon what came before.

The Black subject in Afrofuturism may be some form of transhuman; that is to say, the Black subject may encounter or be fused with some kind of alien life form or have some kind of inborn ability that marks them as different or strange. Of course, this is a hallmark of science fiction. However, in the case of Afrofuturism, the transhuman Black subject's Blackness is usually key to their character.

Writers like Butler and Okorafor take great care to center the transhuman Black subject's Blackness not as a site of tragedy, but as a site of renewed possibilities. These renewed possibilities often occur in the face of tragedy and great challenge, but the subject is not overdetermined by those tragedies and challenges. The transhuman Black subject in Afrofuturism is also not beholden to a particular God or religion; rather, what characterizes the transhuman Black subject is revised and revived notions of spirit and community.

Therefore, Afrofuturistic religious thought must be intersectional. A transhuman Black subject should no longer be controlled by rigid identity constructions. Building upon the work of Butler, Delany, Monáe, Okorafor, and many others, this kind of approach must not only acknowledge but celebrate the diversity of Black bodies, lives, and religious expressions. Those diverse forms are part of a historical and cultural mosaic in which the Black body is reimagined beyond the pain inflicted by white supremacy.

Spirit in Afrofuturistic Religious Thought

Spirit in the case of Afrofuturism is not necessarily a disembodied entity that functions mysteriously and on the behalf of a remote deity. Spirit is the sense of larger and overarching realities, of the possibilities that those realities bring. It is the understanding that connectedness matters and flows from our ancestors. Spirit is that ineffable quality inherent in human life and experiences that enables us to see beyond the material conditions of life and the world, to see the hope that undergirds our narratives regarding human potential. Recovering and remembering African diasporic religious practices in and through Afrofuturism echoes James Cone's early description of Blackness in *A Black Theology of Liberation* when he describes Black people having a "spirit" of Blackness and loving it. He traces this love of Blackness through Aretha Franklin's "R-E-S-P-E-C-T" and James Brown's "I'm Black and I'm Proud." He briefly reads these as representations of a Black spirit that is indomitable, unbowed, and innately connected to a larger sense of self and community. Afrofuturistic religious thought integrates this, centers it, but need not necessarily connect this Black spirit to a Christian God.

Community in Afrofuturistic Religious Thought

Womanist theologians write about community a great deal. Monica Coleman's assessment of the possibilities of a communal theology using Black women's science fiction do not point us toward utopia. Rather, her assessment and this book's assessment of Afrofuturism as a source for revisioning community is part of how Black people in the twenty-first century are utilizing intellectual sources to rethink, revisit, and revise descriptions of Black life.

What this chapter proposes is an Afrofuturistic eschatological approach to Black life. What does such a description of Black futures look like? I propose two dimensions to an Afrofuturistic eschatology.

BLACK FUTURES IN AFROFUTURISTIC ESCHATOLOGIES MUST BE DIVERSE AND INTERSECTIONAL

Any future-oriented discussion of Black life that cites and centers Afrofuturism must be diverse and intersectional. Even at first glance, when considering the architects of Afrofuturism, they have been the Black people who might have been rejected by or failed to "fit" into a mainstream "Blackness." However, it is they who have consistently pushed the boundaries of Blackness forward. These visionaries see the manifold facets of Blackness and work to bring those facets forward. If, for example, we were to consider Prince as an Afrofuturist, we might look at his genius as virtually otherworldly. His music, lyricism, and talent were pansexual, religious, sacrilegious, antiestablishment, and thoroughly Black. Prince played with respectability politics, sometimes seemingly affirming them, and at other times, turning them on their head. It should not be a surprise that Prince became one of Janelle Monáe's mentors. She folded his style into hers, merging them into her Afrofuturistic soundscape. *Dirty Computer* as an album and an emotion picture could easily have fit into Prince's catalog.

Turning to literary Afrofuturism, consider the works of Nnedi Okorafor and N. K. Jemisin. Black women's experience and imagination are at the heart of their epic science fiction and fantasy. A Black future cannot be imagined or come to pass if Black women are marginalized. Further, these Black women at the center of these epics do not exist via the heterosexual male gaze. That is to say, they are not subjects of male fantasies. This does not mean they do not possess sexuality—quite the contrary. However, Afrofuturism shows that Black people can write, draw, record, and film Black worlds into existence that do not repeat the heteronormative patterns of other forms of science fiction and fantasy.

Further, Afrofuturistic works must be diverse in that they reflect, represent and re-present the fullness of the African diaspora. The eschatological dimensions of Afrofuturism do not ignore the effects of slavery on the African diaspora. Indeed, those effects and the attempted erasure of Black lives from history guide the efforts of Afrofuturists. Consider what Nalo Hopkinson says regarding the effects of slavery on the diaspora as well as how she views science fiction as restorative work:

> The experience of slavery is a huge cancer in the collective consciousness of African people all over the diaspora. The ripple effects of it (if you'll bear with a mixed metaphor for a moment) still continue, and they touch the past, the present, and the future. People recognize that about the effects of the Holocaust on Jewish people, but we don't get the same recognition.

We're supposed to have "gotten over it" by now, even though its domino effect still very much straitlaces our lives. Speculative fiction allows me to experiment with the effects of that cancerous blot, to shrink it by setting my worlds far in the future (science fiction) or to metonymize it so that I can explore the paradigms it's created (fantasy). I could even choose to sidestep it altogether into alternate history. Mosley says that sf [science fiction] makes it possible to create visions which will "shout down the realism imprisoning us behind a wall of alienating culture."[3]

Okorafor's *Binti* novellas are an example of her Afrofuturistic eschatological work. What is at the center of her work is the freedom of Black women to break out of rigid societal structures and shape new ways of seeing and being. Okorafor's web page describes Binti's story: "Knowledge comes at a cost, one that Binti is willing to pay, but her journey will not be easy." The future as a backdrop for Binti's story follows the Hero's Journey, but is also statement: Black peoples have not only survived, they have flourished. Further, these novellas as part of an Afrofuturistic eschatology are an example of Okorafor's statement that her writings in some way "experiment with the effects of [the] cancerous blot [of the transatlantic slave trade]." The conflicts between human beings and the Meduse are built upon the history of our real-world global conflicts.

I should note here that Okorafor has recently rejected the term "Afro-futurism" and embraced "Africanfuturism" and "Africanjujuism." This itself is part of the evolving nature of African and diaspora-centered speculative and science fiction. Okorafor's definition of herself as an Africanfuturist is about centering the science fictions that she writes in African contexts instead of centering European conceptions of science fiction. A May 23, 2019, profile of her in the *Chicago Tribune* outlines why she might reject the term in favor of "Africanfuturism":

She calls her work "Africanfuturism," as opposed to the more common "Afro-futurism." The difference, she says, is her books—sometimes with aliens, sometimes with witches, often set in a recognizable, future Africa, with African lineages—are not cultural hybrids but rooted in the history and traditions of the continent, without a desire to look toward Western culture (or even pop culture).[4]

---

3. Rutledge and Hopkinson, "Speaking in Tongues," 592.
4. Christopher Borrelli, "How Nnedi Okorafor Is Building the Future of Sci-Fi from Flossmoor (Being George R. R. Martin's Protege Doesn't Hurt)," *Chicago Tribune*, May 23, 2019, https://www.chicagotribune.com/entertainment/ct-ae-nnedi-okorafor-sci-fi-0526-story.html.

For Afrofuturism as an evolving series of conversations and productions, those of us who are part of this movement must be open to how it is capable of encompassing various Black identities. In this case, Africanfuturism or Africanjujuism can and should stand alongside Afrofuturism as part of evolving visions of diasporic Blackness. Okorafor notes that Africanfuturism is "similar to Afrofuturism" in that both Afrofuturism and Africanfuturism center Black peoples in the diaspora.[5]

BLACK FUTURES CAN DARE TO BE UTOPIAN

One of the challenges in constructing futuristic worlds is the temptation to construct dystopian visions. Indeed, a great deal of late twentieth- and early twenty-first-century science fiction and fantasy is quite dystopian. Indeed, some science fiction theory militates against utopian visions, as those visions have occasionally been linked to real-world dystopian societies (e.g., Soviet-style communism). Those dystopian visions are often tied to whiteness and the anxieties of such in the face of social, cultural, economic, and climate change. As I noted in the first chapter, Black peoples in the African diaspora have already experienced apocalyptic dystopia, the likes of which have been the subject of many science fiction movies and television shows. Abducted en masse by aliens; transported across a vast alien gulf to an alien land; enslaved and brutalized in nearly every imaginable fashion; forced to abandon ancestral customs, religions, and folkways; enduring social, cultural, economic, and environmental discrimination and abuse—Black people have experienced dystopia.

It only makes sense that Black people would dream of better worlds. It only makes sense that Black people would adapt Christian promises of pearly gates and streets of gold, a mansion, a robe, and a crown, and adapt those to a present world. It only makes sense that Sun Ra's Afrofuturism would be in search of a "pure" world where Black people can experience the fullness of being. It only makes sense that African Americans would draw upon African cosmology and aesthetics, Western mythological tropes and themes, and comic book superheroes and create a world that is tantalizing. The vision afforded by Wakanda and the on-screen representation of an unsullied Blackness is the Afrofuturistic eschatological hope. It should not be surprising that Nnedi Okorafor has been tapped to write a Marvel comic book that centers the Shuri, the Wakandan wunderkind who is the smart-

---

5. Okorafor, "Africanfuturism Defined."

est person in the Marvel cinematic universe and is responsible for much of Wakanda's technological prowess. It also should not be surprising that Okorafor remixes this term and calls it "Africanfuturism," as this calls into question what "Afrofuturism" might claim about diasporic identities and sources.

Both T'Challa and Shuri (and the rest of the *Black Panther* characters) are the embodiment of social media hashtags like #BlackGirlMagic and #BlackBoyJoy. Returning to *Black Panther*'s finale, the eschatological hope of such hashtags is evident when they are in Oakland. T'Challa informs Shuri that she is going to oversee the Science and Information Exchange that is part of the first Wakandan Outreach Center. Again, we see traces of Sun Ra's *Space Is the Place* in T'Challa and Shuri's revelation of themselves to a group of Black boys playing basketball. Where Sun Ra materializes in a Black community center and begins to educate the youth, T'Challa says he is going to build an outreach center that will bring Wakanda to Oakland. Both Sun Ra and T'Challa intend to bring technological salvation to oppressed Black peoples—and in T'Challa's case, he also intends to redeem the ground upon which the primordial sin of murder occurred. If Killmonger is the "fallen angel" who wars against heaven out of a twisted desire to do the right thing, then T'Challa at the end of *Black Panther* is the humanistic deity who reveals himself to his distant and estranged relatives. The camera pans to one of the Black youths who is transfixed by the decloaked Royal Talon—perhaps he had dreamed of such things, perhaps he read comic books, perhaps he wanted to be an aeronautical engineer but had been told that such things were beyond his reach. He approaches T'Challa and asks, "Who are you?," echoing the theme of identity that runs through the movie. T'Challa does not have to hide who he is, signifying that the question has achieved an eschatological resolution.

God, the Open-Ended Question

While this book has not attended directly to the concept of divinity or divinities in Afrofuturism, this is not to say that Afrofuturism as a discourse is opposed to the concept of deities or opposed to the interaction with theology. Indeed, we may find deities in many Afrofuturistic productions. As noted in previous chapters, specifically the first chapter, the temptation in Black religious thought is to appeal to the Christian God. However, Afrofuturism is a wide field in which the Christian God (as well as the institutions that purport to represent it) receives robust criticism. It provides speculative backdrops against which the producer and the consumer may explore multiple iterations of divinity.

As I noted at the beginning of this book, this project was not intended to function as a theology. However, the God-symbol in a work on Black religious thought cannot remain ignored. As hinted at in previous chapters, Afrofuturism may offer us resources to move beyond particular Christian conceptions of a monotheistic "God." However, it may also offer resources for reimagining conceptions of God that line up with Christian identities. I do not offer a theology; rather, I think that Afrofuturism in conjunction with Black religious thought gifts us an imaginative insight into what the God-symbol might mean in Black futures.

Here, I return to Daniel Spiro's "Liberating the Holy Name," as well Phillip Butler's recently published "Black Transhuman Liberation Theology." I reiterate these scholars as they all have grappled with the God-concept; admittedly, Spiro is the outlier here as he is not an African American scholar of religion. However, I think his argument against a singular meaning of "God" is helpful here for making sense of Afrofuturistic critiques of Black religion, Afrofuturistic religious thought, and, perhaps, a future attempt at an Afrofuturistic theology. If someone were to write an Afrofuturistic theology as I at first thought, they might be tempted or required to grapple with the classical divine attributes as part of orthodox and liberation theologies. Even process theologies have to contend with those classical divine attributes. Spiro lays out the straitjacketedness of theological debate in the beginning of his work:

> Stated simply, many members of both groups (pro-religion/anti-religion) share an interest in strait-jacketing the debate. They want to keep our choices simple when it comes to religion: accept "God" or reject religion altogether. *What* God you ask? Please, you know the conception I'm talking about. "He" is an omnipotent, omnibenevolent, eternal being who has created the universe and all of its contents in accordance with his own inscrutable will and who has revealed his existence to human beings known as prophets.[6]

For Spiro, theological discussion must move beyond the Christian God or no-religion dichotomy. Such a dichotomy "flattens" the complex nature of discussions about the existence or nonexistence of a god and of how human beings construct their own spiritualities. Spiro's critique of theological

---

6. Spiro, *Liberating the Holy Name*, 5.

debate leads to another compelling recent text by Phillip Butler that seeks to expand Black theological discourse.

Butler's *Black Transhumanism Liberation Theology* seeks to link Blackness, spirituality, and technology in order to craft a liberation theology for Black people that recognizes the possibilities of joining technology and spirituality to create a liberating force for Black people. According to Butler,

> By simultaneously taking on the mantle of liberation and fully immersing one's self into the technological world, one can actually embody a constructed theology that subverts technocratic attempts to control the human body and mind through the enticing makeup of the psycho-realistic virtual world.[7]

His argument is provocative. For Butler, technology is "key to Black revolution and liberation." As he understands our current world, technology is inextricable from Black experiences of the world. To draw on my aforementioned discussions of Black Twitter, Janelle Monáe, and the movie *Black Panther*, it does appear that Black engagements with technology are indeed part of Black cultural productions that can be part of liberationist movements. Indeed, Butler encourages "Black biotechnology to create technological advancements and organizations capable of employing other Black bodies. This tactic is meant to cultivate dignity while accumulating power."[8] Butler sees participation in science and technology as a liberating path for Black people. As I see it, Black people have used Twitter and Facebook as interventions against white supremacy and toward Black liberation. Regardless of the often-racist policies of these platforms' owners, Black people have been able to use these technologies in order to center and lift up Black voices and experiences.

Further, for Butler, the help that Black people need in order to overcome white supremacy's oppressive use of technology will come from within.[9] Liberation requires a "revolt spirituality" that challenges the binary distinctions imposed by colonial frameworks and systems.[10] Butler is also not interested in advancing the descriptions of God as seen in James Cone's theology of liberation. Rather, toward the end of the book, Butler states, "God is us. We are . . . incarnate with life itself."[11] While Butler is not attempting to do

---

7. Butler, *Black Transhuman Liberation Theology*, 14–15.
8. Ibid., 143.
9. Ibid., 129.
10. Ibid., 138.
11. Ibid., 129.

away with the Christian God altogether, he is clear in situating the human being as the effective agent of change and liberation.

What I have gleaned from my own journeys as a science fiction devotee, a former "church kid," an agnostic, an Afrofuturist, and a scholar of Black religion is the capacity to question what "we" even mean when we deploy the word "God." Afrofuturism in all its dimensions has given me new ways of talking about the divine as part of my own Black and nerdy experience. Afrofuturism may resurrect the gods of the African diaspora and give them vitality in the context of technological and fantastical settings. Afrofuturism may even critique the notion of gods by presenting human beings and non-human beings as part of transcendent realities. Afrofuturism as an evolving discourse in Black cultural life possesses the capacity to help us revision the God-concept. It is our gift to use as we will in order to revision Black cultural and religious lives.

An acquaintance posted a reflection on teaching, mentoring young Black men, and the manner in which Black boys and men in America have been socialized to deal with life via aggression. At the end of his reflection, he wrote, "Imagine what the world would look like if we created, nurtured, and facilitated Black men being able to sit with their emotions, learn to manage them, and transcend our traumas?" When I read this, I immediately thought of three things. The first is Essex Hemphill's saying that "Black men loving Black men is the revolutionary act." The second is the loving relationship we saw between Benjamin Sisko, his son Jake, and his father Joseph on *Star Trek: Deep Space Nine*. Finally, I thought of the moments in *Black Panther* in which Black men weep openly and express love for each other. In each of these moments, those who have crafted them have envisioned a Black identity that is not framed by toxic Black masculinity or by dreams of domination.

Afrofuturism and its boundless possibilities enables us to see both Black women and men as fully embodied and complex individuals. The revolutionary relationship between Benjamin Sisko, his son, and his father tells us that in the future that Benny Russell created, a Black man can not only rise to the command of the most important space station in the Federation, he can also maintain close and loving relationships with his father and his son. Further, such relationships are based on mutual understanding, trust, and emotional openness. As Micheal Charles Pounds wrote concerning the third-season episode "Explorers," Sisko himself broke the mold of "traditional" *Star Trek* captains. Captains like Kirk, Picard, and Janeway were larger-than-life figures who maintained emotional distance from their crews. Unlike those captains, Sisko was close to both his father and his son. Further, *Deep Space Nine* took care to show the bonds between three generations of a family. Pounds notes that this episode highlights a core difference in Sisko's character, that of his strength emanating from working with Jake toward a common goal.[1]

Black men being emotionally open was a centerpiece in *Black Panther* as well. Though this book has already discussed the movie at length, it should be noted that one of the most moving scenes in the film is between T'Challa and his deceased father. T'Challa undergoes a ceremony in which he enters into the Ancestral Plane to converse with his father. Overcome with emotion, T'Challa falls to his knees, clutches his father's hands, and weeps. He openly expresses love for his father, and his desire to be a good king. We see the possibilities for Black masculinity in an Afrofuturistic context. Through Afrofuturism, these possibilities are connected to a spiritual realm and practices in which mind, body, and soul are united.

Conversely, *Black Panther* shows us the consequences of toxic masculinity. When Killmonger/N'Jadaka performs the same ceremony that T'Challa did and enters the Ancestral Plane to converse with his father, N'Jobu, he reverts to his childhood self. Because Killmonger never dealt with the trauma of his father's death, he remains trapped in his traumatized childhood. N'Jobu asks, "No tears for me?" to which Killmonger replies, "Everybody dies. That's just life around here."

Killmonger's statement may have been prophetic. As of the writing of this book, the world in general and the United States in particular is in the throes of a pandemic. The novel coronavirus COVID-19 has, to date, killed hundreds of thousands of people worldwide and disproportionately infected and killed Black people in the United States. Further complicating matters in the United States has been the grossly negligent response by the federal government. Additionally, the nation has been gripped by protests against police brutality in the wake of the police murders of George Floyd, Breonna Taylor, and Elijah McClain. In the midst of this, Black trans women have been murdered at near-epidemic rates. The political, sociocultural, and medical landscape of the United States looks every bit the dystopian hellscape that is often presented in apocalyptic media. It has been frighten-

---

1. Pounds, "'Explorers'—Star Trek: Deep Space Nine," 68.

ing to see callous responses to requests that people wear masks in order to help curb the spread of the virus. It has also been frightening to see violent responses to peaceful protests. As of the writing of this postscript, unidentified federal agents in Portland have reportedly been snatching protesters off the streets.[2] The 45th president of the United States repeatedly stoked the fires of white supremacy via Twitter and other public pronouncements. His 2016 campaign was based on a slogan, "Make America Great Again," which was eerily similar to that of Andrew Steele Jarrett, the ultra-right-wing president in Octavia Butler's *Parable of the Talents*. In that book, the fictional U.S. president Jarrett founded his own religious sect, "Christian America," and promised to "make America great again."[3]

Indeed, these concurrent crises might look almost exactly like the dystopian America described in Butler's books and cause one to lose hope. The promise of Afrofuturism is that the Afrofuturist examines the intersections of technology, race, gender, and class and may offer ways to revision Black life and thriving in the midst of crisis. C. Brandon Ogbunu's essay "How Afrofuturism Can Help the World Mend" positions Afrofuturism as a constellation of resources and activities that can help rebuild the world after COVID. Using Du Bois's "The Comet" as a metaphor for COVID and rampant white supremacy, Ogbunu echoes this book's assertion that Afrofuturism is necessary if we want to reform the world.[4]

We need Afrofuturism's ability to revision and reframe Black identities in our toolbox in order to reimagine Black selves. We need Afrofuturism alongside other intellectual projects to help us understand that if *all* of us do not get free, *none* of us get free. As I noted earlier, this book began as a way of me using *Star Trek: Deep Space Nine* in order to cope with the ongoing litany of Black names we must recite in the face of white supremacist violence and then expanded into a larger reflection on the intersections between Afrofuturism and Black religious thought. What I have found in Afrofuturism and Black science fiction is another set of tools that helps me frame Black lives and make all Black lives actually matter.

2. "Unidentified Federal Agents in Camo and Rented Minivans Are Grabbing People off Portland's Streets," *The Week*, July 17, 2020, https://theweek.com/speedreads/926070/unidentified-federal-agents-camo-rented-minivans-are-grabbing-people-portlands-streets.

3. Butler, *Parable of the Talents*, 20.

4. Ogbunu, "How Afrofuturism Can Help."

BIBLIOGRAPHY

Alleyne, Allyssia. "How 'Black Panther' Costume Designer Ruth E. Carter Wove an Afrofuturist Fantasy." *CNN*, February 21, 2019. Accessed December 19, 2020. https://www.cnn.com/style/article/black-panther-costumes-ruth-e-carter/index.html.

Anderson, Reynaldo, and Charles E. Jones, eds. *Afrofuturism 2.0: The Rise of Astro-Blackness*. Lanham, MD: Lexington Books, 2016.

Anderson, Victor. *Beyond Ontological Blackness: An Essay on African American Religious and Cultural Criticism*. New York: Continuum Books, 1995.

———. *Creative Exchange: A Constructive Theology of African American Religious Experience*. Minneapolis, MN: Fortress Press, 2008.

Barksdale, Aaron. "10 Experiences That Every Black Nerd Can Relate To." *Huffington Post*, November 12, 2015. Accessed December 19, 2020. https://www.huffpost.com/entry/10-experiences-that-every-black-nerd-can-relate-to_n_56441b4fe4b045bf3dedceob.

Barnes, Steve. *Star Trek Deep Space Nine: Far Beyond the Stars*. New York: Pocket Books, 1998.

Barr, Marleen S., ed. *Afro-Future Females: Black Writers Chart Science Fiction's Newest New-Wave Trajectory*. Columbus: The Ohio State University Press, 2008.

Battlestar Galactica. "Daybreak: Part 2." Directed by Michael Rymer. Written by Ronald D. Moore. Aired March 20, 2009, on the Sci-Fi Channel.

Bell, John. "A Charles R. Saunders Interview." Black American Literature Forum, 18, no.2 (Summer, 1984) 90–92.

Bengal, Rebecca. "'You Don't Own or Control Me': Janelle Monáe on Her Music, Politics and Undefinable Sexuality." *The Guardian,* February 22, 2018. Accessed December 15, 2020. https://www.theguardian.com/music/2018/feb/22/you-dont-own-or-control-me-janelle-monae-on-her-music-politics-and-undefinable-sexuality.

Bould, Mark. *Science Fiction.* London: Routledge, 2012.

———. "The Ships Landed Long Ago: Afrofuturism and Black SF." *Science Fiction Studies* 34, no. 2 (July 2007): 177–86.

Brode, Douglas, and Shea T. Brode, eds. *The Star Trek Universe: Franchising the Final Frontier.* Lanham, MD: Rowan & Littlefield, 2015.

Brooks, Kinitra. "Myrtle's Medicine." *Emergence Magazine.* Accessed December 19, 2020. https://emergencemagazine.org/story/myrtles-medicine/.

Bruggemann, Walter. *The Prophetic Imagination.* Minneapolis, MN: Augsburg Fortress, 2001. Kindle.

Burnett, Zaron. "Why Black 'Game of Thrones' Fans Need #DemThrones." *Mel Magazine.* Accessed December 19, 2020. https://melmagazine.com/en-us/story/why-black-game-of-thrones-fans-need-demthrones.

Butler, Octavia. *Bloodchild: And Other Stories.* New York: Open Road Integrated Media, 2012.

———. "Lost Races of Science Fiction." In *Octavia E. Butler,* by Gerry Canavan, 181–86. Urbana: University of Illinois Press, 2016.

———. *Parable of the Sower.* New York: Grand Central Publishing, 1993.

———. *Parable of the Talents.* New York: Grand Central Publishing, 1998.

———. *Seed to Harvest: The Complete Patternist Series.* New York: Open Road Integrated Media, 2012.

Butler, Phillip. *Black Transhuman Liberation Theology: Technology and Spirituality.* London: Bloomsbury Academic, 2020.

Calhoun, Jordan. "An Open Love Letter to Every Blerd." *Black Nerd Problems.* Accessed December 19, 2020. https://blacknerdproblems.com/an-open-love-letter-to-every-blerd/.

Canavan, Gerry. "The Octavia Butler Papers." *The Eaton Journal of Archival Research in Science Fiction* 3, no. 1 (November 2015).

———. *Octavia E. Butler.* Modern Masters of Science Fiction. Urbana, IN: University of Illinois Press, 2016.

Coleman, Monica A. *Making a Way Out of No Way: A Womanist Theology.* Minneapolis, MN: Fortress Press, 2008.

Cone, James. *A Black Theology of Liberation: Twentieth Anniversary Edition.* Maryknoll, NY: Orbis Books, 1986.

Coogler, Ryan, dir. *Black Panther.* 2018; Burbank, CA: Buena Vista Home Entertainment, 2018. DVD.

Cowan, Douglas E. *Sacred Space: The Quest for Transcendence in Science Fiction Film and Television.* Waco, TX: Baylor University Press, 2010.

Dayfloat. "Janelle Monáe Speaks on Sexuality on Sway in the Morning." *Okayplayer.* Accessed December 15, 2020. https://www.okayplayer.com/news/janelle-monae-sway-in-the-morning-interview-sexuality.html.

Delany, Samuel. "Racism and Science Fiction." *New York Review of Science Fiction,* no. 120 (August 1998). https://www.nyrsf.com/racism-and-science-fiction-.html.

Douglas, Kelly Brown. *Stand Your Ground: Black Bodies and the Justice of God.* Maryknoll, NY: Orbis Books, 2015.

Du Bois, W. E. B. "The Comet." In *Dark Matter: A Century of Speculative Fiction from the African Diaspora,* edited by Sheree R. Thomas, 5–17. New York: Warner Books, 2000.

———. *The Souls of Black Folk.* New York: Signet Classics, 1995

Dyson, Michael Eric. *Reflecting Black: African American Cultural Criticism.* Minneapolis, MN: University of Minnesota, 1993.

Easton, Lee, and Randy Schroeder, eds. *The Influence of Imagination: Essays on Science Fiction and Fantasy as Agents of Social Change.* Jefferson, NC: McFarland & Company, 2008.

Ellsworth, Scott. *Death In A Promised Land: The Tulsa Race Riot of 1921.* Baton Rouge: Louisiana State University Press, 1982.

English, Daylanne, and Alvin Kim. "Now We Want Our Funk Cut: Janelle Monáe's Neo-Afrofuturism." *American Studies* 52, no. 4 (2013): 217–30.

Epsicokhan, Jamahl. "Star Trek: Deep Space Nine: 'Far Beyond the Stars.'" *Jammer's Reviews.* Accessed December 15, 2020. https://www.jammersreviews.com/st-ds9/s6/stars.php.

Evans, Curtis J. *The Burden of Black Religion.* New York: Oxford University Press. 2008.

Finley, Stephen C. *Esotericism in African American Religious Experience: "There Is a Mystery."* Boston: Brill, 2014.

———. "The Meaning of Mother in Louis Farrakhan's "Mother Wheel": Race, Gender, and Sexuality in the Cosmology of the Nation of Islam's UFO." *Journal of the American Academy of Religion* 80, no. 2 (June 2012): 434–65.

Fitz-Gerald, Sean. "Read How Martin Luther King Jr. Affected *Star Trek* and Nichelle Nichols's Career." *Vulture,* July 31, 2015. Accessed December 14, 2020. https://www.vulture.com/2015/07/mlk-jr-star-trek-nichelle-nichols.html.

Florio, Angelica. "Janelle Monáe's 'PYNK' Video about Female Sexuality Will Make You Feel Like a Goddess." *Bustle,* April 10, 2018. Accessed December 15, 2020. https://www.bustle.com/p/janelle-monaes-pynk-video-about-female-sexuality-will-make-you-feel-like-a-goddess-8746306.

Forman, Bill. "Pop Sensation Janelle Monáe Uses Science Fiction to Convey Stark Realities." *Colorado Springs Independent,* June 10, 2010. Accessed December 14, 2020. https://www.csindy.com/coloradosprings/pop-sensation-janelle-monandaacutee-uses-science-fiction-to-convey-stark-realities/Content?oid=1739497.

Francis, Consuela, ed. *Conversations with Octavia Butler.* Jackson: University Press of Mississippi, 2010.

Geraghty, Lincoln, ed. *The Influence of Star Trek on Television Film and Culture.* Critical Explorations in Science Fiction and Fantasy, edited by Donald E. Palumbo and C. W. Sullivan III. Jefferson, NC: McFarland & Company, 2008.

Gerlach, Neil, and Sheryl N. Hamilton. "Introduction: A History of Social Science Fiction." *Science Fiction Studies* 30, no. 2 (July 2003): 161–73.

Gonzalez, Juan, and Amy Goodman. "Science Fiction Writer Octavia Butler on Race, Global Warming, and Religion." In *Conversations with Octavia Butler,* edited by Consuela Francis, 222–25. Jackson: University Press of Mississippi, 2009.

Gray, Herman. *Watching Race: Television and the Struggle for "Blackness."* Minneapolis: University of Minnesota Press, 1995.

Greven, David. *Gender and Sexuality in Star Trek: Allegories of Desire in the Television Series and Films.* Jefferson, NC: McFarland & Company, 2009.

Hairston, Andrea. "It's Our Time: The Women of Wakanda." *Los Angeles Review of Books,* September 8, 2018. Accessed December 19, 2020. https://lareviewofbooks.org/article/time-women-wakanda/.

Handlen, Zack. "*Star Trek: Deep Space Nine*: 'Far Beyond the Stars'" *AV Club,* November 14, 2013. Accessed December 15, 2020. https://tv.avclub.com/star-trek-deep-space-nine-far-beyond-the-stars-1798178688.

Harrison, Rosalie G. "Sci-Fi Visions: An Interview with Octavia Butler." In *Conversations with Octavia Butler,* edited by Consuela Francis, 4–5. Jackson: University Press of Mississippi, 2009.

Holmes, Barbara A. *Race and the Cosmos: An Invitation to View the World Differently.* Harrisburg, PA: Trinity Press International, 2002.

Imarisha, Walidah, Adrienne Maree Brown, and Sheree Renee Thomas. *Octavia's Brood: Science Fiction Stories from Social Justice Movements.* Oakland, CA: AK Press, 2016.

Irwin, William, ed. *The Matrix and Philosophy: Welcome to the Desert of the Real.* Chicago: Open Court, 2002.

Jackson, H. Jerome. "Sci-Fi Tales from Octavia Butler." In *Conversations with Octavia Butler,* edited by Consuela Francis, 43–48. Jackson: University Press of Mississippi, 2009.

Jackson, Sandra, and July E. Moody-Freeman, eds. *The Black Imagination: Science Fiction Futurism and the Speculative.* Black Studies and Critical Thinking, edited by Rochelle Brock and Richard Greggory Johnson III. New York: Peter Lang, 2011.

Jemisin, N. K. "How Long 'til Black Future Month? The Toxins of Speculative Fiction, and the Antidote That Is Janelle Monáe." September 30, 2013. Accessed December 19, 2020. http://nkjemisin.com/2013/09/how-long-til-black-future-month/.

Jindra, Michael. "Star Trek Fandom as Religious Phenomenon." *Sociology of Religion* 55, no. 1 (Spring 1994): 27–51.

John Hope Franklin Center at Duke University. "Left of Black with Jonathan Gayles and Alondra Nelson." Season 2, episode 7, October 24, 2011. YouTube. https://www.youtube.com/watch?v=ElOWrWGH8hI&t=775s.

Kai, Maiysha. "Whose World Is This? *Black Panther* Production Designer Hannah Beachler Walks Us through Wakanda." *The Root,* February 21, 2018. Accessed December 19, 2020. https://theglowup.theroot.com/whose-world-is-this-black-panther-production-designer-1823105143.

Kappell, Matthew Wilhelm. *Star Trek as Myth: Essays on Symbol and Archetype at the Final Frontier.* Jefferson, NC: McFarland & Company, 2010.

King, Debra Walker. *African Americans and the Culture of Pain.* Charlottesville: University of Virginia Press, 2008.

Lieb, Michael. *Children of Ezekiel: Aliens, UFOs, the Crisis of Race, and the Advent of End Time.* Durham, NC: Duke University Press, 1998.

Lightsey, Pamela. *Our Lives Matter: A Womanist Queer Theology.* Eugene, OR: Pickwick Publications, 2015.

Lock, Graham. *Blutopia: Visions of the Future and Revisions of the Past in the Work of Sun Ra, Duke Ellington, and Anthony Braxton.* Durham, NC: Duke University Press, 2000.

Lomax, Tamura. *Jezebel Unhinged: Loosing the Black Female Body in Religion and Culture.* Durham, NC: Duke University Press, 2018.

Lorde, Audre. *Sister Outsider.* New York: Ten Speed Press, 1984.

Maloney, Devon. "How The First Wakandacon Escaped the Fan Convention Curse." *The Verge*, August 13, 2018. Accessed December 19, 2020. https://www.theverge.com/2018/8/13/17677296/wakandacon-convention-chicago-black-panther-wakanda.

Manigault-Bryant, LeRhonda, Tamura A. Lomax, and Carol B. Duncan, eds. *Womanist and Black Feminist Responses to Tyler Perry's Productions.* New York: Palgrave Macmillan, 2014.

Mar-Abe, Alice. "Ferguson Is the Future." *Nassau Weekly*, October 11, 2015. Accessed December 19, 2020. http://nassauweekly.com/ferguson-is-the-future/.

Matiluko, Oluwaseun. "Sun-Ra's Space Is the Place: A Radical Black Reimagining of a Better Future." Project Myopia, May 6, 2019. Accessed December 19, 2020. https://projectmyopia.com/sun-ras-space-is-the-place-a-radical-black-reimagining-of-a-better-future/.

McCaffery, Larry, and Jim McMenamin. "An Interview with Octavia E. Butler." In *Conversations with Octavia Butler*, edited by Consuela Francis, 14. Jackson: University Press of Mississippi, 2009.

McCormack, Michael Brandon. "'Your God Is a Racist, Sexist, Homophobic, and a Misogynist . . . Our God Is Change': Ishmael Reed, Octavia Butler and Afrofuturist Critiques of (Black) American Religion." *Black Theology* 14, no. 1 (April 2016): 6–27.

Miller, Jim. "Apocalyptic Hoping: Octavia Butler's Dystopian/Utopian Vision." *Science Fiction Film Studies* 25, no. 2 (July 1998): 336–60.

Mohdin, Aamna. "The 'Wakanda Forever' salute has become a symbol to celebrate black excellence." *Quartz*, March 13, 2018. Accessed December 19, 2020. https://qz.com/quartzy/1227759/black-panther-the-wakanda-forever-salute-has-become-a-symbol-of-black-excellence/.

Moon, Mariella. "Facebook Accused of 'Empowering' a Racist Company Culture." *Endgadget*, November 9, 2019. Accessed December 19, 2020. https://www.engadget.com/2019/11/09/facebook-accused-racist-company-culture/.

Morris, Susana M. "Black Girls Are from the Future: Afrofuturist Feminism in Octavia E. Butler's 'Fledgling.'" *Women's Studies Quarterly* 40, no. 3/4 (Fall/Winter 2012): 146–66.

Muhammad, Elijah. *Message to the Blackman in America.* Atlanta: Messenger Elijah Muhammad Propagation Society, 1997.

———. *The Mother Plane.* Atlanta: Messenger Elijah Muhammad Propagation Society, 1992. Kindle.

Nama, Adilifu. *Black Space: Imagining Race in Science Fiction Film.* Austin: University of Texas Press, 2008.

Neal, Ronald B. "Spike Lee Can Go Straight to Hell!: The Cinematic and Religious Masculinity of Tyler Perry." *Black Theology* 14, no. 2 (August 2016): 139–51.

Nelson, Alondra. "Introduction: Future Texts." *Social Text 71* 20, no. 2 (Summer 2002): 1–15.

Ogbunu, C. Brandon. "How Afrofuturism Can Help the World Mend." *Wired*, July 15, 2020. https://www.wired.com/story/how-afrofuturism-can-help-the-world-mend/.

Okorafor, Nnedi. "Africanfuturism Defined." *Nnedi's Wahala Zone Blog*, October 19, 2019. Accessed December 19, 2020. http://nnedi.blogspot.com/2019/10/africanfuturism-defined.html.

———. *Binti: Home.* New York: Tom Doherty Associates. 2017.

Parker, Ryan. "'Black Panther': Ryan Coogler Reveals What Happened to Killmonger's Mother." *Hollywood Reporter*, May 4, 2018. Accessed December 19, 2020. https://www.hollywoodreporter.com/heat-vision/black-panther-what-happened-killmongers-mother-1108754.

Parrinder, Patrick, ed. *Learning from Other Worlds: Estrangement, Cognition, and the Politics of Science Fiction and Utopia.* Durham, NC: Duke University Press, 2001.

Patterson, Orlando. *Slavery and Social Death: A Comparative Study.* Cambridge, MA: Harvard University Press, 1982.

Pearson, Anne Mackenzie. "From Thwarted Gods to Reclaimed Mystery?: An Overview of the Depiction of Religion in Star Trek." In *Star Trek and Sacred Ground: Explorations of Star Trek, Religion, and American Culture*, edited by Jennifer E. Porter and Darcee L. McLaren, 15–17. Albany: SUNY Press, 1999.

Pearson, Roberta, and Máire Messenger Davies. *Star Trek and American Television.* Berkeley: University of California Press, 2014.

Pinn, Anthony B. *The End of God-Talk: An African American Humanist Theology.* New York: Oxford University Press, 2012.

———. *Why Lord?: Suffering and Evil in Black Theology.* New York: Continuum Publishing Company, 1995.

Pinn, Anthony B., and Benjamin Valentin. *Creating Ourselves: African Americans and Hispanic Americans on Popular Culture and Religious Expression.* Durham, NC: Duke University Press, 2009.

Potts, Stephen W. "'We Keep Playing the Same Record': A Conversation with Octavia Butler." In *Conversations With Octavia Butler*, edited by Consuela Francis. 65–73. Jackson: University Press of Mississippi, 2009.

Pounds, Micheal Charles. "'Explorers'—Star Trek: Deep Space Nine." In *The Black Imagination: Science Fiction, Futurism, and the Speculative*, edited by Sandra Jackson and Julie E. Moody-Freeman, 47–80. New York: Peter Lang, 2011.

Pulliam-Moore, Charles. "Janelle Monáe Explains How *Dirty Computer* Connects to the Rest of Her Afrofuturist Discography." *io9*, October 29, 2018. Accessed December 14, 2020. https://io9.gizmodo.com/janelle-monae-explains-how-dirty-computer-connects-to-t-1830079331.

Ramsey, Guthrie P. *The Amazing Bud Powell : Black Genius, Jazz History, and the Challenge of Bebop. Music of the African Diaspora.* Berkeley: University of California Press, 2013. http://search.ebscohost.com.libproxy.furman.edu/login.aspx?direct=true&db=nlebk&AN=562942&site=ehost-live.

Reed, Anthony. "After the End of the World: Sun Ra and the Grammar of Utopia." *Black Camera* 5, no. 1 (Fall 2013): 118–39.

Renault, Gregory. "Science Fiction as Cognitive Estrangement." *Discourse* 2 (Summer 1980): 113–41.

Ringer, Christophe D. "Afrofuturism and the DNA of Biopolitics in the Black Public Sphere." *Black Theology* 14, no. 1 (April 2016): 53–68.

Rollefson, J. Griffith. "The 'Robot Voodoo Power' Thesis: Afrofuturism and Anti-Anti-Essentialism from Sun Ra to Kool Keith." *Black Music Research Journal* 28, no. 1 (Spring 2008): 83–109.

Rouse, Carolyn Moxley, John L. Jackson Jr., and Marla F. Frederick. *Televised Redemption: Black Religious Media and Racial Empowerment.* New York: New York University Press, 2016.

Roussos, Eleni. *The Art of Marvel Studios: Black Panther.* New York: Marvel Worldwide, 2018.

Rutledge, Gregory E., and Nalo Hopkinson. "Speaking in Tongues: An Interview with Science Fiction Writer Nalo Hopkinson." *African American Review* 33, no. 4 (Winter 1999): 589–601.

Sales, Ruby. "Racial Injustice and Religious Response from Selma to Ferguson." Plenary Panel, American Academy of Religion annual meeting, Atlanta, GA, November 21–24, 2015. Audio recording.

Saltzman, Stephanie. "Janelle Monáe's Response to This Sexist Tweet Is Perfect." *Allure,* April 14, 2015. Accessed December 14, 2020. https://www.allure.com/story/janelle-monae-twitter.

Sarantis, Julia. "How Janelle Monáe's Visual Album 'Dirty Computer' Explores What It Means to Be Free." *KultureHub.* Accessed December 14, 2020. https://kulturehub.com/janelle-monae-dirty-computer/.

Smith, Ayana. "Blues, Criticism, and the Signifying Trickster." *Popular Music* 24, no. 2 (May 2005): 179–91.

Sneed, Roger A. *Representations of Homosexuality: Black Liberation Theology and Cultural Criticism.* New York: Palgrave Macmillan, 2010.

Sommerlad, Joe. "Octavia E, Butler: Who Was the Black Science Fiction Writer Who Overcame Prejudice and Poverty?" *The Independent,* June 22, 2018. Accessed Saturday, March 27, 2021, https://www.independent.co.uk/arts-entertainment/books/news/octavia-e-butler-black-science-fiction-writer-bloodchild-xenogenesis-parable-a8411566.html.

Spanos, Brittany. "Janelle Monáe Frees Herself." *Rolling Stone,* April 26, 2018. Accessed December 14, 2020. https://www.rollingstone.com/music/music-features/janelle-monae-frees-herself-629204/.

Spiro, Daniel. *Liberating the Holy Name: A Free-Thinker Grapples with the Meaning of Divinity.* Eugene, OR: Cascade Books, 2014.

Star Trek: Deep Space Nine. "Far Beyond the Stars." Directed by Avery Brooks. Written by Ira Steven Behr, Hans Beimler, and Mark Scott Zicree. Aired February 11, 1998, on Paramount Television.

Star Trek: The Next Generation. "Devil's Due." Directed by Tom Benko. Written by Phillip LaZebnik and William Douglas Lansford. Aired February 2, 1991, on Paramount Television.

———. "Who Watches the Watchers?" Directed by Robert Wiemer. Written by Richard Manning and Hans Beimler. Aired October 14, 1989, on Paramount Television.

Star Trek: The Original Series. "Charlie X." Directed by Lawrence Dobkin. Written by D. C. Fontana. Aired September 15, 1966, on Paramount Television.

Stout, Daniel A. *Media and Religion: Foundations of an Emerging Field.* New York: Routledge, 2012.

Stucky, Mark D. "He Is the One: The Matrix Trilogy's Postmodern Movie Messiah." *Journal of Religion and Film* 9, no. 2 (October 2005): 2.

Szwed, John F. *Space Is the Place: The Life and Times of Sun Ra.* New York: Da Capo Press, 1998.

Thomas, Sheree R. *Dark Matter: A Century of Speculative Fiction from the African Diaspora*. New York: Warner Books, 2000.

Tymn, Marshall B. "Science Fiction: A Brief History and Review of Criticism." *American Studies International* 23, no. 1 (April 1985): 48–49.

University of Maryland College of Behavioral and Social Sciences. "Ezekiel's Wheel Ties African Spiritual Traditions to Christianity." Accessed December 19, 2020. www.https://bsos.umd.edu/featured-content/ezekiels-wheel-ties-african.

Vaatanen, Paivi. "Sun Ra: Myth, Science, and Science Fiction." *Fafnir—Nordic Journal of Science Fiction and Fantasy Research* 1, no. 4: 39–46.

Wallace, Alicia A. "You Should Have Been Listening to Octavia Butler This Whole Time." *Electric Literature*, June 19, 2020. Accessed December 14, 2020. https://electricliterature.com/parable-of-the-sower-octavia-butler-listen-to-black-women/.

Wanzo, Rebecca. "Apocalyptic Empathy: A Parable of Postmodern Sentimentality." *Obsidian III: Literature in the African Diaspora* 6/7, no. 1/2 (Fall/Winter 2005–Spring/Summer 2006): 72–86.

Weisenfeld, Judith. *New World A-Coming: Black Religion and Racial Identity during the Great Migration*. New York: New York University Press, 2016.

West, Cornel, and Eddie S. Glaude Jr., eds. *African American Religious Thought: An Anthology*. Louisville, KY: Westminster John Knox Press, 2003.

Westhelle, Vitor. *Eschatology and Space: The Lost Dimension in Theology Past and Present*. New York: Palgrave Macmillan, 2012.

Whitbrook, James. "Donald Glover's Mom Warns Him Not to Mess Up Lando for Her." *io9*, October 27, 2016. Accessed December 14, 2020. https://io9.gizmodo.com/donald-glovers-mom-warns-him-not-to-mess-up-lando-for-h-1788279602.

Wilford, John Noble. "Ezekiel's Wheel Ties African Spiritual Traditions to Christianity." *New York Times*, November 7, 2016. Accessed December 19, 2020. https://www.nytimes.com/2016/11/08/science/ezekiels-wheel-ties-african-spiritual-traditions-to-christianity.html.

Wittung, Jeffery, and Daniel Bramer. "From Superman to Brahman: The Religious Shift of the Matrix Mythology." *Journal of Religion and Film* 10, no. 2 (October 2006): 11.

Womack, Ytasha. *Afrofuturism: The World of Black Sci-Fi and Fantasy Culture*. Chicago: Lawrence Hill Books, 2013. Kindle.

Young, Thelathia. "'Uses of the Erotic' for Teaching Queer Studies." *Women's Studies Quarterly* 40, no. 3/4 (Fall/Winter 2012): 301–5.

Youngquist, Paul. *A Pure Solar World: Sun Ra and the Birth of Afrofuturism*. Austin: University of Texas Press, 2016.

Zaki, Hoda M. "Utopia, Dystopia, and Ideology in the Science Fiction of Octavia Butler. *Science Fiction Studies* 17. no. 2 (July 1990): 239–51.

Zamalin, Alex. *Black Utopia: The History of an Idea from Black Nationalism to Afrofuturism*. New York: Columbia University Press, 2019.

INDEX

Abraham, Alton, 118

Africa, 9, 14n3, 80, 92, 93, 94, 97, 98, 100, 103–4, 107, 108, 126, 155; cosmology, 156; diaspora, 20, 21, 23, 24, 26, 151, 153, 154, 156, 160; encounter with Europe, 14; mythological past, 100, 101; South Africa, 34, 111

African Americans, xi, 10, 18, 21, 27, 28, 29, 30, 44, 48, 56, 79, 81, 93, 97, 125, 128, 135, 136

African Methodist Episcopal church, 126

African spiritualities, 108

African traditional religious practices, 136

Africana esotericism, 117, 127, 128

Africana esoteric studies, 127, 128

Africanfuturism, 155–57

Africanjujuism, 155–56

Afrocentricity, 139

Afrofuturism, xii, 1–3, 6–9, 14, 20, 21, 23–30, 33–38, 42, 43, 46–48, 52, 60, 62, 66, 71, 73, 75–77, 92, 97, 98, 103, 106, 110, 111, 121, 123, 131, 132, 134, 141, 143–47, 149, 150, 152, 153, 154, 156–58, 160–63; Black masculinity and, 9, 98, 161, 162; Black religious thought

and, xii, 26, 28, 37, 98, 132, 148–49, 152, 157, 158, 163; eschatology and, 9, 33, 111, 117, 119, 123, 125, 132, 139, 153–55; humanistic Afrofuturism, 135, 157; intersectional Afrofuturism, 7, 8, 36, 42, 43, 45, 46, 48, 57, 60, 62, 110, 149, 153, 154; spirituality and, 48, 97, 106, 133, 159; theorizing, 66, 134, 149, 151; utopia and, 9, 23, 26, 41, 55, 59, 106, 110, 117, 119, 150, 156

Afrofuturism listserv, 141, 147

Afrofuturist, 3, 7, 21, 23, 24, 26, 34, 46, 103, 123, 132, 135, 147, 154, 160, 163

Afrofuturistic religious identity, 146

Afrofuturistic religious thought, 149

Afropessimism, 116

Allah, 127, 130

Alpha Quadrant, 78, 81

American Academy of Religion, 2, 97

Amsterdam News, The, 84

ancestors, 99, 105, 107, 109, 141, 153

ancestor veneration, 106

ancestral plane, 101, 106, 109, 110, 162

Anderson, Victor, x, 2, 3, 20n17, 28, 145

Andrews, Dale, 33

Walking Dead, The, 142

Washington, Isaiah, 15

Weisenfeld, Judith, 9, 30, 135, 136, 137

West, Cornel, 14

Westhelle, Vitor, 117

white supremacist imaginary, 24, 88, 91, 93

white supremacy, xi, 8, 9, 14, 19, 23, 28, 37, 41, 46, 62, 72, 74, 117, 136, 153, 163; Black liberation theology and, 115, 116; Black Panther and, 97, 98, 100–102, 104, 105, 108, 112, 131; "Far Beyond the Stars" and, 78, 79, 82–84, 87, 89, 90, 91, 94; the Nation of Islam and, 123, 126, 137; social media as tool against, 159; Sun Ra and, 118, 120, 122, 137; Toni Morrison on, 150, 151

Williams, Delores, 28

Witten, Taylor, 138

W'Kabi, 104, 107, 108, 110

Womack, Ytasha, 6, 7, 21, 23, 24, 43, 134

womanist theology, ix, x, 30, 31, 32, 35, 36, 52, 53, 148, 153

Wonder Woman, 96

World Fantasy Convention, 139

World War II, 127

Yahweh, 83

Yoruba mask, 94

Youngquist, Paul, 7, 118, 119, 21

Zamalin, Alex, 22, 26

"Zekiel Saw the Wheel," 125

Zen, 70

Zicree, Mark Scott, 82

Zuri, 98

NEW SUNS: RACE, GENDER, AND SEXUALITY IN THE SPECULATIVE
Susana M. Morris and Kinitra D. Brooks, Series Editors

Scholarly examinations of speculative fiction have been a burgeoning academic field for more than twenty-five years, but there has been a distinct lack of attention to how attending to nonhegemonic positionalities transforms our understanding of the speculative. New Suns: Race, Gender, and Sexuality in the Speculative addresses this oversight and promotes scholarship at the intersections of race, gender, sexuality, and the speculative, engaging interdisciplinary fields of research across literary, film, and cultural studies that examine multiple pasts, presents, and futures. Of particular interest are studies that offer new avenues into thinking about popular genre fictions and fan communities, including but not limited to the study of Afrofuturism, comics, ethnogothicism, ethnosurrealism, fantasy, film, futurity studies, gaming, horror, literature, science fiction, and visual studies. New Suns particularly encourages submissions that are written in a clear, accessible style that will be read both by scholars in the field as well as by nonspecialists.

CPSIA information can be obtained
at www.ICGtesting.com
Printed in the USA
JSHW060204140722
28040JS00003B/5